Himmler's Jewish Tailor

Religion, Theology, and the Holocaust
Alan L. Berger, Series Editor

Himmler's Jewish Tailor

The Story of
Holocaust Survivor Jacob Frank

Mark Lewis & Jacob Frank

Syracuse University Press

First Edition 2000

00 01 02 03 04 05   6 5 4 3 2 1

The paper used in this publication meets the minimum
requirements of American National Standard for
Information Sciences—Permanence of Paper for Printed
Library Material, ANSI Z39.48-1984. ♾

Library of Congress Cataloging-in-Publication Data
Frank, Jacob.
Himmler's Jewish tailor : the story of Holocaust survivor Jacob
Frank / Mark Lewis and Jacob Frank.
p. cm. — (Religion, theology, and the Holocaust)
Based on Mark Lewis's taped interviews with Jacob Frank.
Includes bibliographical references (p.   ) and index.
ISBN 0-8156-0606-0 (cl. : alk. paper)
1. Frank, Jacob. 2. Jews—Poland—Lublin Biography.
3. Holocaust, Jewish (1939–1945)—Poland—Lublin Personal
narratives. 4. Lublin (Poland) Biography. I. Lewis, Mark, 1968–.
II. Title. III. Series.
DS135.P63F635 1999
940.53'18'092—dc21
[B]   99-40004

Manufactured in the United States of America

Sometimes, sometimes, I wouldn't want to forget. Who can forget something like this happened? The whole ink what there is in this world, with paper, you cannot write what this was that really happened. I was in all kind of concentration camps for five years and nine months, and every day from the beginning was happening something else. So who can remember, who can write this everything that was really happening? Even today, after fifty years, not talking about other people, I still cannot understand *that this is true, because it's impossible to understand—the brains couldn't swallow that something like this* could *happen.*

—JACOB FRANK

Mark Lewis was born in 1968 in Cleveland, Ohio, and was raised in Charlotte, North Carolina. He has published several short stories and a work of fiction titled *Suspicions Among the Thoughts I May Contribute* (1995). He has worked as an editor, reporter, and freelance journalist for newspapers, magazines, and online media. Currently he is writing a novel titled *The Discovery of the Amputees.*

Jacob Frank was born on January 3, 1913, in Lublin, Poland. He ran away from home as a boy to become a tailor rather than fulfill his father's wish that he become a rabbi. After the Nazis invaded Poland in 1939, Frank was randomly chosen to head the clothing factory at the SS-run Lipowa labor camp, managing 450 tailors by the end of 1943. His position put him in contact with such notorious SS officers as Heinrich Himmler, Adolf Eichmann, and Odilo Globocnik. A witness to the total liquidation of the significant Lublin ghetto, Frank was the only survivor of his sixty-four-member family. After Lipowa, he was interned in a prison and three other concentration camps, including Natzweiler and Dachau. He emigrated to the United States in 1946, becoming a successful clothing designer and tailor in New York City.

Contents

20. Officers   135

21. The Airport Rebellion   146

22. Schama Grajer   151

23. Schama Grajer's Wedding   154

24. The Liquidation of Majdan-Tatarsky   160

25. Dora and Nunyek   169

26. Dora's Return   180

27. The Lublin Prison   183

28. The Safe Haven of Despair   204

29. The Chicken Coop   214

30. "This Is the Last Stop of Your Life"   222

31. A Contact from Inside   228

32. The Dachau Shower   240

33. The Remains   253

34. The Reversal   257

35. The Mob   265

36. The Consequences of the *Gela Later*   273

37. Final Words and Thoughts   282

     References   291

     Index   293

Illustrations

Map

Introduction

Entering Memory

IN THE SUMMER OF 1994, I visited New York City to embark upon an extensive set of conversations and discussions with Jacob Frank, a Jewish tailor and clothing designer originally from Lublin, Poland, who was imprisoned in four labor and concentration camps during the Nazi Holocaust of 1939 to 1945. Two months of interviews and meetings form the basis of this book, comprised of Mr. Frank's oral history and many discussions that probe his experiences. Mr. Frank's stories and recollections cover his servitude in the Lipowa labor camp in Lublin, incarceration in a prison in Lublin, and internment in three other camps—the Radom labor camp in Poland; the Natzweiler-Vaihingen concentration camp in Alsace, near Strasbourg; and the Dachau concentration camp outside of Munich.

While still in high school, I knew of Mr. Frank as a Holocaust survivor, a tailor, and the father of one of my mother's friends. I didn't know anything specific about his time in the camps, either because I didn't have the opportunity to inquire or wasn't present when he told some of his stories to my mother. Four years later, my mother suggested I write a book about Mr. Frank's experiences, but the project seemed too straightforward and realistic for my imaginative impulses, which had steered me toward experimental literature. When Mr. Frank turned eighty, however, my thinking had matured, and my investigative propensities were alerted to that fact that if Mr. Frank's account of Lublin were not recorded, it might be lost.

This, however, didn't turn out to be entirely true, as Mr. Frank had been videotaped for the Fortunoff Video Archive for Holocaust Testimonies at Yale University, and some fifteen years earlier he had recorded some autobiographical cassettes. Interestingly, some of these audio documents are diaries that were made on the spot; he recorded one of them, for example, in his hotel room in Hamburg, (West) Germany, in 1973, when he was testifying in an extensive war crimes investigation of Lublin SS and police forces. The Hamburg tape describes his emotions upon returning to German soil and seeing Lipowa camp officials again, thirty years later. Mr. Frank turned these five cassettes over to me during the course of the interviews, which helped me outline his narrative and provide the backdrop for more extensive discussions.

Before I had the opportunity to watch the Yale tape, I had already started to research Lublin and the Lipowa camp. When I did finally see the tape, I recognized that the brief interview didn't explore the totality of Mr. Frank's experiences or draw out all he knew about the various camps where he was imprisoned. This was partly due to the nature of the archiving project, which wasn't devoted to in-depth biographies of the interviewees, and also because the interviewers didn't possess enough specific background information to delve into camps and figures that were unknown at that time.

It was not only to add to the historical record that I urgently wanted to present Mr. Frank's history. There is now a significant number of historical works, films, and archives about the Holocaust that have documented the genocide and offered interpretations of its causes. What inspired me, however, was Mr. Frank's voice and the rarity of experience it represented. As soon as I heard his undeniably rich, authentic Yiddish accent over the telephone, insisting that there were no other living survivors from Lublin who could relate what he did, I knew that it would be a worthy challenge to document the words of one survivor whose memories had not reached more than a select circle of family and friends. Unless one attempts to talk to all sorts of people and discover what they think and how they express themselves, one doesn't recognize how much a single individual has to reveal, whatever his or her circumstances. While some people are more articulate than others, some more perceptive, some privy to events and knowledge that we consider more important than others, there are voices that cry out with indelible recollections; they speak from a point-of-view that a traditional history is not often able to capture.

Prior to the Nazi invasion of Poland in September 1939, when he was twenty-six, Frank was a very successful tailor in Lublin, designing clothing in the modern style and counting both prominent Gentiles and Jews among his clients. When he was forced to begin working in the Lipowa labor camp, he was classified as a *Schutzhaft Jude,* or "protective custody Jew." The sentence of protective custody meant detention in a concentration or work camp for an unspecified period of time. The protective custody prisoner had to be protected—but from whom? Against what? The term was standard doublespeak for state-security repression: a person could be thrown in jail or a camp not for committing a criminal offense[1] but because that person was undesirable and was viewed by the State as likely to engage in agitation or dissent. Many protective custody prisoners were not sent to camps because they held seditious political views or disseminated radical intellectual ideas, but because they belonged to an ethnic group or religion that the Nazi state opposed.

The practice of protective custody followed the logic of penal practice that arose after most European nations abolished the official use of torture by the end of the 18th century[2]—a prisoner was no longer punished to exact vengeance but supposedly to protect others. Although the actual Nazi program was more extreme than social repression, calling for the execution of the mentally ill, persons with congenital diseases, deaf people, Jews, Gypsies, homosexuals, Jehovah's Witnesses, and the clergy, the term "protective custody" was a deceptive euphemism for the first measures used to single out those groups and rid the rest of society of them. Though it was not a designation for murder, as "special treatment" was, the phrase demonstrates that already in 1933, when the term was coined, the Nazis used code words to obscure repression and to justify it legally.

Mr. Frank, born on January 3, 1913, in Lublin, is perhaps the only person to have survived the entire existence of the labor camp at 7 Lipowa Street in Lublin (first an independent camp, later a branch camp of Majdanek)—meaning that he was in the camp from its beginning in 1939 until its liquidation in November, 1943. Lipowa was Lublin's main labor camp, located right in the city and directly controlled by the SS, which ruled the camp under three regimes of com-

1. A protective custody regulation of 1937 states that it was not to be used for the purpose of punishing criminal offenses. It was a "coercive measure of the Secret State Police to protect the State against subversive activity and may be applied to persons whose behaviour endangers the existence and security of the people and State" (regulation translated in Distel and Jakusch 1978, 42).

2. England's abolition in 1640 was one of the first, and its early reform was followed by Prussia (1754), Saxony (1770), Austria/Bohemia (1776), South Netherlands (1787–94), and the Dutch Republic (1795–98).

manders.[3] Starting in January 1940, two groups were forced to work in the camp as slave laborers: general laborers who were picked up by the SS when they made raids on the Lublin ghetto, and skilled trades-people that the local Jewish Council (called the *Judenrat*) were forced by the Nazis to select.[4] By late 1940 through January 1941, the camp also included approximately 1,350 Jewish prisoners of war who had served in the Polish army. These POWs were used for projects outside the camp, including clearing snow and building barracks,[5] while civil-ian Jewish prisoners built the Lipowa camp compound, then worked in camp factories to produce army uniforms, boots, and saddles. Through 1941 and 1942, there were several new infusions of Jewish POW labor, as well as civilian Jews who were transported to Lublin from Germany and Warsaw, Poland,[6] as the Nazis proceeded with deportations.

Starting in August 1940, the camp was commanded by the highly successful combination (in Nazi terms) of *SS-Untersturmführer* Horst Riedel and his adjutant, *SS-Untersturmführer* Wolfgang Mohwinkel.[7] Riedel concentrated on making business deals, which led to the eco-nomic success of the camp, while the "restless, arrogant, and tireless" Mohwinkel[8] implemented a brutal regime of discipline, including beatings, hangings, and shootings; many of these criminal actions were carried out without provocation on the part of the prisoners and were not punishments for "violations" of the camp disciplinary code. These crimes were actually not new to the camp, as an earlier com-mandant, *SS-Obersturmbannführer* (Lieutenant Colonel) Dolp, also employed brutal methods and tortures and permitted his henchmen

3. Investigation of the SS and Police Leaders in Lublin, 8365–68. These court documents, stored at the *Zentrale Stelle der Landesjustizverwaltungen zur Aufklärung nationalsozialistische Verbrechen* in Ludwigsburg, will hereafter be abbreviated as *SSPF*. For specific information about commanders and their underlings, see Chapter 20, "Officers."

4. Hilberg writes that Jews selected from the ghettos for forced labor were sent to SS-controlled labor camps and private company camps: "All Jews who had left the ghettos were labor prisoners of the SS. . . . The SS labor camps were subjected to a constant consolidation and weeding out process, from which the company camps re-mained largely immune" (Hilberg 1985, 531).

5. *SSPF*, 8373.

6. *SSPF*, 8370–74.

7. An *Untersturmführer* is the equivalent of a second lieutenant.

8. *SSPF*, 8366–67.

to do the same, until he was removed from his post due to alcoholism in June 1940.[9]

In February and March 1941, the camp's business and economic planning were taken over by the German company *Deutsche Ausrüst-ungswerke* (German Supply Establishment), although in reality, this company was an SS subsidiary (or front) headed by Riedel and ultimately controlled by the notoriously corrupt *SS-Obergruppenführer* and Higher Police Leader Odilo Globocnik. In November 1941, Globocnik relieved the business-savvy Riedel from his post, supposedly because of his arrogance,[10] and the highly dedicated Mohwinkel took over as commandant until November 3, 1943; this is the date when all Jews in Lublin work camps were murdered in a mass execution, code-named the *Erntefest*, or "Harvest Festival."[11]

Mohwinkel had helped develop a forced labor camp in Lemberg under the DAW organization,[12] and he applied the model to Lipowa, speeding up the production of down jackets for *Wehrmacht* troops fighting in Leningrad. According to a German court biography of Mohwinkel, he was "very committed to building the Lipowa camp and made it one of the most important DAW organizations outside the German Reich by his total lack of thought about consequences and by using Jewish labor without concern"[13] for their health or safety. It cannot be overemphasized, however, that the extreme violence and pressing pace of work at Lipowa cannot be attributed to Mohwinkel alone; it required the cooperation of his staff, which, for example, resumed raids on the Lublin ghetto in November 1941 so that there would be enough workers to meet higher production quotas.

9. According to German court documents, Dolp's first name wasn't known, and his surname is a phonetic spelling. He served under Ludolf von Alvensleben, the Lublin *Selbstschutzführer* who was the first Lipowa commandant. Because he wasn't particularly interested in running the camp, he allowed Dolp to administer it. In the Lublin war crimes investigation, Mr. Frank deposed that he witnessed Dolp murdering Jewish prisoners (*SSPF*, 5694). Dolp was killed in shelling in Romania in 1944 and was never tried for his crimes (*SSPF*, 8402).

10. *SSPF*, 8368.

11. The German court records aren't always so direct when discussing this final liquidation in Lublin. It is sometimes only referred to as the "action of November 3, 1943," in which "the camp lost its labor force" (*SSPF*, 8368).

12. *SSPF*, 8368.

13. *SSPF*, 8368. The reader will find numerous examples of this in Mr. Frank's account in the course of this book.

During Mohwinkel's reign, 2,815 to 3,000 workers[14] lived in impoverished conditions in the camp barracks, barely subsisting on rations that were constantly being reduced; besides this physical burden, all of their families were murdered when the Lublin ghetto was liquidated in April 1942. Nevertheless, the productivity of Lipowa and a similar camp that housed clothing shops at the old airport, *Plaga Lashkewicz*,[15] inspired *SS-Reichsführer* Himmler and Globocnik to expand the SS slave-labor enterprises in Lublin.[16] The planned SS business empire had to be built and operated, so they decided to open the even larger Majdanek concentration camp to provide the manpower.[17]

One cannot say with absolute certainty that Mr. Frank is the only survivor of Lipowa because there may be other survivors of Lipowa who have not published their testimonies, others of whom researchers

14. *SSPF*, 8376.

15. The camp was also known by the German appellations *Flughafen* Lublin and *Flughafenlager* (Lublin Airport and the Airport Camp, respectively). Goldhagen, who researched the camp based on the SSPF records, reports that the camp was founded in the autumn of 1941 and contained a small "Main Supply Camp" and a larger SS Clothing Works (run by the *Deutsche Ausrüstungswerke*). The Supply Camp's core population was approximately twenty-five prisoners, supplemented by work crews of around 100 prisoners who came from nearby camps; they loaded and unloaded freight cars and built barracks. The Jewish prisoner population in the Clothing Works was between 3,500 and 5,000 Jews (around two-thirds were women); these prisoners sorted the valuable possessions collected from Jews murdered in the Aktion Reinhard killing operations. The clothing, linen, watches, jewels, and money were valued at over 178 million Reichsmarks.

In both the Supply Camp and Clothing Works, extreme beatings were the norm (many of which resulted in death); prisoners were kept severely undernourished; typhus and dysentery repeatedly spread through the camps; public hangings were common, and Jews were shot on the spot or sent to the Majdanek gas chambers. The brutality was so regular and immense that Goldhagen uses the camp as an example of how the Nazis subjected the Jews to this treatment to exterminate them, rather than use them as a profitable workforce (Goldhagen 1997, 300–311).

16. Arad 1987, 15. In Chapter 8 ("The First Leather Coat"), Frank recounts a story of Himmler's tour of Lipowa in July 1941 with Globocnik and other SS leaders.

17. In September and October 1941, Frank recalls that work brigades of Jewish prisoners of war went from Lipowa to Majdanek every day. In 1942, Frank spoke with a prisoner of war who told him he had seen ovens being installed there. Frank reports that in late '42 and early '43, it was common knowledge that the work brigades were digging long trenches at Majdanek, and although these ditches were purported to be crude bomb shelters to be used in Russian air raids, prisoners doubted that this was their actual purpose.

are not aware, or survivors who were imprisoned in Lipowa during its existence but were later transferred and killed elsewhere. While a handful of Jewish soldiers in the Polish army escaped from Lipowa[18] and some Lubliner Jews escaped the overcrowded and hunger-ridden conditions of the ghetto to hide in Russian-occupied eastern Poland, Mr. Frank believes that no other civilian survived the camp's final *Erntefest* liquidation on November 3, 1943.

Mr. Frank is probably the only living survivor who can extensively describe Lipowa's structure, operations, and events in great detail.[19] An account of his imprisonment in Lipowa is important because it occurs during the period of crucial transitions in the Nazi policy toward the Jews and the development of the Nazi extermination policy. Nearly all of the events that he relates are eyewitness accounts of major Nazi policies and atrocities. He recalls the eviction of Jews from their homes in Lublin, the squalid ghetto where they were sequestered, and the overcrowded conditions in the camp when it became flooded with deportees. He remembers in detail how the SS factory operations functioned within the labor camp system. He tells disquieting stories about how the Majdanek killing center was constructed.

An intelligent, at times pensive man with a startling memory, Mr. Frank is a valuable historical source for his knowledge of the Lublin ghetto. As a native of Lublin, rather than a Jew deported to the Lublin "reservation" from Germany or from a small Polish town, Mr. Frank is knowledgeable about Jewish cultural life in Lublin before the German occupation. He also gives an elaborate account of the phases

18. Gruber (1978) reports some of the conditions and central figures at Lipowa. However, because prisoners of war left the camp each day to work on building and cleaning projects on the outskirts of Lublin, Gruber (a POW) did not have knowledge of the construction and organization of the camp, its inner workings, civilian prisoner conditions, or the Lublin ghetto to the extent that Frank did.

19. Lipowa is rarely mentioned in the historical literature. Yahil (1990) only mentions that it was a camp for Jewish prisoners of war from Western Poland. Feig states that Lipowa was one of two branches of Majdanek in Lublin but does not go into detail about it. In the most in-depth historical survey to date, Goldhagen describes the formation, structure, and brutal discipline of the camp, drawing from a postwar legal investigation of the Lublin camps (Goldhagen 1997, 295–300). Outside of the court records (at the *Zentrale Stelle der Landesjustizverwaltungen,* 208 AR-Z 74/60), he notes that he only found material about Lipowa and the old airport camp in "fleeting references and an occasional brief mention in a memoir" (Goldhagen 1990, 573n. 9)

of ghettoization in Lublin, from the sealing of the Lublin ghetto to its reduction into the Majdan-Tatarsky ghetto in March 1943.[20] While historical works on the Holocaust mainly treat Lublin as a transport center and examine the region, not solely the city, in the context of Nazi resettlement projects and deportations,[21] there are no firsthand survivor accounts in English that describe Lublin's cityscape, the history of the Jewish quarter, its business and religious communities, or the unfolding progress of genocide within the ghetto. Documentary testimony about the Lublin ghetto is very slight, and historical works in English have revealed only a few of its major cataclysms.[22] There is a similar paucity of information about the Majdan-Tatarsky ghetto, where the families of Lipowa workers lived after the large Lublin ghetto was destroyed.

Mr. Frank's account is even more extraordinary because of the position he held at Lipowa. Since he was the head of the 450–75-man clothing factory, he is a fount of information about the camp's layout, its conditions, its role in the German war effort, and the SS officers, guards, and other shop leaders in the camp. Mr. Frank had daily dealings with camp commandant Mohwinkel[23] and many other officers for whom he had to make clothes. He intimately knew the dominating but dependent relationships Nazi officers had with the Jews they utilized for slave labor. He describes how the workers kindled the hope that their industry would save them; painfully and without irony, Frank returns many times to the fact that it did not. His knowledge of beatings, torture, and murder in the shops, through which the Nazis sought to assert their power instantaneously rather than simply sate sadistic urges, was valuable enough to warrant his testifying in the war crimes trials of Mohwinkel and other Lublin SS officers in Hamburg in 1973. Regarding Adolf Eichmann, Mr. Frank witnessed his round-

20. Confirmed in Apenszlak 1982, 96.

21. Hilberg 1985, 206–7, 210–11; Levin 1973, 178–84, 189–90.

22. Hilberg only notes that the ghetto was established in April of '41 (1985, 221) and that it could not be sealed (228). For a study more specific to the Lublin district, see Browning 1993, an author who studied a police battalion that carried out the *Erntefest* liquidation and many mobile killing missions in surrounding towns in the Lublin region. While his work corroborates many events of which Frank was aware, its focus is not the Lublin ghetto or Lipowa.

23. On July 26, 1974, in Hamburg, Mohwinkel was sentenced to life imprisonment for his part in the murder of Polish Jews in the camp. He was then sixty-two years old. (*London Times* July 27, 1974, page 1A.)

ing up 118 children and sending them to the woods of Trawnik in 1942. Frank was forced to help load the children into trucks; he then rode with them into the woods and saw the Nazis prepare to execute them in a clearing.

Mr. Frank was also forced to make iconographic, gray leather coats for many Nazi figures, including Mohwinkel, Amon Göth, Himmler, Eichmann, and Globocnik. Frank explains how the coats created a fearsome, unchallengeable appearance, how they were sought after by low-ranking, status-seeking officers, and how Nazi officers gave the coats as gifts to high-ranking officers, commandants, and police leaders to secure alliances and ensure recommendations.

Mr. Frank is a source of rare information about a prison in Lublin on Zamkawa Street, where he was held captive from November 3, 1943, until July 24, 1944. The Lublin Prison was a penal institution that had a criminal population as well as a separate population of approximately 300 Jews, who were supervised by the Gestapo. The Jewish inmates were mainly skilled craftspeople and their families, as well as a few Jewish prisoners-of-war from the Polish army who had sorted the clothes of prisoners executed at Majdanek. In the case of the craftspeople, high SS and Gestapo leaders had privately retained these Jews as their personal tailors and shoemakers and did not want to relinquish these relationships when deportations and liquidations pressed forward. SS and Gestapo officers, therefore, arranged for their personal "slaves" to be removed from Polish cities and ghettos about to be liquidated and placed them in prison for "safekeeping."

While in the prison, Mr. Frank was required to finish a leather coat for Globocnik, but in a severe paralysis of demoralization following the murder of his entire family, he saw no reason to continue complying with Nazi orders. He refused to complete the coat, and as a reprisal, the prison commandant, Dominik,[24] threatened to kill all the Jewish prisoners if Mr. Frank would not work. In debates between Mr. Frank and other Jewish tailors who represented the prisoners, Mr. Frank argued that the prison situation was futile and death was imminent for all the prisoners, while the spokespeople urged the group's survival and argued against what they viewed as Mr. Frank's pessimism. In my discussion about this incident with Mr. Frank, readers should note that the Nazis did not only use torture, starvation, and discipline to ensure submission, but they were equally effective in ma-

24. Dominik is a phonetic spelling based on Mr. Frank's pronunciation.

nipulating a community into putting psychological pressure on its members. This complemented the well-known system of offering special privileges to certain prisoners in order to make them compliant and to fracture group solidarity.

After weeks of prolonging the work on Globocnik's coat and then finishing the job, Mr. Frank was not given any new projects. Idleness suffused the large common room where the craftspeople lived, circulating stale news from the Polish jail-keeper, who made his blood money selling cyanide pills. One of the ways the prison community had urged Mr. Frank to work was to give him a small private room and have a young Jewish woman, whom Mr. Frank had known before the war, move in with him. While they were spared grueling physical labor and cooked their meals in a private corner, their new familial ties were mainly cemented by inner pain and futility. Mr. Frank went to sleep praying he would wake up dead, but he no longer thought of genocide, perhaps because he was powerless against it. "Why was I only the one from my family what was still alive?" he ponders. The other craftspeople were already thinking competitively about their survival, weighing in their minds whose "protector" was more influential. Would Himmler's tailor be spared but Gestapo Chief Worthoff's tailor be killed? Thirteen people were taken out of the Lublin prison, not knowing if their protectors or the usefulness of their skills had anything to do with their selection. Mr. Frank's last memories of the prison are of heads slumped over tables—suicides—and 287 prisoners in the prison courtyard wrapped with wire in a ganglionic mass.

Following a brief stay at the Radom labor camp, Mr. Frank was next interned at Natzweiler, the only death camp in occupied France (Alsace). Yahil mentions that Auschwitz prisoners were gassed at Natzweiler; their corpses were used in anatomy classes at the University of Strasbourg and their skulls for "ancestral heritage" research.[25] Feig's survey of the camp is somewhat more complete, as it includes topographical information, a chronology, and some explanation of atrocities committed there,[26] but treats only the central camp, not its seventeen subsidiaries. Mr. Frank provides original information for the branch at Vaihingen, where he was imprisoned from August 15, 1944 until March 25, 1945. In addition to slight information about Vaihingen's layout, labor projects, and everyday life, Mr. Frank's oral history

25. Yahil 1990, 537.
26. Feig 1981, 217–26.

is valuable for an explanation of how the Jewish authority structures of *Kapos* and leaders of the prisoners were transplanted from the Radom camp. Of further interest is the sympathetic way Mr. Frank was received by the father of the camp commandant's mistress, a man who prolonged Mr. Frank's visits to his house on the pretext that Mr. Frank needed to finish more tailoring work for him and his daughter. The reader may compare these meetings to the outside contacts Mr. Frank had in other camps, recognizing that war, propaganda, and hatred did not create uniform relationships between Jews and non-Jews. Mr. Frank experienced master and slave relationships and relationships of social rejection and acceptance, as well as relationships of staged equality and pseudo-acceptance where he was invited to join in polite social intercourse about "what the Germans were doing to the Jews."

Mr. Frank's account concludes with his final days at Dachau, when he no longer had his family or the more protected status of head tailor; it was a period filled with rumors about what the Nazis would ultimately do with the prisoners they were relocating from camps threatened by Allied forces. Mr. Frank's final six weeks in Dachau were relatively empty and uneventful, marked by one lucidly remembered event. After the group of prisoners in his barracks was taken to a shower on the pretext of disinfection before possibly being relocated to another camp, Mr. Frank secretly exposed himself for several hours to the freezing, late-winter air in an attempt to make himself ill. As Mr. Frank tells the story, many complexities become apparent. He himself cannot say why he was trying to catch a chill: was this the seed of a suicide attempt to annihilate the five years of hopelessness in the camps? During the barracks roll call the next morning, he tried to be admitted to the hospital: a bed in the hospital might have meant a safe haven while the rest of the camp prisoners were liquidated, as was rumored. But it was also possible that admittance to the hospital was tantamount to a death sentence. In the camp system, where expediency was practiced assiduously, the sick were expendable, and Mr. Frank believed that they were executed in the Dachau hospital. Mr. Frank is still uncertain about his motives: did he envision this as a plan for survival, or was he pushing himself toward a situation that could mean death, just so he could bring about some change in the routine of being moved from camp to camp? As for the other prisoners in his barracks, Mr. Frank does not know if they were killed by the Nazis, relocated, or liberated by the American Army when it arrived a few days later.

Readers of literature, persons interested in the Holocaust, and even survivors should prepare for some stylistic idiosyncrasies in *Himmler's Jewish Tailor*. Mr. Frank's oral history is not presented in abridged, conventional English with proper grammatical form and punctuation. One adamant editor informed me that this "phonetic reproduction" served no purpose. To be accurate, the written representation of Mr. Frank's English locutions, influenced by Yiddish, isn't an attempt to reproduce his pronunciation phonetically; instead, I strove to capture Mr. Frank's accent, his grammar, his syntax, and the way his personality emerged in our conversations. It's impossible that Mr. Frank's voice will read on paper exactly as it sounds in life; the reader has no way of knowing the quality and timbre of his voice, what his tone of voice was at a given moment, or how long his pauses before he answered. Nevertheless, I've tried to offer something that is more authentic than ghostwriting. The reader should recognize that comprehending his accent will require some adjustment, but it becomes easier as the reader goes along and recognizes that there are patterns in Mr. Frank's speech. He often uses "what" for the modifiers "that" and "who;" he says "only the one," rather than "the only one;" he sometimes substitutes the future tense for the conditional; and he uses compound tenses infrequently, substituting the present or past tense and indicating time by other phrases. The reader may also wonder whether I have corrected Mr. Frank's English in other instances. He correctly uses "with whom," and refers to both genders in certain statements he makes.

Mr. Frank's extemporaneous speaking is a valid mode of expression, not a lower grade of writing; thus, some fragments, changes in narrative pace, and digressions are intentionally left in the book. I have organized the material somewhat chronologically, in some cases combining many conversations to create a composite portrait or narrative, much in the same way a documentary filmmaker splices together interviews to produce a new work. For many episodes, it was only by conversing with Mr. Frank over several days that I, as a listener, could piece together such a composite version, and I often outlined on paper what exactly took place so that I could present it in a form that the reader could grasp. Moreover, my goal was to bring Mr. Frank's descriptions and remembrances together with greater force, rather than have certain details about a camp or event, for example, lose impact by being dispersed over many pages. The oral biography and dialogues are not in a completely raw form, then, but they have not been distorted or falsified. The occasions that inspired a particular topic, the manner in which Mr. Frank developed his account, and reiterations of opinions and contradictions among them have not been expunged.

When judging the extent to which contradictions in a survivor's account affect its validity, it's useful to study how witnesses sometimes change their stories as they make several pre-trial depositions and then testify again in the courtroom. One notices that witnesses sometimes contradict themselves when questioned by prosecutors a second or third time; they might also expand their accounts or correct an earlier version of testimony, stating that they were mistaken before but now have hit on the way it actually was. Do these numerous versions of the truth destroy their credibility, as deniers of the Holocaust might allege? In Mr. Frank's account, there are enough precisely remembered events to overrule this objection. Nevertheless, in cases where Mr. Frank did present different versions of a story, I tried to sort them out with further questioning as much as possible. One must remember that, when Mr. Frank first described some of these events to German prosecutors in the '60s, twenty years had passed since the camps; even though some events were unforgettable, there were others that didn't come as easily but were essential to remember as completely as possible in order to prosecute the Lublin SS officers on trial. By the time I talked with Mr. Frank, another thirty years had passed, and he was then eighty-one, so it's undeniable that he would forget certain details and only gradually remember others over multiple conversations. Because this too is part of the documentary process, I made note of these things rather than cover them up.

Readers may also be curious why I left some of the question-and-answer-type discussions in the book, rather than remove them to create a seamless narrative of Mr. Frank's account. After watching and reading many interviews with survivors and examining memoirs that were ghostwritten and turned into tidy stories, I decided that a conventional Holocaust memoir, which uses a silent amanuensis, isn't the most accurate form of Holocaust testimony. Because history is transmitted between individuals in a process, it's important that the testimony records this process: how the survivor recollects his or her experiences and how both the survivor and listener interpret the events. By following the interviewer's questions, the reader may better understand the workings of the process. The reader can see what kind of questions were asked and why they were asked; additionally, the reader can grasp that the way the survivor relates his or her story gives clues about what he or she believes, even if those beliefs are unstated. By following how the survivor broached a certain subject, espoused a view, contradicted himself or herself, or broke off from a discussion when he or she was tired or disinterested, the reader can understand that the oral history didn't follow one trajectory, cleanly cut and punched out. By following the exchanges, the reader may experience what was behind the scenes, finding out along the way what the survivor was willing (and not willing) to discuss and how he or she discussed it.

Second, because some of the dialogues are left in the book, the reader can observe Mr. Frank's moods and emotions as he spoke about his experiences and reacted to my questions. If, for example, the reader was presented with a straightforward retelling of how Mr. Frank's wife and one of his sons were shot and pushed into a ditch, the reader might believe that Mr. Frank related this stoically or even mechanically, not knowing the shame and sense of obliteration Mr. Frank felt as he recalled their dehumanized murder. Holocaust experiences aren't the everyday conversational material between two individuals, especially if one of them was not in the camps and ghettos. Because the survivor experiences feelings of shame, helplessness, disillusionment, and despair, he or she often finds it easier to quarantine the memories in isolation; for some survivors, it took decades before they found people interested in their experiences and were ready themselves to talk about them. On the other side of the relationship, when the listener learns of horrifying events, such as an SS man who killed a child by picking her up by her legs and slinging her against a brick wall, he or she feels an imperative to respond. When sitting face-to-face with the survivor, there is no way to avoid difficult silences or to simply turn a page or keep watching a film, hoping for a change of scene. As uncomfortable as this process is, it is a real part of the experience of learning first-hand about the Holocaust, and I hope to bring some amount of this to the reader.

But is this significant for the reader, who is not learning about it first-hand, but through the writing in this book? The reader can observe how I, the listener, interpreted Mr. Frank's experience, and can explore the ways in which he or she interprets it differently. Many of the first readers of this book expressed very different viewpoints about Mr. Frank's overall attitudes and reactions; this can be attributed, in part, to the way those attitudes were presented and how his reactions were explored.

I often began our dialogues with a question about Mr. Frank's underlying psychological state at the time of a particular event. Mr. Frank would retort, not mockingly but emphatically, that reflecting on how one felt was totally impossible when a gun was thrust in one's face. This in turn might lead to a discussion about how his ability to reflect on his experience was deadened suddenly in some cases but more gradually in others. Mr. Frank and I also discussed whether his understanding of human nature changed as different events occurred. When he found no reason to live, why did he not see simple dichotomies between comrades and enemies, but a spectrum of human tendencies and interests? Why did tragedy cause him to sink into himself without accusing all humanity of fundamental brutality? Did Mr. Frank attempt to find rational explanations for the predatory and base human acts that he witnessed?

Mr. Frank usually showed great urgency when speaking about these questions, but occasionally I encountered attitudes other than openness. Sometimes, Mr. Frank's usually free way of digressing dissolved into defensive deafness. He reacted strongly, for example, when I asked him, without any overtone of judgment, to compare his conditions with those of other prisoners. For a few moments, an episode of self-vindication ensued because Mr. Frank did not want me to view him as receiving special privileges and favors that gave him an advantage in the camps.

To address this question of special treatment and advantage, one must understand that the treatment, respect, and type of work that the prisoners received in a camp truly varied according to their classification—political prisoner, professional criminal, emigrant, Jehovah's Witness, homosexual, Jew—and according to the type of job he or she had. Beatings, torture, inanition, lack of medical treatment, and a paucity of contacts with the outside world all attacked the foundations of the prisoner's self, making it more difficult for the prisoner to act on impulses of goodwill, and making him or her suspicious of other prisoners' intentions and motives. Since none of the prisoners (except civilian criminals) had committed any real offenses, and because their imprisonment in the camps was for an indefinite period of time with no legal process of appeal, they experienced feelings of severe entrapment and psychological debilitation. The latter fact was particularly true for Mr. Frank, since his position of power as factory manager didn't guarantee that he would be immune from punishment. If there is one theme that I found to be clear in his recollections, it is that for all his uniqueness as a highly skilled tailor, it was not the key to his escaping death. As he says, there was no reason—it was an accident that he survived.

As head of the clothing factory at Lipowa, Mr. Frank was fortunate to work in an area that was covered and was not subject to the elements. Furthermore, he was skilled in a trade that the Nazis temporarily intended to exploit, although the genocidal program eventually took precedence over the value of Jewish labor. While at Lipowa, Mr. Frank had the unusual privilege of being allowed to bathe in private bathhouses in Lublin so he wasn't subject to lice, fleas, and sores; he also had separate accommodations from the rest of the prisoners, so he was less likely to get typhus. As a manager, he was bound, under the threat of death, to follow the commands he was given, but he was also able to alleviate some, but not all, of the acts of violence in his shop by befriending the SS supervisor Langfeld and making clothing for him. He was able to periodically leave the camp confines for camp business, but did not possess an open pass to come and go freely; he could be challenged by SS and police personnel outside the camp at any time. He was able to perform small favors for workers in the shop, though in his own estimation many of these actions were a common kind of sharing that didn't require great sacrifice. Instead of taking credit for performing these favors, Mr. Frank believes that he did what any ethical person (in his mind, a good Jew) would have done. Yet if someone were being tortured or beaten in the camp office or outside the shop on the lot, he was powerless to intervene.

He received some extra food, and occasionally alcohol or cigarettes, in the packages of material that officers brought him for their clothing. These gifts of appreciation increased his caloric intake, offered relief from the stresses of camp life, and allowed him to share with those closest to him. Even though Mohwinkel forbade him to make any clothing without his approval, Mr. Frank still undertook unofficial work; on the one hand, he knew the officers who wanted clothing could beat him or kill him if he refused, and on the other, he recognized that doing a favor might be useful for the future (although no Nazi ever became an ally whose assistance he could rely on). It's important to note that there was no standard economic system or set price for this unofficial work; it was the officer's fiat whether he de-

cided to give Frank anything. Thus, Mr. Frank couldn't be assured
that continued moonlighting would secure his survival or eliminate
day-to-day uncertainties and actions against prisoners.

Overall, then, Mr. Frank's standard of living at Lipowa was higher
than other prisoners there, but he was not immune to violence and
had no certainty that he or his family would live because of his position. His authority during that time doesn't explain why he survived,
as he was in a number of situations later where his skills and former
positions had absolutely no bearing on what happened to him; his
transport to Vaihingen instead of being executed in Auschwitz is one
such example. Later, in the Lublin Prison, Mr. Frank, like other prisoners, was not molested by guards and supervisors. The minimal work
he had to do could be stretched out, the rations were reduced but sta-
ble, and there were facilities for bathing. The prisoners were under
fewer physical stresses, but when all but thirteen of them were executed, the cleaner conditions and nourishment they'd had didn't save
them.

I sensed that Mr. Frank was reticent or defensive at the least hint
of comparisons to other prisoners, because to him, it was likely that I
would find his living conditions and privileges were superior to those
of other prisoners and thus determine that his survival was unfair. In
the simplest terms, many prisoners did whatever they could in order
to survive; sometimes their schemes, positions, and choices helped
them, but for most, these factors could not overcome the tightly organized system of extermination. As Lawrence Langer explains in his
book *Holocaust Testimonies: The Ruins of Memory,* our normal rules of
ethics don't apply when we judge a survivor, because our moral judge-
ments are based on the assumption that the prisoner always had the
opportunity to evaluate choices and select the best option, the one
that would keep the prisoner and his or her family and neighbors alive.
The prisoner confronted many situations that did not present this type
of moral choice with one best solution. Often the prisoner had no
choice at all; every choice would lead to some type of further suffering
or loss, or the situation would later change in a completely unforesee-
able way, overriding the prisoner's decisions and plans. Furthermore,
the prisoner had no way of knowing if the way the Nazis presented a
situation was the truth or a deception, making it impossible to know
whether a logical course of action would lead to survival. There are
numerous examples of situations like these in this book, from the
times Lipowa prisoners were randomly selected at roll call and exe-

cuted, to the unpredictable events leading to Frank's wife being taken
to the Majdanek death camp.

Another problem encountered in our dialogues was the occasional
absence of nuances and the tendency toward generalization, as we discussed different personalities, motives, and behavior. On the one
hand, to Mr. Frank, the Nazis with whom he had constant dealings
were representative of all Nazis, and all Nazis, he said, wanted to become "good killers." But contradictions emerged: he found there
were differences between the older and younger generations of Nazis,
between the educated and the uneducated, between the killers and
those reluctant to kill during the period of 1940 to 1941. Mr. Frank
didn't characterize the Nazis as personifying theological evil, but he
did metaphorically speak of them as "devils" whose schemes could be
intuited, if not predicted. His reluctance to unconditionally accept
that there were nuances in individual Nazis' behavior is understand-
able in light of the injuries and losses he sustained; if he admitted that
some Nazis weren't as bad as others, it would have seemed that he
were giving some of them the benefit of the doubt, when in fact, he
made it very clear that he found it impossible to explain how extreme
and horrible their crimes were. Because Mr. Frank found that mass extermination required the cooperation of German society, he was more
likely to lay blame at the feet of all Nazis and civilians than to concede
that certain individual Nazis were apathetic functionaries in the system, while others were more interested in the proceeds of expropri-
ated property than in murder.

Yet Mr. Frank often showed a marked perceptivity when I asked
him to contrast situations that he had already related. In these dialogues, he would scrutinize a situation as he didn't originally. For example, he spoke several times about what influenced him to consider
suicide and what dissuaded him from committing it: I mentioned several events in different camps when he was consumed with futility and
asked him to compare his thoughts on suicide in those different situations. In other cases, when he spoke about Jews like himself who became permanently confused about the meaning and existence of God
during and after the Holocaust, versus those who became more fer-
vently religious, our discussions catalyzed new explanations for the
phenomenon.

In summary, the discussions complement Mr. Frank's narrative by
adding new dimensions to the testimony and biography. They represent the passing down of history more accurately, elucidating the con-

tradictions and psychological pitfalls in the survivor's recollection of factual and deeply traumatic events. They examine multiple angles of Mr. Frank's experiences, which any sound interview should do, but with the added benefit of showing his initial reactions and how he developed his thoughts. Overall, the bulk of *Himmler's Jewish Tailor* is still the story of Mr. Frank's labor and concentration camp experiences, with which the reader can grapple as he or she is willing. Almost all of Poland's Jewish population was destroyed, the Lublin region's significant community included, and we are fortunate to be able to look directly into the maw of Nazi destruction by reading a Lublin survivor's rare testimony.

Several people are deserving of special commendation because they have given of their time and themselves in helping me complete this book. I express my greatest gratitude to Jacob Frank. At eighty-one, he committed himself to explaining the events and situations of his camp experiences during an arduous interviewing process. Relating memories of ghettoization, torture, and murder is dispiriting and disquieting, and I know it affected his moods, dreams, and physical health during the time of my visit. I hope he is pleased that this the book of his experiences contributes to the mounting documentation about the Holocaust and that his testimony brings more attention to Lublin among those cities whose Jewish populations were decimated.

My mother, Betsy Rosen Metzler, initially suggested this project when I first graduated from college, and she later encouraged me to undertake it when I began to consider it seriously. Since she and Mr. Frank's daughter are friends, she first heard some of Mr. Frank's stories before I did and recognized their uniqueness. Professor Lawrence Langer welcomed me, a stranger, into his home in Boston when I was on my way to New York to interview Mr. Frank; his advice ranged from the practical ("Make sure you have a reliable tape recorder"), to the historical ("Find out everything"), to the critical ("There are other memoirs in the world besides Primo Levi's and Willenberg's; you must read those other books"). Kimi Reith wonderfully wielded the critical magnifying glass through multiple readings and discussions, and a thimbleful of praise and appreciation in an acknowledgment does not begin to measure up to her contribution. I will have to return it both in love and in kind. Sue and Dougall Reith served both as excited first readers and referees of style; they also generously donated the cassette tapes I used for the interviews. While I interviewed Mr. Frank, Chapin Walker Day III gave me Manhattan lodgings in an unusual arrangement of excess rooms, thereby granting the closest thing to institutional support that this project received. I also want to express my sincere thanks to Alex Thomas, who translated German court documents and enthusiastically discussed the actions of the Lublin SS and the decisions of the court.

Himmler's Jewish Tailor

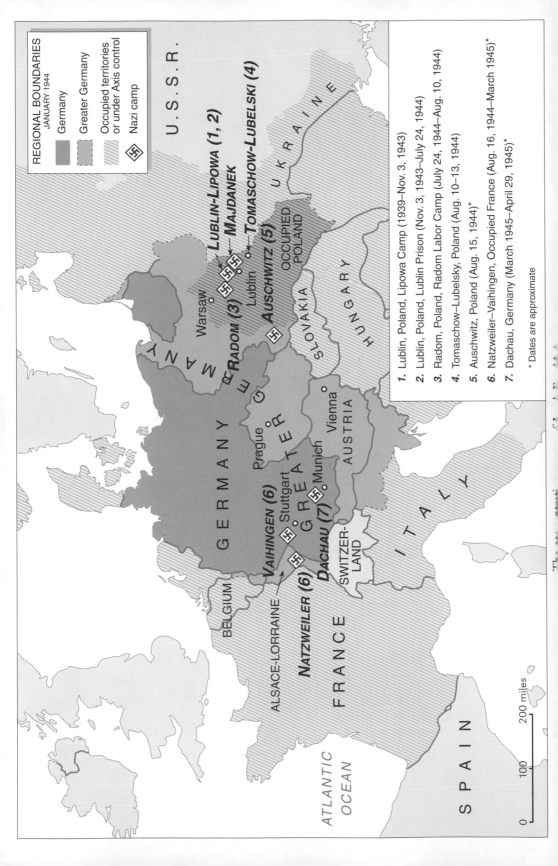

REGIONAL BOUNDARIES
JANUARY 1944

- Germany
- Greater Germany
- Occupied territories or under Axis control
- ⌗ Nazi camp

1. Lublin, Poland, Lipowa Camp (1939–Nov. 3, 1943)
2. Lublin, Poland, Lublin Prison (Nov. 3, 1943–July 24, 1944)
3. Radom, Poland, Radom Labor Camp (July 24, 1944–Aug. 10, 1944)
4. Tomaschow-Lubelsky, Poland (Aug. 10–13, 1944)
5. Auschwitz, Poland (Aug. 15, 1944)*
6. Natzweiler-Vaihingen, Occupied France (Aug. 16, 1944–March 1945)*
7. Dachau, Germany (March 1945–April 29, 1945)*

* Dates are approximate

U.S.S.R.

UKRAINE

LUBLIN-LIPOWA (1, 2)
MAJDANEK
TOMASCHOW-LUBELSKI (4)
AUSCHWITZ (5)

Warsaw

RADOM (3)

Lublin

OCCUPIED POLAND

SLOVAKIA

HUNGARY

G E R M A N Y

Prague

G R E A T E R

Vienna

VAIHINGEN (6)

Stuttgart

Munich

AUSTRIA

NATZWEILER (6)

DACHAU (7)

SWITZER-LAND

BELGIUM

ALSACE-LORRAINE

F R A N C E

I T A L Y

ATLANTIC OCEAN

S P A I N

0   100   200 miles

1
—

The Young Needleman

1925

WHEN I WAS TWELVE or twelve-and-a-half years old, my father want me to be a rabbi or something more in the Jewish way of life. My upbringing was in a very Hasidic home; my father was a Talmudic, all the time with a prayer book in his hand. In the middle of the night, he used to wake up and sit by a candlelight or a kerosene light, to sit for two or three hours and to pray and to study, and then he went back to bed. I was one boy from six girls, and I was watched by him that I shouldn't do something to hurt myself or do wrong, and I went to the *yeshiva*. Being twelve years old, looks like, I don't know if I was so smart, but the Dean from the *yeshiva* said to my father that I would need to go to another *yeshiva* what this is a higher education there. And the higher education school was outside Lublin, about twenty or twenty-five miles, with the name Mezzrich. *Mezzriche Yeshiva* was known not just in Poland but in other parts of the world, because there was also there students from the United States, from England, from France, and my father wants me to go there.

My father signed me up to go away to this *yeshiva*, but I was very attached to my family, especially to my mother. I had six sisters, and they always was after me to watch me wherever I went, telling me to walk slow or to eat slow. Being attached so much to them, I felt this was hard to go away from them, and I couldn't take my home with me.

Before I left, my father prepared me with a whole wardrobe, the Hasidic way how I was dressed, and I was supposed to go away in a couple of days; everything was prepared. Before I had to leave Lublin, my father put me to bed that I should take a rest—I had to travel by horse and buggy for ten or fifteen hours. He undressed me and he covered me with the blanket and he went down to the synagogue to

3

make the evening prayer. He figured when he'll come back, he'll dress me, and I had to leave by eight o'clock in the evening.

So the moment when my father left for the synagogue, I was making believe that I am sleeping, I dressed myself, and I escaped from home to an uncle of mine, my mother's brother's nephew. He was a tailor. I knew that I am doing a terrible thing to my father, but being attached to my mother and the six sisters, I couldn't take this moment to go away to be separated from them, and that's what made me escape from home. My father, when he came back and he didn't find me there . . . he was very, very disturbed and very angry. He was looking for me but he didn't know where I am. Then later when he found out, in a day or two, he said I am no more his son—he don't want to see me anymore before his eyes.

I couldn't go home that my father should not see me for a year and a half. I was by the uncle; I came home only to see my mother with the sisters during the time when my father was not home—I know in the morning he went to *schul*, to *daven*, to make the prayer— so this was only the time when I could come into the house. He didn't see me; I didn't see him.

In a year and a half, I learned the tailoring trade very quick. In that time, I was about thirteen-and-a-half years old. I decide I'll leave Lublin to go to Warsaw because my father had a sister in there, and I figure I'll be able to stay with her, and from there I'll go to work already in the trade what I learn in a year and a half.

I went to Warsaw; before I left I wrote a letter that I am coming. They was waiting in the train station, they picked me up, my aunt and uncle, they was very pleased to see me, they didn't know the circumstances that I didn't see my father, and he didn't want to see me, so I came home to them. They liked me very much—they gave me a separate room for myself, we start to talk, and I tell them the story. My aunt, she became a little bit cooler from how she was an hour before, but I'm still her brother's son, so she didn't show that she is not so happy.

The next day my aunt and my uncle start to have a talk with me, what my plans are, what I want to do, when I decide to go back home. I told them that I don't think that I'll go back home because my father doesn't want to see me, and I can't stay in the house where my father doesn't want me . . . "My plans are if I can stay here with you, my aunt and uncle. I am a tailor now, I learned my trade, this is already a year and a half that I am in this line, and I know very well this line, and I would like to go to a tailor to go to work. If I can stay here, I will even pay how much for food and for the room what this has to cost, because I know that if I can get a job, I will make a nice salary here"—because the wages in Warsaw for the working people was much higher than in Lublin.

She said, "Well, you have a very nice plan. This is nothing wrong to be a tailor. And I think your uncle, my husband, knows some people in this line, and he'll see to find some place for you to go to work." Didn't take too long, and in a couple of days, my uncle told me that he has somebody, he is a very, very good tailor, and if I would like he can take me there. I said, "Sure, I would love to." I came over to this tailor place, and my uncle took me in to this man, and he interviewed me and asked me what I knew about this trade. I tell him much, much more than what I really knew, but he tells me he'll try me out, and the next day I came and they gave me something to do, and it looks like he likes the work what I am doing, and I had a job.

I was there for a year and a half, and from there I went to another tailor. I told him . . . what this was not true . . . he asked me what I know about tailoring and I tell him I can make a jacket by myself because I know the whole trade.

But this was not true, because in the old place they didn't trust you to do work before you was ready . . . you had to be on a contract for three years, and I was there only a year and a half. But I learn in a year and a half, I tried to learn the trade what another boy would have to work for three years or four years.

And I remember he said, "OK, let's see what you can do." So he told me to come the next day in the morning.

I came in, and he gave me a bundle, a jacket—what this is cut pieces—and he told me to make the jacket . . . to prepare a first fitting, so everything was to order, a custom tailor.

They gave me this jacket what was already cut, and I made the first jacket, and I brought in the jacket from the shop to the showroom, where he had his desk. He was sitting there waiting where the customers came in there . . . and I went in with the jacket on the hanger. He examined the jacket, and he said, "Everything looks good, but this is not so . . . this is not the way what I like it to be." This is not the way from the work what he is doing, so he says, "It's *not* so good, but I see you have an idea, so if you'll be here for a couple a weeks or couple a months you'll learn—you'll do the way what I want you."

I was working in this place for four and a half or, I think, five years, and in that time, I was making a salary that in Lublin, they didn't believe; when I tell them how much I made a week, they said that I am a show-off, so much money I made. I used to make seventy-five *zlotys,* was like here seventy-five dollars a week . . . like a fortune with money in that time, and I was in that time only sixteen-and-a-half years old.

But before the high holidays, I decide to go home to Lublin. Two days before *Rosh Hashanah,* I came to Lublin; I didn't see my father this same day. In the meantime, in all the years, I was writing to my family, I was writing also to my father. He never answered me. He couldn't forget and to forgive me for what I really did. In his way, I think, he was right. He had one boy what he was raising for all his life, and he wants me to be a rabbi, and all of a sudden I became a tailor. So the first day I didn't see him, but a day later, *Erev Rosh Hashanah,* my father came back from the morning prayer from the synagogue, and I was in the other room and I heard him coming in. When he was starting to eat breakfast, I went over to the table and I said, "Good morning, Father. I know that you're not so happy maybe to see me, but now that this is *Erev Rosh Hashanah,* a whole year, the Jew has sinned. He goes to the synagogue and he says to God, 'I have sinned, and please forgive me for the wrong things through all the year.' And God is listening to him, and he is forgiving him. So I come to you, Father, I know that I did something terrible in that time, but there are so many years, I always went in the right way, I *davened* every day, and I'm doing my prayer every day, please forgive me what I did three or four years ago."

My father stood up from the chair, and he took me around the shoulders, and he start to cry, and he said, "You are my son. I am forgiving you. You did something that hurt me very much, but you are still my son and I loved you all the time, even when I didn't see you, and let's forget what this was. Tomorrow is the first day of *Rosh Hashanah.* Let's be a family together like this was before."

Twelve or thirteen years later, with this hell, when the extermination start—in the beginning, we didn't know if this is an extermination, but the conditions was very bad—and before my father went with my whole family in the line to go away, about three or four hours before, we was together, and we was talking . . . they gave an order that everyone from the ghetto has to come out,[1] and my father doesn't think that he'll see me anymore. Before they went out to go to the line, he said, "My son, I'm sure you'll be the one that'll survive

---

1. The liquidation of the Lublin ghetto in April 1942.

and you'll tell the world what really happened with us. I don't know what will happen with us, if we are going to live or we're going to die, but I can tell you, I had the feeling, that you will be there, you will survive, and you will tell the world what really happened to us, to the Jews."

ML: When you decided to leave home, was that a momentary impulse, because you were too afraid to leave and you didn't want to leave your mother and your sisters, or did you have a plan in your mind where you were going and what you were going to do?

JF: I think I had a plan because I had boys, friends, there in the neighborhood, but they was not so religious like in my home, like I was in that time. And I was a little bit not so . . . I was afraid to go away because I was attached to the family, but in the other way, I had in my mind I wouldn't want to be a rabbi or another clergyman like my father want me to be, I want to be more like the other boys. This is the answer what I can give you.

ML: That experience of deciding yourself who you wanted to be—did you ever think about that in light of your experiences in camps where choice was limited or you had no choice of what happened to you? To me there's a contrast between deciding what you can be yourself and then living in a very violent and rigorous world where it's decided for you.

JF: In that time in Europe, a father, when he told you something, you had to obey. That's how the upbringing from the religious home was. Being in that time twelve or twelve-and-a-half years old, I didn't agree with this type of thinking. At that time I was already thinking that I am entitled to say something what I want to be or to do.

ML: Later on, under the Nazis, you had no choices—you were taken to places against your will, your family was split apart—how did you see the world at that time? Did you believe that the camps operated with a *Führer* principle: the leader is all-important? Did you ever have feelings that this bore a resemblance to your father's authority, or did you see that here, in these later experiences, these dealings with authority were very different?

JF: I think the answer to this is, being in camp, again, you had to do what they want you to do. You couldn't decide the way what you want to do, because you couldn't escape. There was no way to escape somewhere else except if there was a way to run out from the camp, but we was living in a country what even if you run out from the camp and you'll do what you want to do—Poland was a very anti-

Semite country—they'll catch you and they'll give you over to the
Germans. There was no way to escape. In the time when I escaped
and I was twelve or twelve-and-a-half years old, I had a way to go to
an uncle, or from an uncle to go to Warsaw. I had ways where to carry
out my will. But in the time from the war, if something happens, you
couldn't do anything what you want to do, but you had to do what
you are told to do.

When I was growing up in the city Lublin, even as a little boy,
when it came to a Polish holiday, a Christian holiday, Christmas, the
Jewish children was afraid to go out in the street, because we was
afraid for the Polish boys what they'll beat you up or even they'll kill
you, because this Polish child heard the Jews was kidnapping Polish
children and that they sucked their blood for the holidays. This was
the way how the *Polaks* brought up their children.

This was the way what I was thinking when I was a small . . . in
the city where I was born . . . to always to be afraid. Not only this—
there was times when I was already a grown-up man what I was thinking in this way. When we was walking in the street and across the
street was a policeman walking, you notice you didn't do anything
wrong, but you was afraid that he can accuse you that you did something wrong, to come over to arrest you or beat you up—that's the
way how Jews was brought up in Poland.

ML: What do you remember as the differences between the Warsaw Jewish community and the Lublin community?

JF: The Warsaw community comparing to the Lublin Jewish community was a big difference. Warsaw was a big city; was almost a million
people, or 750,000, I don't know exactly, but was more the big city, was
not so anti-Semite. Maybe was the same, but they didn't show out because everybody was busy with rush, running, running, running, a little
similar to New York . . . in that time, the difference from a small to a big
city. The Jew in Warsaw was living more freely than the Lublin Jew.

ML: Were there fewer rumors about ritual murder and Jews suck-
ing the blood of Christians for holidays?

JF: Not what I heard in Warsaw. You see, in Warsaw, the people
was more occupied to improve their lives. And to improve their lives,
they had to work harder. And to work harder, they was always more
occupied, not to think about other things. In the smaller places what
they didn't know this better life, they had time to think about things
like anti-Semitism . . . what they was thinking was: if you'll think bad

about the Jew, you'll take away from him, and you'll have better. If you'll make more miserable his life, you'll improve your life.

It also has a lot more to do—I am talking from Lublin, what I remember as a child—has much more to do with the teaching from the church, from the clergy about the Jews, because the Polish men or women was attached to the life of the church, and they was listening more to the priest. And the way what the clergy from the church was teaching in that time was not so good for the Jew.[2]

ML: How do you know what the Polish clergy was teaching?

JF: How we know? Because when you was playing with the little boys, with a Polish little boy, and when he said something what made you think this is not the way what this should be, you asked him, the little boy, "Who told you that?" He said, "The priest told me this." That's how you know.

There was times not only from the little boys, when you played with them . . . even much before the war broke out, in the early thirties, '31, '32, if you went to the movies, and the Jewish woman was sitting watching the movie, she was wearing a fur coat. Behind her back was sitting a Polish guy, a Polish boy, a youngster . . . with a razor blade he cut. When the woman went home, she saw her fur coat, her Persian lamb coat was cut. She didn't even feel it . . . but she knew somebody behind her did this. He was doing this to destroy, not to steal.

---

2. A number of other factors contributed to Polish anti-Semitism. Poland suffered a loss of exports to the new Soviet Union in 1919, and Poland continued to carry a considerable national debt through the 1930s; thus, the Polish economy was suffering. After the First World War, when Poland waged war in 1920 against Lithuania and the Ukraine in order to aggrandize territory, the Russians, Austrians, and Germans in those areas persecuted Jews who settled there. Additionally, the Polish-Russian border shifted many times in the decades preceding the World War II, and the Jews residing there (the highest concentration in Europe) bore the blame for economic hardships and the condition of the peasant-serfs. Former Russian Jews were suspected of not holding true allegiance to the Polish state. "[U]nemployment . . . , insufficient credit, and unstable currency and inexperienced administrators" were all obstacles to Polish modernization (Levin 1973, 167). Besides practicing a different religion, Jews had the appearance of, and in fact were, an insular community who spoke their own language and practiced their own legal tradition from the Talmud; their dress, businesses, and associations were easily identifiable (Levin 1973, 165–69). While cultural differences and economic depression alone are not causes of violence, they form a basis for xenophobia and nurture the perception that a group can be victimized and used as a surrogate target for frustration and resentment.

2

Tailoring in Lublin

1931–1938

BEFORE THE WAR, when I came back from Warsaw to Lublin, I decide to open a shop. In that time, I was maybe about seventeen or seventeen-and-a-half years old. I was young and I didn't know how to start. So I went down in mine home where I was born, and I start to talk to people from the neighborhood, where they know me when I was a little boy from twelve or thirteen years old. I told them the story, "I just came back from Warsaw, and I am a very good tailor, maybe you know somebody he needs a suit." Talking with people, we were standing in the street . . . one had a store, he was dealing in flour. So he said, "If you say that you came from Warsaw, and you are so a good tailor, how about you make me a suit?"

And he asked me, "How much will you charge?"

"How much you think the suit will be worth it, so much you'll pay me."

He bought some material and I bought a machine, and I put up a shop—a machine with a table in the house where my parents was living. There was a couple of rooms there, and I took a place in the kitchen. We didn't have too many rooms there—was three rooms—in Europe, they didn't count the kitchen, so if you want to count, it was four rooms. Four rooms and we was seven children, but in that time when I came back from Warsaw, two sisters was already married, so only was five children with me. I took away a piece of space in the kitchen, and I made a shop there. I made the suit ready—it looks like he was very, very pleased, and he send a cousin or another relative, and I start to become busy.

Across the street from where I was born was a little store what they had things for tailor trimmings—buttons, threads, other things,

10

and this store was run by a young woman and her sister. When I made a suit, I went in the store to buy some buttons, and the sister, her name was Dora, was helping out, and that's how I met my wife. After a couple of times what I come over to buy trimmings for the suits, I ask her out for a date, and she accepted. We start to date, and after a year—was not even a year—I married her.[1] After a year later, we had the one boy, and after three years the other boy.

Her father was not so happy that his daughter fell in love with me, and that I fell in love with her, because, you know, he didn't like me. He didn't like for his daughter to have a son-in-law for a tailor because he was a businessman, and in that time, he was not a poor man. But so happen, his wife became sick, she had cancer, and she died. She was the businesswoman—the whole business was on her shoulders, and after a certain time, he had to give up the business because at that time, everything was sold on credit. Their business was wholesale, and all the businesspeople bought merchandise from them. When they heard that the head from the business died, they didn't pay the bills, so he lost all his fortune. When he lost everything, so he accept me.

Her father was the president from a synagogue with the name *Kockler schul*. I really don't know the meaning from this word *Kockler*—the congregation was mostly businesspeople, and also the intelligentsia, the lawyers, doctors, their children. In this synagogue, you couldn't get a place except if somebody died—the son took over the seat, or another relative took over this place. When I became the son-in-law from the president, I became a member also from the *schul,* because before, they wouldn't let me in because I was a tailor.

Working in my parents' apartment for about a year, my parents didn't let me spend money—food and other things didn't cost me, so I kept the money what I made, and in a year I made a nice bundle. In that time, I had maybe about seven, eight hundred *zlotys,* the value what I am figuring from today, here, was like maybe seven, eight thousand dollars. I was a rich young man.

From there, I had already a whole clientele, Jewish customers. Most of the businesspeople, they was in the flour business. I found out to have a Polish clientele is a little more important than a Jewish clientele. You couldn't make a lot of money from Jewish men because most of them, they was poor. They couldn't afford to pay a price what you could make if you'll go for yourself, so I start to look around for a

1. In 1932.

place outside the Jewish community. Looks like in that time I was not big, eighteen years already, but they told me I am a smart boy. I rent a place, two rooms, one small room and the other a little larger. I moved the shop to this place, and this was on the Krakow Street, in a hotel—they also rented some rooms for business . . . the English Hotel, the *Hotel Angelsky* they called this in Polish.

You know, I had a couple of suits already in the work . . . I used to sit by myself and to work there in the hotel. The windows looked out, was like a main street, so I left the light burning a whole night—I figure the people will see that the light is burning, so I am busy, very busy. I didn't have nothing else to do; I only took with me two or three suits from the customers from the Jewish community. The tailors across the street—if you didn't put in Venetian blinds or if you didn't cover the windows, you could see inside the shops—so even the tailors used to talk between them—I found out later when I joined the union.

"You are a young Fritz, you are a young man, and right away you are so busy you are working day and night?! The whole night I see the light in your windows!"

They start to be jealous of me, and this was just a made-up story. But I still was figuring how to get in a Polish customer. I had to pay rent and in that time, even the rent was not so high, but for me, not doing too much business, I had to do something to be able to keep up this place. Across the street was another hotel with the name *Hotel Sasky,* and over there was a store from yard goods. The yard goods from the store came from Yankowsky, a mill from a special place in Poland, they call this Bieliz, *Bielsko*—a whole town was factories what they used to make yard goods, men's goods. The factory Yankowsky had there their own store. Here also in the United States, many designers have special stores what they are selling only their goods.

Saturday morning, I went down and I was standing almost by the door from the store, to watch the people what they're going in, and what they will buy when they go out with packages, how many cuttings of suits or pants they are buying. I was standing maybe about ten or fifteen minutes, or maybe longer, and to watch people going in and out, some of them buying, some of them not. One man bought maybe about five or six suits, and the salesman made a package, and he packed this in nice wrapping paper, with the name Yankowsky, and he paid, or he didn't pay . . . I was waiting that he should come out.

I made up my mind to do something. What I did is, when the

man went out from the store, I went over to him and I said to him, "I am a very good tailor and I saw that you bought I don't know how many suits. I have my shop across the street, and I just moved in here not too long ago. I would like you to try me; I would like to make a suit for you. And the price? I don't know who is your tailor, but I assure you the suit will be as good as what your tailor is dressing you in. It will cost you much cheaper, and if you wouldn't like it, if you wouldn't like my work and the suit wouldn't be to your satisfaction, I'll pay you back for the material."

He was standing with me, and it took five or six minutes, and I am talking to him, and he is standing and listening to what I am talking to him. He said, "You know, I like how you approach somebody to go out from a store and to tell them so a story what you told me. I'd like to go over with you, what you told me was across the street, I'd like to see your shop."

I was very happy to hear this, and I took him over to my shop. I opened with my key the door, there was nobody there, and he saw there a mannequin, and one suit hanging what I brought with me when I had an order from the Jewish customer from the old shop. He looked at the mannequin where the jacket was hanging . . . he didn't know too much if this is good or not; if he likes it, I didn't know. But he said, "You know, I'll take the chance, I'll leave you one cutting to make me a suit." He unpacked the package what he bought across the street, and he left one suit material.

I took the measurement from him, and I tell him, "I am a little bit busy now"—this was not true—and I gave him a time to come for the first fitting in the next week or almost two weeks, and he said to me, "You think you'll be able to finish?" Before he went over to my shop, he looked down at me because he was tall and comparing to him I was very little and very thin, and he said, "You are sure that you can make a suit for me?"

I said, "Please, you try me, and if the suit will not look good, like I said before, I'll pay you for the material. You couldn't risk too much, and you'll save money, I'm sure you'll save a lot of money." He didn't ask me the price.

I kept the suit for three or four weeks after I finished, to show that I am busy. Also, I have to say, when he came into my shop, nobody was there. I opened the door, he said, "Nobody is working! Where is your shop?" I said, "Today is Saturday. I am Jewish. I'm religious; I am not working Saturday."

"But you're taking orders?"

I didn't know what to say, so I had to find something to tell him.

I knew that I know my trade, I know that he'll be pleased, and he tried on the suit. The showroom was with three mirrors, and he looked around and he turned in this side and that side and all the sides, and he looked at the slacks—in that time we used to make a three-piece suit—trousers and a vest and a jacket. Looking at him, how he stays in the three mirrors and he turns in every side, I saw that he likes it. I ask him, "How do you like my work? How do you like the suit?"

He said, "It looks OK."

"Only OK? I think the suit looks beautiful."

"Maybe if you want to use this word, 'beautiful,' then I am very pleased. How much is the suit?"

I ask him, "Who was your tailor till now?" He gave me the name from his tailor—a Polish tailor—his name was Adamchek. I knew the Adamchek, I knew his shop, and Adamchek was not really so a good tailor: I knew that I am better than he was. I knew already how much the Adamchek is charging for a suit—I don't know how much he's charging *him*, but I know the general price . . . I belong already to the union—so when he asked me the price, I tell him with 25 or 30 percent less than what the Adamchek is charging.

I ask him, "Is this not too much?" He said, "No," and he took the suit.

The same day what he took the suit home, in two or three hours he came back with the whole bundle, with the whole four cuttings from material what he was buying, to make for him a whole wardrobe. He was a head from a city government office—from the agricultural office. When he brought me this bundle, he told me, if I'll have time, I should rush with these suits because he has something in his mind, to do for me something, business-wise. So when I had already four suits, and I had about two suits from before what I took with me from the Jewish customers, I advertise for a helper. Two people came and I put two people to work. I cut the four suits—I had the pattern what I cut from the first suit—and I was in business. I start to be busy with two people working.

Took about two months, I was busy with the four suits, because everything in that time was not like here—here you have machines, line stitch machines, other machines—everything was made by hand, every stitch in that time. I made for him the four suits and he came and picked up—not all four suits together—every two weeks or three weeks he picked up another suit. I knew that he was very pleased.

He said, "You will have me for a customer forever."

I ask him, "You told me that you have something in your mind, to do for me something business-wise. I remember you told me a couple weeks ago."

"Yes, I want to talk with you about this. I am the head from a big office." By the way, his office was on the Sklodowsky Street, what was in the same street what the Nazis took away buildings from the Poles, from the city government, and they made offices[2]—but this time what I am talking was in the early thirties, '32 or '33, I think. He told me he is the head from the agricultural office, he has a lot of people working in this office . . . he is wearing the suits to the office, and they already admire the suits what he is wearing. And he told them the story that he found a tailor and that I have my shop there—but they cannot buy four or five suits like he bought, or to pay cash, you know, right away, but if I want, he'll send me all the people what are buying material by the Yankowsky. He has a deal with the Yankowsky too, the same deal he wants to make with me: every office-man what he is working, when he needs to buy suit material, he goes in there to the Yankowsky store, he gives him a written paper from the office that the head is responsible for the money, and he buys the suit material or two suits or for his wife, and the man gives him out the suit material. The suit material what he is buying, he doesn't charge him; he sends the bill to the head from the office. And every month, the head takes off from the office-man's salary, and to Yankowsky he sends every month payment for the material. The same thing he was doing with the Adamchek . . . the Adamchek is also tailoring for his office people what is working for him, and also when they have to pay money for the suit to Adamchek, the Adamchek also sends the bill to him. If I would like to do the same thing, he can take some office people what they is working there and send me some customers, and he'll be responsible for the money. Instead to give the customer the bill, I should send him the bill and every month I'll get a part for how many *zlotys* a month he is taking off from their salary.

So in that time I start to be very, very busy. I hire another two men—I had four men already working for me. Every first of the month, I receive a check in the mail from all the names, from three or

2. See Chapter 19, "Majdan-Tatarsky."

four or ten, and later, the whole office I was working for them. Instead to have from one customer ten dollars or fifteen dollars a month, I receive $150 or $200 from all the customers, the names . . . he paid so-and-so much. My wife helped me with the bookkeeping, and I was in business.

In that time, before I opened the shop . . . this I forget to tell you . . . before I opened this place in *Hotel Angelsky,* I decide to go to Germany. Was in 1932, I heard that there is a school, they have a system for designing men's suits. The system is so you don't have to work very hard with the fittings to charge too much. You see, when you take the measurement from a customer, you watch his figure, how he is, and the system gives you all the knowledge how to get the cutting and the fitting right. So I went to Germany . . . we didn't know from a Hitler in that time. I was there four weeks, and I came home, I start to look for this place, the *Hotel Angelsky,* and I start to be very busy.

I had a whole book with names from Polish customers. They was really better than the Jewish customer, because the Jewish customer, like I said, he couldn't afford, and he was a harder customer to please than a Pole, I have to say . . . and this went on till 1938. From there I moved from *Hotel Angelsky* to an apartment with six rooms, with a balcony—this was the main street, in the corner from the Krakowsky Street, the *Platz Luketka.* I had a big room for the shop and a big showroom. Till 1938 I was very, very busy. I had a very, very beautiful home. I became known as one from the best from the young tailors in Lublin. Was very, very good tailors, but they was much older than I was, and people, they used to look for my type of work because it was more modern.

In 1937 or 1936—I don't remember when I moved—there came out an order from the Polish government that all judges and all prosecutors and all lawyers, they had to wear special uniforms in the court. They used to wear all civil clothes, but if they'll appear in court for a trial, they all have to wear special robes over their clothes. In Polish they call this a *toga.* In the front of the robe, used to be a pleated—I don't know what you call this in English—the judge was wearing a pink one . . . in Polish a *jabot,* pleated, pinned on the robe. The prosecutor was wearing blue, the lawyer was wearing white or another color, but nobody from the tailors could make the robes. When I was in Germany in 1932, they taught us to make so a robe that was pleated with a yoke on top, and from the yoke was pleated the back and the front, and I was only the one in Lublin what I knew how to make.

When the order came out I was reading the paper, and I had a customer, he was a Jewish lawyer, his name was Hochgemeine. I just was reading in the paper there came out the new law, and I learned in Germany in 1932 how to make, because over there in Germany they used to wear already the robes and coats. So the Hochgemeine came in, I made for him the suit, and I tell him the same day I bought the paper that a lawyer or a prosecutor or a judge wouldn't be able to sit in the courtroom without a robe. And I said to him, "Mr. Hochgemeine, I know how to make this." I had a book with all the sketches what I made in the school in Munich—in *München*—and I brought in the book, and I put up the page what the robe was there.

"Yes, you're right! This is exactly what we'll have to wear. I'll go and buy material. I'll be the first you'll make me so a robe."

And this was the case. It was black material, a very thin material, and I made him the robe. From this robe, most of the lawyers and the judges, they became my customers. I became busy with making the robes, I was busy for months and months to make . . . in that time, I had four or five people working for me. Like I said in the beginning, 90 percent I had a Polish clientele, but after when I made the first robe, the lawyer Hochgemeine, he send a lot of friends, also lawyers. In that time, I start to have a mixed clientele, Jewish lawyers, gentile lawyers, judges—was not too many Jewish judges, but lawyers, there was some.

I had one lawyer, his name was Litsky. He was one from the best lawyers, not in Lublin, but in Poland. They used to use him also in France. It went around between the people in Lublin—if somebody is sentenced to death, he freed this guy from the death sentence. This Litsky became my client. So I start to have a better clientele, lawyers, judges, accountants, bookkeepers, office people . . . I start to be very known as one from the best young tailors in Lublin . . . till 1938.

I had some customers from the publishers from Polish papers. I had the publisher from the Polish paper *Glos Lubelsky*, the *Words from Lublin*. This was a fascistic, an anti-Semitic paper, a right-wing paper. From most of the papers, if they had something bad to write about Jews, you could find in this paper. The publisher from the paper—I forgot his name—was my client, from 1935 or 1934, for many years. But in 1938, start to be articles in this paper, or in other Polish papers, that the Polish people shouldn't go in to Jews to buy goods, or to have things made by Jewish people. In 1938 they start also to be very friendly with Hitler Germany. Every day was getting more articles in this paper about Jews, about how Polish people shouldn't go in Jewish stores. In that time when I read the articles in papers, I was figuring I am so a good tailor, they will have to come to me, even when they write in the papers not to go to a Jewish tailor or other Jewish businesspeople. Looks like I was mistaken.

I still had a suit in the work for the publisher from the paper what he was writing the anti-Semitic articles.

ML: He was writing some of the articles too?

JF: I don't know if he was the writer, but he was the publisher—he was responsible for the paper, what this is in the paper, no? That's what a publisher is.

The same client has to come for a fitting, to fit a jacket, the first or the second fitting, and I receive a telephone call from him that he will appreciate if I can come with the jacket to make the fitting in his house. He was the first what I heard this—but I understood what he means because of the articles in his paper not to go into a Jewish business to buy something or to go into a Jewish tailor. He was afraid that somebody from the Polish side will see him coming in . . . like I said, I had my shop on the second floor: he'll go in the hall and he'll go up on the stairs, and maybe someone will see him that he is going up to a Jewish tailor.

I said to him, "I am sorry, I cannot come to you because I am very busy—this is the one thing. And the other thing"—this is the first time what I receive so a call from a client—"If you don't feel good, I made you many suits, you have suits to wear, so I'll wait for you when you feel better, and you'll come and fit the jacket."

This was my answer. In that time, I could afford to answer in this way, because my name was Mr. Frank, in Polish it's *Pan Frank*. *Pan Frank*—the "a" is an "ah" in Polish. After the telephone call, I went into the other room where my wife was there, this was not the business place, but the living quarters. And I told her the story . . .

"You know, Dora, I think that's the answer from the articles. He didn't want to come to fit the jacket because he doesn't want some *Polak* to see him come into a Jewish tailor," and I tell her what I told him and she says, "You did the right thing."

I was figuring that because he is the publisher from *Glos Lubelsky*, maybe that's why he doesn't want someone should see him. But looks like later on, many other Polish customers, they was afraid to come to me, and this business starts to fall down . . . from the Polish clientele went down maybe 90 percent. But I still had a mixed clientele—Jewish intelligentsia, the lawyers, prosecutors, judges. So business-wise was not for me so bad, but I had also five or six people working for me, so I had to release two or three because the amount of orders fell down.

What they was printing in the paper not to go into Jewish stores or to Jewish craftspeople . . . they used to put up people, with signs, like here when there is a strike. They had signs on the front on the chest:

"DON'T GO IN! IT'S A JEWISH STORE!"

This was in the end of '38, in the beginning of '39, and they already felt something cooking, that a war would break out, but they didn't think about . . . the anti-Semitic way was more important than to think what will be if a war will break out. Not only this—they used to picket most of the Jews, not most but all Jewish stores . . . not only to carry the signs not to go in Jewish stores—was restaurants what belonged to Polish owners, and was big signs in the window:

"A JEW AND A DOG ARE NOT ALLOWED TO COME IN THIS RESTAURANT."

ML: How do you say that in Polish?

JF: *Zhyt n sou* . . . I forgot the Polish language. I'll say this in German:

"JUDEN UND HUNDS IST DIE EINTRICH VERBOTEN."

This is:

"JEWS AND DOGS, THE ENTRANCE IS CLOSED FOR THEM."

This was the way from before, very, very close before the Second World War broke out. The anti-Semitism was so big in Poland, not just in Lublin. In Poland. There they didn't think . . . 1938, the Germans, they are sending over spies, and they'll be finished in a couple of days, a couple of weeks, there'll be no Poland anymore.

3
—

Invasion, Escape, Entrapment

September 1939–Early 1940

I WAS LIVING IN LUBLIN in the Krakowska Street; this was outside
the Jewish community. I had my business place there. In Europe, was
a system not like here . . . here a tailor has to have a store on the
ground floor in the front from the sidewalk or from the street in the
lower part. But in Europe, there was some craftspeople what they had
their business downstairs in stores, but most of the craftspeople, you
could have your shop, your business place, in your apartment two or
three floors higher than where you live.

Across the Krakowska street when I looked out the window, was a
tall building, the fire department was nearby. And I don't know how
to describe this place: was a tower, with a big clock, and everyday
eight o'clock in the morning, came out a fireman with a —what do
you call this when somebody died from the army and they blow the
horn? He came out and he blowed out a hymn . . . it was time to start
the day's work, eight o'clock.

I was on the second floor with a balcony in the front . . . the balcony with the windows. When I went out on the balcony, I could see
the time from the clock and I could see the fireman blowing the city
hymn . . . the sound, the way, I don't know how to describe this . . .
he played out something everyday.

Before the war broke out, the Polish city government said that
every block has to have a committee. Two or three months before we
know that any day the war would break out, we have an idea. They start
to organize committees from every block, that if there'll be a bombing,
we should be on top of the buildings, for the air raid, with some sand.
To extinguish the fire before the fire department came in, we should
take care of it! But this was ridiculous . . . but that's what was.

20

The Germans had spies what they prepared from months and months before, so when the German aeroplanes was flying, some from the spies show this place from the tower, from the fire department, and they bombed the tower. I was across the street maybe five hundred or six hundred feet, maybe a thousand feet. They bombed the building where I was with my family, but the bomb fell down on the sidewalk, and it didn't explode. When we start to run down to hide ourselves, we saw the bomb was maybe about fifty or twenty-five feet below; in the grave, in the ground, was lying the bomb.

After the first day when I saw they bombed, the whole neighborhood there where I was living was straightened out to the ground from the bombs—with the tower, with the fire department, everything was gone. After a couple hours when we went down from the hiding place lower in the basement somewhere, me and my wife . . . in that time I had two boys, what they was named Monyek and Nunyek,[1] when we came out from the hiding place we saw this mess, with so many dead, the ambulances start to speed around . . . was a wreck, was a mess, we didn't know what to do.

My parents and the whole family was living close by in the Jewish section. More of the places they are bombing there was nearby buildings what belongs to the city government, so I was afraid again they'll come to bomb. They did come the next day too; so I took my family and we went down to live where my parents was living.

ML: And what was your family's impression of the time? I'm assuming it's complete chaos, no one knows what's going to happen . . .

JF: So what kind of question could you ask . . . you was waiting all to be killed or maybe the war will come to an end, that was the impression! You didn't think, you didn't have something else to think, where could you go?

ML: What about food?

JF: Everybody before, like I said, we had an idea, two months before the war broke out, everybody was preparing themselves to go out to buy how much they could. Everybody had food prepared. But over a couple of weeks, when the Germans was already there and occupying Lublin, they gave out rationing cards, and that's how you could manage with food . . . but it was not enough.

ML: And Jewish grocers and butchers were supposed to accept

---

1. In Hebrew, "Moshe" and "Noah."

these ration cards and only give out a certain amount of food. Do you remember people complying with that?

JF: They was complying, they was complying, they knew this is no other way than to comply with the orders because we know this is not the fault from the bakery or the butcher, he has only so much food to give . . . and everybody can get so much what the law told them to, from the rationing cards what they are entitled to get. So was not a thing to fight or to argue with this. Was some times, some places when they came in with the cards and they was standing in line, and they came in to the door, or to the window, was no more food, so they went home without food. What could you do? So you was waiting for the next day, or the next second or the third day.

It was not pleasant even before they start to exterminate us . . . not a pleasant life. But after a couple of days, you get used to it. And especially a Jew—a Jew says, "God wants it this way, so we have to believe that's the way it should be, but God will help us to live, to live with hope, that the next day, the next week, it'll be better." But was not this way the next day or the next week—it became worse.

———

Lublin was from the first cities what the Germans occupied. The moment when they came in, the 18th of September, 1939, looks like they knew right away where the Jewish community lives. I'm sure that the Poles helped them in this. They called out through megaphones that all the Jewish men from fourteen to sixty years old had to come out from the apartments. They took us together on the street . . . was in that time about five or six thousand people. Only the men—the women with the children, they said they can stay home. They put out tables there, a lot of Nazis went around with reflection lights, and they concentrate all the Jews . . . in that time, there was also not just the Jews, they took everybody, Poles, the Polish-population men too.

Under the gun, they took us to a certain place with the name Lipowa Street. This was what they used to have horse races there, or the circus when they used to come, Barnum and Bailey from the United States. The lot was connecting the Lipowa and the Sklodowsky Streets, was about five or six blocks, the length and also the width. From the Jewish community till Lipowa Street for a mile we walked in the line. When we came there, a German Nazi came out: the name from the Nazi was Gunst;[2] his rank was a *Standartenführer*, this is the rank in English like a colonel. He made a speech and he said that all the Poles should go to the right side, and the Jews to the left side.

After two to three hours they released the all Polish men, and they kept us for two days and two nights without water, without food outside in the lot. Even though was September was not so cold, but the couple of days what we was there, was very windy, very cold . . . a lot of Jews, they died from heart attack, from fear, from cold, from hunger, from thirst.

Then they registered us. They was working late in the whole day, late in the night, they registered everybody. They didn't give you no reasons for the registration . . . the reason was you have to do what I am telling you to do . . . right away from the beginning. If you didn't walk fast enough, they show you the reason that you should walk. They gave you with the gun over your shoulders, over your head. And you fall down, or somebody was killed, the others should see what they did to him so you know you have to run—this was the reason.

You didn't know with whom you were sitting—just with Jews. You was so occupied in your mind what will be the next moment, the fear was so big, was so great, you didn't see even the next one, the next man to you. Was some from the neighborhood, but when they tell you to go down, when you came down from the house, they start to run you with the guns:

"*Run! Run! Run! Run! Run! Quick! Schnell! Schnell! Schnell! Fast!*"

You didn't have time to look, even if you know somebody near you is your next neighbor, you didn't see him, he didn't see you, because you was occupied from thinking what'll be the next minute, if they'll kill you or if they'll shoot you.

It so happened that I was together with my father, but also I had about six brother-in-laws, what they went—but we was separated. We didn't discuss nothing . . . when we was there for the two days, was no discussion one with the other at all. We was sitting like mutes, like we don't have voices. Everybody was sitting with the head down and to look nearby, some was with a heart attack, some was dead. That's all what we saw.

2. For more information about Gunst, see Chapter 20, "Officers."

But after two days, two nights, another SS man came out, and he spoke through the megaphone.

"All of you that was registered here, you'll be released soon after this, and when we need you we'll call you. And if you wouldn't appear on this lot to work, we have your addresses and your names and you'll be shot with your family." [3]

After the speech they opened the gates, and they let us go home. I don't know what happened to the people what they died there. It's like in a war on the front when the soldiers run and one falls dead; the next line runs again and the dead is lying there. The same system was like in that time with the dead.

We was only relieved, we came home to cry and to laugh and to kiss and to hug our families, the wife or the children or the parents— was like a Jewish holiday . . . we survived. But the surviving was not for too long.

The Nazis wanted a Jewish council, but they didn't select; they had an order, and they put out the posters on the walls that the Jewish people should know. The community decided on twelve people, and the Nazis said, "You'll be the *Judenrat*. You'll represent all the Jews from Lublin. You'll be responsible for the orders what we'll give out, and you have to carry out the orders." [4] They chose one from the twelve, his name was Kestenberg, and they told him, "You will be responsible for the twelve and for all the Jews from Lublin from the orders what we'll give you. We'll talk only to you."

Kestenberg was a very known citizen from the Jews in Lublin. He had a business from writing things, from books to sell, all kind of things what you write, a very big business. Not like here a stationer's . . . but special . . . frames for pictures, typewriters, more for school things, one from the biggest. This kind of business he had off the main street, the Krakow Street, like here the Fifth Avenue, the Madi-

3. Mr. Frank recalls that the registration took place in September, soon after the invasion, while German court documents give a later date of December 4, 1939. The documents also state that Jewish males as young as twelve had to register; Frank remembers the minimum age of fourteen (*SSPF,* 8369).

4. According to Mr. Frank, the *Judenrat* in Lublin was derived from the *Gemeinde,* the previously existing body of leaders in the community. Because the Nazis allowed the Jewish community to choose its own representatives, the Nazis fed the Jews' illusion that they still had some measure of self-determination. By believing that compliance with Nazi orders would give them room to maneuver and save more people in the long run, Jewish leaders established a fatal pattern of acquiescence.

son Avenue. He was a very, very respected citizen; I am talking from before the war . . . that's why the Nazis chose him, because they was looking for information from who was before the war the knowledgeable, respected citizens. They was looking for the intelligent Jews. They kept them to carry out their orders, and then later they killed them when they didn't want the intelligent part to lead the Jewish people from Lublin.[5]

The next day, the *Judenrat* start to work. They start to receive orders from the SS headquarters . . . by the way, the headquarters from Hitler and Himmler's staff for the whole Poland was in Lublin, on the *Kruel Leszcynskiego* Street, this is in English King Leschinsky Street. The main leader to exterminate the Jews was from the beginning, from 1939, the *Obergruppenführer* Odilo Globocnik. This was the mass murderer what he was in charge to liquidate the Jews from Lublin, and from around Lublin.[6]

So the *Judenrat* start to receive orders from the Nazis. The liaison officer from the SS was the *Standartenführer* Gunst. He was living on the Shopena Street; this was one block from the Lipowa. He gave an order to Kestenberg that everyday the SS need a thousand Jews to send to work . . . for cleaning projects, other projects. After a couple days was an announcement near the building from the *Judenrat* that Jews have to come to register to go to work, and if they wouldn't come, then the Nazis will come to take them and it will be much worse.

The *Judenrat* organized a labor office and a Jewish police. The Jewish police guys, they went into the houses, and they act like police from other nationalities. They used to go to every house and take a

5. Terrorizing and eliminating the potential leaders made it difficult for the community to organize revolts. The Nazis also researched the members of the community who had the greatest wealth.

6. Austrian Odilo Globocnik, Higher SS and Police Leader for the Lublin region, was in charge of setting up and directing the SS and police posts in the East. He founded a network of labor camps in Lublin for private profiteering under the umbrella of the *Ostindustrie* company. Since all population transfers to Lublin were under his supervision, he could use people from those transfers for manpower in his industries, until the time came when they had to be exterminated. Under Himmler, he served as chief of the massive Jew-killing program in Poland, called Operation Reinhard. Earlier, in 1940, he was in charge of the execution of Polish intelligentsia, and planned and initiated the eviction of the Polish population from the Lublin region. Globocnik became head of the Treblinka, Belzec, Majdanek, and Sobibor killing centers in 1941, founding the last three (Marszalek 1986, 37–8).

couple of men out between the ages twenty and twenty-three everyday to work, then they escorted the Jewish workers to the places
where the Nazis want them to come. They was there a whole day
working, and in the evening they let them go home. From the thousand workers became two thousand, and three thousand later, and so
on and so on. This went on for two or three months.

The Jewish police were helping the Nazis in their work, but they
didn't create division in the community, not entirely . . . was a little
bit of resentment from the Jewish community to the police, because if
there was a selection—a selection means they concentrate some Jews
to send away to labor camps or to concentration camps—and if they
want to have a thousand or two thousand Jews, and the policeman
saw in the group a relative from him or a friend, he took out, he saved
him or her, and he put in his place or in her place, another Jew. But
the police didn't do special things—to beat or to kill. I never saw a
Jewish policeman do this. Only when there was a selection, if they can
exchange somebody, they will do it; they will save them for a certain
time.

About the Jewish police, we think that nobody should do this
kind of thing, even if this meant death, but this will mean death if you
wouldn't carry out the order from the Nazis. When the Jewish police
did something, this was most of the time under the command from
the SS, from the Nazis standing by and to see how the police works. If
a policeman was too lazy to carry out what the Nazi wants . . . not because he was lazy, but because he didn't have his heart to do, so the SS
guy gave with a stick or with a gun over the policeman's head too.

After we was released, we went back to our old routine what we
did before. This was the beginning; nobody was bothering us for a
short time, so everybody went on with their work . . . you couldn't
work—but you're sitting and thinking. If somebody had a store, they
went back and they opened the store, and nobody came in to buy
something.

I had my tailor shop where I lived, on the Krakowska in the Gentile
section. I had four rooms, so in two rooms I had my living quarters—
in one room I had the shop, and in one room I had the showroom. So
I was sitting there and thinking what happened, and then I start to
think what will be, what will happen . . . nobody came in.

The equipment was there, but the materials . . . this is another
story . . . when we start to talk, you're reminding me, you're asking
me about materials. . . . In the showroom where I used to live was

some shelves made—I had a lot of materials—and the shelves was with
sliding doors. When a customer came in, I moved the sliding door and
took out some material to show the customers to choose what they
want. When the Nazis occupied Lublin and they bombed the
Krakowska Street, I had a lot of goods, imported English wools, some
fur pieces . . . I was thinking what to do with the materials.

I called up a couple of Polish customers what I had. I had one customer what he was the publisher from a Polish paper,[7] and this was a
customer for the last ten years. I called him up, and I tell him that I
would like to give him some materials to keep for me, and maybe if
the war will come to an end, maybe I'll get them back from him. He
used to be a very nice gentleman, and I dress all the whole family,
him, his wife.

He said OK, and I gave him a lot of the imported goods, the
wools to hide, and also I called up another two or three in that time,
and I gave all away the materials, but I left on one shelf a couple of
pieces of material, because I figure . . . if some Nazi will come in and I
have so many bare shelves . . . all the walls, the shelves was mounted
on the walls, and if they will open the sliding doors and they would
not see the material, they'll ask me, "Where is the material what was
here?" So I left a couple of pieces, and I open a little bit one shelf that
they should see that there is some material.

So happened that a couple of weeks later two SS men came up,
and they knocked on the door. I opened the door, they came in, and
they looked around. They ask me, "Where is the material what was
here?"

I said, "Some military people was here before, and they took out
all the materials except they left two or three pieces—that's what is
left."

In this apartment was two entrances. Was one entrance where the
showroom was and was another entrance to come in where my living
quarters was. So they was in the showroom. From the living room was
a door to the showroom . . . my wife opened a little bit the door to
see; she saw the two SS, the two Nazis, and them asking me where the
material is. One went over—before I want to tell him that the military
people was here and they took away the material—and one hit me in
my face.

7. This was a different publisher than the one from *Glos Lubelsky,* referred to in
the previous chapter.

My wife came out from the room and went over to them. She was standing in front of me, and she said to the Nazi what he punched me, "Officer, you can do with me anything what you want—but my husband, he is the father of my two children . . . if you'll do to him something he would not be able to feed my kids."

In the meantime when she went in my front of me, I managed to open the door, and I jumped; I jumped one flight from the stairs, from the entrance from the showroom. They start to shoot; one was running after me, and he was standing above me in the stairwell. I was almost already gone from there: I made one jump from a whole flight and was there two floors. I went around to jump down the other flight of stairs and I escaped. They went after me, but they couldn't catch me. I was running down to my parents where they was living in the Jewish section, to hide myself.

After a day my wife came down from the Krakowska Street and we both decide, we all decide, that I should run away. At that time, was an opportunity to go to the Russian side of Poland. The Russians had a pact with the Germans, and they divide the Polish territory,[8] and the Russian border was standing seven kilometers from Lublin. My parents, they was not for this and they was not against, because they didn't want to be separated from me—I was only the one boy from six girls—but to save my life, they didn't say anything.

We decide . . . my wife decide most of the thing for me, that I should leave her with the two children and I should go over to the Russian side. She is sure that they will come back because they couldn't catch me, and they'll kill me or they'll arrest me—she don't know what they'll do. We figure this way: the women and the children, what interest would they have to harm them? But with the men, the Nazis will do what they want to do.

I took a warm coat and some food with me, and I went to the Russian side. There, many Jews escaped a week before or even before the war start—maybe a million Jews or maybe less than a million. And on the Russian side was very bad—not bad what the government, the Russian soldiers or the officers did to you something, but the conditions was very bad to live there. There was no houses. A family, what they had an apartment from three or four rooms, and they was four or five people, they took in refugees what they came over, what they escaped from Poland. Everybody took into their homes some Jewish

8. Hitler and Stalin signed the Nonaggression Pact on August 23, 1939.

men. We was sleeping on the floors, they didn't have no place for us. So they gave us one room—maybe was six or eight men lying on the floor. Crowded . . . the lice start to eat us . . . terrible things.

Somebody took me in their house, and I was lying on the floor to sleep . . . in the morning we could go out. Everybody had some money with them; I had a couple of pieces of gold what I sewed on in my shoulders, maybe if I need some money I'll sell the five ruble gold piece to keep alive. In the daytime, was not so bad . . . the restaurants was full with the all refugees; everybody had a couple of *zlotys*. But in the evening to go back to the crowded room and the lice . . . but was generous from the other Jews to take in so many people what they didn't have no place to live.

One day I went out on the street to take a walk, and somebody came across me, and he said, "Mr. Frank! You are here? You are here too?" I had some customers from out of town, and this was a Polish customer of mine; a year before I made for him some suits. So happened that in my trade, in my town, I was very known as a good tailor, so I had a richer clientele. He was a clerk in a bank, and he had an apartment, his own one-family house, five or six rooms.

He asked me, "Where are you staying?" so I tell him how I live.

He said, "You are coming with me. You will be with me, Mr. Frank."

So I was like newborn. He took me into his house. He gave me a small, little room, with an electric light, was a couch there, and they feed me. I was there for two and a half months. When I came out on the street, people what they saw me, I couldn't tell them where I was living. This was a secret, because if the others will hear, they'll maybe ask to take them in and he would not be able to refuse them, so nobody should know this that I am there.

Being there for two and a half months . . . in the nighttime when I lie down on the couch, I start to think, and many, many nights I couldn't sleep at all, but some nights I slept for only two hours or three hours. Most of the time I was lying there and crying in the nighttime. I was talking to myself: "What kind of person are you? You have there a wife with two children . . . you are here and you are living like a king—they feed you and you go out and have a couple glasses of beer—what kind of man are you? What kind of human being? You left a wife with two children."

I talked over with the people what they took me in, and I tell them I decide to go back to Poland on the German side to my family.

They couldn't talk me out from this . . . they start to talk me out: "What can you do for them? Like I hear, it's very bad there." They didn't know the atrocities what is going on there. The Russia was friends with the Germany, so the news didn't come to you to tell you how this is on the other side. But the customer of mine told me, "We don't know nothing from there what's going on, but we heard before the war, before Hitler occupied Poland, what they did with the Jews in Germany, so I'm sure this is not there a picnic, and I don't know if you'll be able to do something for them." My feeling was that I must go home, but he was right. Later I found out that he was right—many, many years later.

It was very hard to go back to the German side because of the border. You had to hide from the border patrols what the Russians and Germans had there. If they'll catch you on the border, they'll take you for a spy, and they'll kill you anyway. Luckily I came over the German side, and from there I used to hitchhike. The town what I crossed the border, the name was Wlojimyesch . . . some Polish farmers, I pay them, I still had some money left, and I came back to Lublin.

The 16th of December, 1939, I came back to my house, and my older boy was sick. He had an infection in his throat—streptococcus. He had in that time 104, 105 temperature. My wife told me the doctor was here about two hours or three hours before I came, and he said he doesn't know if our boy will survive, because even if he'll survive, he'll be brain-damaged from the temperature. And the doctor said, "Twenty-fours hours from now, this will decide his life—if he'll survive or not."

You can imagine at what time I came back. Sitting and listening to my wife what she is telling me the story of what the doctor said . . . the boy was lying in bed for two or three days in a coma—he didn't open his eyes.

I was sitting with my wife and I hear a voice—"Daddy, you are home?"—from my boy. He opened his eyes, and he start to . . . we both didn't know . . . like when I am talking now to you, my hair, my skin from my head with the hairs was standing up to remind myself how this was. He opened his eyes, he turned around and he looked at me, and I said, "Yes, Monyetchku"—Monyek was his name—"Yes, Monyetchku, I am home."

We called the doctor the next day in the morning. He said, "You are lucky. This was the breaking point from the twenty-four hours."

———

Two days later, December 18, 1939, I went down to buy some food. I saw a poster hanging up on the walls that everybody should wear an armband with the star of King David. This was the first thing what I learned when I came back. If somebody was caught not wearing the armband, they shot you or they arrest you, and they tortured you till you was dead.

In two days, this was the 20th of December, two policemen came up with one from the *Judenrat:* they have an order, they need five tailors; they had to come to the SS Headquarters. I couldn't say no, so I went with them to the office from the *Judenrat*. There I met four other tailors, Gerishon Klein, Saul Gootmacher, Fernandt and one other. Klein and Gootmacher, they was two guys what I knew them for years before the war. We lived in the same section on the Krakow Street, and they had their clientele, their business, and I had mine. Always in the evening, once or twice a week, we used to meet each other in the union. We used to play dominoes or have a meeting after working hours, for an hour or two to mingle and to talk.

Three or four blocks from the Lipowa 7 was the street Shopena. Shopena Street 17 . . . this was temporary headquarters from the SS. They took us for a tour in the basement . . . was there special-made torture tools, special benches with cuffs . . . you kneel down, and they attach your arms and legs, and so when they give you some lashes, you cannot move your body. We was standing on the side, five tailors with the two policemen and the one from the *Judenrat*, for an hour or two hours. On the ground floor, a very, very large office with six or eight chairs, the Nazis was sitting there. A German Nazi came down from the first floor, and he looked us over, the five tailors. He came over to the line what we was standing, and he point with his finger to me.

"You will be the leader. We are building tailor shops and other shops, and you will be the leader for the tailors. If you will have an order, you will be responsible. And if you will not carry out, you will get killed with your family." [9]

9. By decree of October 26, 1939, Jews were interned in forced labor camps under the Higher SS and Police Leaders; in Lublin, they fell under Globocnik's jurisdiction. According to Levin, there was neither a census nor classification of labor beforehand. Arguing that the Nazis never viewed the Jews as a permanent slave-labor force, she finds that while a high percentage of Polish Jews were skilled in trades, by the end of 1941, only eighty thousand were employed in labor camps and private

Civil people could only walk on the streets till five o'clock—after five o'clock if they caught somebody they killed him, or they arrest him, not just Jews but even Poles. They kept us for a couple of hours, this was after five, so two SS men took us in the back of a van. When we was sitting, we was talking why they took us down to the basement to show the torture tools . . . to intimidate us if we wouldn't carry out the orders, so we can expect they know what our address is and what they'll do with us.

———————

January 1940, Mr. Kestenberg received an order from the SS commandant, his name was Riedel. Riedel wants him to start to establish the tailor shop on the Lipowa Street.[10] They had some buildings on the lot, stables from horses what was before. The SS wants to build barracks, but until the barracks would be built, they want to have the tailor shop and a shoemaker shop in what was before the stables from the horses. The *Judenrat* has to supply all the tools, machines, scissors, press irons, and other things; they are responsible for all the tools what they need to make up the tailor shop and the shoemaker shop.

They organized . . . they appealed to every Jew. They put up posters in Yiddish or in Polish, the same in two languages. They knew who was before the war a builder, who was before in the lumber business or in the hardware business, so they knew every Jew what he did. The Jewish community, the *Gemeinde*—we called them this before we called them *Judenrat*—every Jew was registered in this office. They appealed to them to see that they help to carry out the order what they received from the SS.

Was a lot of Jews what they was better off than some others, what I am talking from the building line or in the hardware line or in the other lines, so they signed over their businesses to Polish people, to customers there or to people what they were before dealing with them. These people what they signed over, they was figuring that maybe when the war will come an end, maybe the Poles will give them

---

industry using prison labor (Levin 1973, 155). Hilberg effectively argues that even though portions of the Jewish labor force were preserved for a time for heavy weapons production, and that Himmler sought to profit from SS-controlled factories, in the final balance, "economic factors were truly secondary" (Hilberg 1985, 542). While the Nazis stood to gain from looting private property and saving food supplies by deporting the people who would consume them, genocide was the ultimate goal.

10. For background on Riedel, see Chapter 20, note 7.

back their business. But in that time, in the beginning, they still had a voice, and even when the business was not theirs anymore and in the name was by somebody else, by the Polish name, they was still respected to make the decisions from the business. So they donate all the building things what they need to build the barracks.

I had three machines. Because Lublin was bombed, and no one needs suits, I had no customers anymore, so I gave away one machine. Every tailor . . . was a couple thousand tailors in Lublin, so you could have a couple thousand machines—what you don't need so many even. Later I gave away another machine, and I left myself with one machine—maybe I'll need for me, for the family to mend clothes. But later on, you didn't need the machine at all.

ML: What I'm confused about is, were the tailors giving their machines because the *Judenrat* requested them, or did the *Judenrat* say, "If together we don't come up with this equipment, the Nazis are going to punish us"?

JF: They didn't say the Nazis will punish us. If you would not give, if we would not supply the Nazis what they want, they'll come and they'll take it—not a punishment—they'll come and they'll find the way how to get the equipment themselves. Then, God forbid, because of the tools, we start to lose our lives. So we start to feel that is true what especially Kestenberg was talking about.

From time to time was meetings, not just from the *Judenrat*, but they invite some people from outside. They was talking about what they need the next day to deliver, and they went out and they spread around the word by the Jewish population. We knew that if we have, we will give them—some of us start to understand that sooner or later they'll take away everything, even our lives, because for any little thing, they shoot, they kill, they beat up people, so we saw what situation we are living. If you had something, was not a problem anymore to keep.

The main problem was to be able to keep yourself alive. This was the only thought what everybody was thinking . . . maybe, maybe the next week, maybe the next day, maybe the next month the war will come to an end.

———

After Kestenberg received the order, in January '40, to open shops, he called me over to the *Judenrat* office . . . I was living not far from there.

"We have an order to start to build the tailor shop, and the SS wants to have a hundred tailors. We need you, Mr. Frank, to organize the tailor shop."

In that time, I had some friends, tailors, and I start to talk with them, and they agreed that they'll work with me, but was very hard to find a hundred tailors. Most of the tailors, they hide themselves because they was afraid. I figured they was hiding because when I went out to find the hundred tailors . . . I knew them from the union or from the synagogue when we went on Saturday to pray . . . I'm talking from before the war.

I came to their homes to tell them, "Will you go with me? They will open shops."

The wife told me, "My husband is not home."

So when I ask her, "Where is he?" and she says, "I don't know," I figure I can go back another day—the SS gave an order to find them in ten days. The first day I could find nobody. Every tailor, I went from street to street, where I knew they lived, the wife said, "He's not at home."

"Well, where is he? I was here yesterday; I was here before yesterday. I can never find him here. I would like to talk with him. . . ."

I tell his wife . . . I talk with her freely . . . "I know that you are afraid that they'll take away from you your husband, your breadwinner; they'll do to him something. I am in the same ship, the same way. Why can't you tell me where he is? I'd like to talk with him."

She said, "I really don't know."

They didn't trust even me. They know me all the years; but because I was before chosen from the Nazis to be the head, they lost their faith.

When I couldn't find any tailors, the *Judenrat* sent the Jewish police to find where they are, and they find out they are hiding. They find a couple of them . . . I went over to the *Judenrat,* and I saw the five or six the Jewish police brought, and we start to talk. We had a conference with some of the *Judenrat,* and they explained that the Nazis want to open shops, and they'll give out rationing cards, the *Verpflegung,* for everybody what would have a working permit. Who would not have the permit would not get the rationing cards, and they would not be able to get food for themselves or for their families.

A couple days later, they start to come out from their hiding places. They come up to me where I was living, and they start to volunteer.

They call me Jack . . . "Jack, I'll volunteer, I'll go with you . . . you take my name . . . I want to take the risk. What will be will be."

SS-Obergruppenführer Odilo Globocnik (second from right) with other SS officers in Lublin. In addition to serving as head of the SS in the Lublin region, he was in charge of the extermination of Jews in Poland and founded killing centers at Belzec, Majdanek, and Sobibor. Mr. Frank came to Globocnik's office every day to pick up uniforms for cleaning and pressing. *Courtesy of Yad Vashem, Jerusalem.*

Was there ten or twelve, and my wife wrote their names and their addresses. The next day, more came, more than a hundred for what I need . . . they was ready right away to go to work to receive the *Verpflegung.*

I had the hundred tailors, and we got the shop ready. And we were sitting and waiting again for new orders: what kind of work to do and what to make.

From all the shops, I was only the one what was selected to be the head, because in that time there was only an order from the Nazis to Kestenberg that they want to have a tailor shop; they didn't talk about other craftspeople. Then later, after a month, they came out with an order that they want to have all kind of shops and craftspeople. The heads from the shoemaker shop, the saddler shop, the carpenter shop, the blacksmith shop what they put horseshoes on the horses, the capmaker shop to make soft caps and stiff round hats for the officers, they was not selected by the Nazis. They select the heads between themselves. I knew single people that they'll be in the shoemaker shop, but who will be the head from the shop I didn't know. I met the leaders there on the Lipowa six months later when the shops was ready.

The Nazis said that the tailor shop will start to repair the uniforms for the SS, to clean them, to press them, and this was the work what we start to do. I start to become busy. The commandant from the Lipowa with the name Riedel, he was an *Untersturmführer,* a second lieutenant, he called me in his office, and he gave me an order: every day I have to go to *Kruel Leszcynskiego* where the headquarters was from the big bandits, where the big Nazis was, and to pick up every day the uniforms from the *Obergruppenführer* Globocnik and from the SS people what they are around him. Every morning, eight o'clock, I was there in the office, with two other tailors. An SS man with a car, he brought us over there, and we brought the uniforms to the shop . . . we start to clean and to press.

In early 1940, we still was living in our homes. We came to work eight o'clock in the morning, and after five, we walk home. In the same time, they start to build the Lipowa camp—the permanent barracks. The *Judenrat* had to supply the tools . . . they didn't have all the tools what they need; they had to build with their own hands. Fifteen-hundred Jews was coming to work to build. A lot of them was wounded on the job, and they took them to the hospitals . . . some from them died.

4

The Lublin Ghetto

1938–Late 1940

IN 1938 THEY TRANSFERRED Jews from Germany to Poland and
the destination was Lublin. You see the Jews what I am talking about,
they was not German Jews, they was Polish Jews living in Germany
. . . they was not German citizens, even if they became German citizens later. They was not born in Germany—they was there fifteen or
sixteen or seventeen years, but they still considered them as not German citizens . . . they were citizens from other countries, from
Poland, from Czechoslovakia. So these Jews from other countries
came over on the Polish border; they brought them to Lublin—most
of them, not all. Some of them went to other states—to Warsaw or to
Krakow, but most of them they came to Lublin.

I remember when the German Jews came with the women and
the children; all families; the Nazis told them to take with them more
expensive things to carry with them, so they had valises with jewelry
and diamond earrings. But later, when Lipowa was built, they took
most of the German Jews, they had lists of who came to Poland, they
look them up and they send them over to the Lipowa Street with the
same valises, with gold, diamonds, pins, other things. When they came
on the Lipowa, they took away everything, and this was the end from
the German Jews what they send over in 1938.

Everyday they brought Jews from somewhere else, from around
Lublin . . . we didn't know even from where they came. From the beginning, after 1939, after the war broke out, I don't remember they
brought from other countries except from Germany. They brought
from other countries to other cities, but to Lublin I remember only
German Jews they brought after 1939.

In the end of '39 or in the beginning of '40, in January or Febru-

37

ary when they opened the camp Lipowa, they brought the Professor David.[1] He was a German . . . his grandparents was born in Germany! His whole family—real Germans! He was in the First World War a high-ranking officer . . . he was a good fighter . . . he received the highest medal, the Iron Cross, the highest medal from Germany in that time.

ML: Do you know how one German Jew among many German Jews transported to Lublin became Jewish commandant?

JF: He was the teacher from the chief from the Gestapo, Worthoff. He gave him piano lessons. The chief from the Gestapo was a little boy in that time, and the Professor David . . . after when this became so bad for the Jews in Germany, because he had the Iron Cross, so he was still allowed to teach, to give lessons. Before he was teaching in all kind of universities, conservatories, teaching conductors how to conduct, and later he became a teacher from children, and because he was so with the Iron Cross, so he taught piano lessons to Worthoff. So when they brought him to Lublin, the chief from the Gestapo, I'm sure that he knew he is coming; he paid him back and gave him a job to make him commandant from the camp.

Most of the Jews what the Germans expelled from Germany . . . I figure was forty-some thousand Jews, forty-two or forty-four, I'm not sure—most of the Jews from Lublin, everybody took somebody in. If somebody had more rooms they took in a whole family, and if somebody had only two rooms, a family of two with a child, they took in one person or two people . . . and many of them from the German Jews was separated because one family couldn't all go in to whomever could take them in, because was crowded. Most of the Jews in Lublin was poor, even before the war, so they was living like five or six people in two or three rooms, and they still took in somebody.

In our family was nine people—seven children and my father and my mother. All the sisters had husbands and children, but they didn't live with us. In that time one or two was not married, so was only four people. So we took in a family from three people—two parents with a little girl, seven or eight years old. They was not too long with us, about three-and-a-half months. They find some relatives . . . this was outside Lublin. When the relatives in a smaller town heard that the Germans send over people what they was Polish citizens before, so

---

1. A German Jew who was made head of all the Jewish civilian prisoners. Frank refers to him as the "Jewish commandant."

they was looking for them, and they found them, what I am talking about this family of three, and they took them in.

While they was by us they didn't do anything . . . after some time, they start to find work—also people start to give them some work to exist. They was very miserable, because in Germany, before Hitler came, they had a better life than the Jew in Poland, because Germany was more cultural-minded. But the Nazis changed their culture to a killing system . . . I don't know how exactly to express this in English. They took their culture from all the scientists, from all the writers, from all the conductors from music, they took all the culture, and they changed this to kill, especially Jews. They called them rats.

"They are a rotten nation, a rotten people; they shouldn't exist."

And this was the policy from the beginning. Didn't start so very harshly, but systematically, we was all liquidated—that was the end.

———

Grodzka Street was between the Kowalsky Street and the Shiroka Street . . . a short distance from there most of the Jewish people had their residence. At the beginning of the Grodzka Street there was a tower, and through the tower was hanging a chain, across the tower from one side of the street to the other so that nobody can pass through this tower. The very heavy chain was made hundreds and hundreds of years ago when the law was the Jews could live only to this point starting from the tower, and this was the chain what the Jews couldn't pass by. This chain was in the middle of the tower; but also from both sides, from the left side and from the right side was two narrow openings what you could go through, but there was two watchmen.

Before the war there was some merchant Jews what they was dealing in business with the Poles, and they had to go into the Gentile section, where the Gentile businesspeople, the Poles, used to live. They call the Jewish section a ghetto from my time . . . so if a Jew had to pass by to the outside from the Jewish community, he had to show the guard a special pass by the two small openings. And after five hundred or six hundred years later from when the chain was built, the Polish government liquidate the chain from the tower what I was talking before, so Jewish people could live on the other side.

When the Nazis made the ghetto, there came out an order in 1940—all the Jews what they are living in the Polish section, they have to move to the community where the Jews was living hundreds of years ago. All Jewish people should be concentrated between the

The entrance to the Lublin ghetto in June, 1941. The German sign above the door on the left warns of infectious diseases. Photo by Max Kirnberger. *Courtesy of the Deutsche Historisches Museum, Berlin, and Yad Vashem, Jerusalem.*

Shiroka and Kowalsky Streets, starting at the gate on the Grodzka Street. Before was about five thousand Jews living in the Jewish quarter; there the Nazis put in all the Jews from Lublin from all the streets. In the ghetto, thirty-eight thousand or forty-two thousand Jews was living there. My parents, my six sisters . . . every sister was married and had two or three or four children . . . all of them had their homes in the ghetto because they lived in the Jewish community.

  Was not a mass moving all at once. You couldn't see nothing. They just moved, a normal moving like you move here in the States from one city to another or from one street to another. You saw sometimes a big wagon with two horses to carry furniture. We know if you saw a wagon, someone was moving from the Gentile population to the Jewish community. When it start to be a mass moving, or a mass marching, when you concentrate all the people . . . they gave you a week, or sometimes in the beginning they gave you four weeks, so you had time to pack, not to move all in one time, all the people.

  ML: In the beginning, when there were orders issued and things would be a certain way for a week or two weeks, and then something else would change, and people were still given some time to plan and get ready, do you think this made people less suspicious than they would have been? Was it a scheme to make them less knowledgeable about their fate?

JF: I know what you're asking. Some people, they was thinking this way . . . maybe this'll get a little better, because they see we carry out the orders what they give us; if they want us to move, we move; if they want more people to work, in shops or outside to clean the streets or to do something, we are doing. But most of us, most of the Jewish population, we found out with the time, we found out that this is only schemes.

All the people had to move to the Jewish section except the heads from the shops—they will have to live outside the Jewish community in some apartments what the SS opened on 16 Grodzka Street, because . . . you asked me why the Grodzka Street. They don't want the heads from the shops, when they have to take measurements, to take orders, to deliver some work or to take some work to the labor camps, they shouldn't mix with the general population because of cleanliness. They shouldn't catch from the ghetto . . . there'll be lice there in the ghetto or other insects. That we shouldn't be infected with diseases, we shouldn't live with the other Jews in the big ghetto. That's why they gave us the special places to live, away a couple of thousand feet.

Was also another reason why I think they want us to live away from the big ghetto. Most of the time, the SS used to come in the ghetto in the nighttime to some houses, and they took out people . . . we didn't know every time what happened there in the ghetto because there was a gate, and we was almost separated from them. But especially the leaders from the shops, we had a chance sometimes to go in and mix with our relatives, but not to be too long there. To sleep, we had to go back. We found out that certain nights they took out some Jews—they never returned.

Most of the time they took out the intelligentsia . . . doctors, lawyers, more or less what they was occupied in politics, Zionism, all kinds—they call them socialists, even Zionists they call socialists, communists, whatever names the SS want to call them. The Nazis put up signs on the houses from the shop leaders, on the Grodzka Street, that the SS should never enter in the nighttime . . . to control the houses . . . the idea was not to interfere with the nighttime rest, because we have to go to work in the morning. If they sometimes came in to check in the houses, they had to have a special pass from Globocnik, the General from the SS. They gave us special houses so that they should also have us concentrated, the heads from the shops in one place, separate from the general Jewish population.

ML: So for that last reason you're giving, because all the leaders were concentrated together it made them easier to control too. It meant there was less conversation, less discussion within the community.

JF: That's right. This *was* the reason, because a year and a half later in '42 when they liquidate the ghetto and get ready to put the Jews in the small ghetto outside from Lublin, at Majdan-Tatarsky,[2] they had put SS all around the four sides of the ghetto, and they had the people all together, so was not too much work for them to do. They put the SS with machines guns all around, and they gave the Jews in the ghetto an order to get out, and they brought them all in the nighttime to the Grodzka Street. The Grodzka Street was a very long street, maybe about a mile long, and at the other end, there was the very tall tower with the clock, where it starts the Gentile section. Before the war, thousands of Jews was living with the Gentiles to the same houses, the same streets.

In August of 1940, around the ghetto, the Nazis made a gate on the Grodzka Street, about a thousand or fifteen-hundred feet from the Shiroka Street. The gate was watched by the Jewish police in the beginning. Later, the SS start to watch who is going out . . . if somebody had a working card and they had to go out to work, so they let them out. To let them in, they had to show a pass. The Jews what they went out to work from the ghetto, they was not allowed to walk on the sidewalk. They had to walk on the middle of the road together with the horses. If they saw a German, they had to greet him to take off their hats, their caps. Sometimes if a Jew didn't see the German, and the Nazi saw that he didn't raise his cap, he stopped him, and he had to count a hundred times to raise his hat from his head, and to count loud, and if he missed one he had to count over. This was the punishment for not greeting them . . . this was not so bad, but this was the start.

Later, for any little thing, they arrest them and take them to SS

2. Approximately three thousand Jews were sent to live in small, ramshackle farmhouses on the outskirts of Lublin. The reduction of a large ghetto into a smaller one was a common intermediate stage before complete annihilation, retaining for a time a small section of the population for work. Frank explains the Majdan-Tatarsky ghetto in greater detail in Chapter 19, "Majdan-Tatarsky."

headquarters on Shopena 17, the torture place. Some of them didn't come out; they beat them to death, and if they came out, they was so beaten they couldn't even move to go away.

In '40 and '41, during the time of the large ghetto, we received the rationing cards from the *Judenrat*. The Germans supplied to the *Judenrat,* and we picked up the rationing cards there. Everybody saved money under the mattress . . . was not a system in Europe in that time to have money in the bank, so if you have some money, you keep it under the mattress. When they made the ghetto, my father didn't work, but before the war, he was like a furrier—he made hats for *Hasidim,* for rabbis. Do you see the fur hats what the rabbis are wearing? This was one trade what he had, and the other thing what he made money was . . . he was a very smart man . . . they call this in Yiddish a *daiyan,* was like a judge, not a regular judge from a court, but he straightened out businesspeople if they had some arguments between them. They paid him for his service.

ML: Your parents had enough money to last for nearly two-and-a-half years?

JF: A lot of people, they died from hunger—what do you think? Till they locked up the ghetto and you couldn't go out, was not a long time, about eight months or ten months or six months . . . I don't know . . . so you can survive with less to eat and to hope that maybe, maybe this war will come to an end. This gives you a way to live, not eating normally. But everybody had something to sell, a fur coat, a diamond, a pair of earrings, so when you didn't have the money, you start to get connections with Polish people and sell something. That's how you managed.

When the ghetto was locked up with gates, and the SS was watching the gates, people smuggled from outside. In the beginning, the penalty for smuggling was a couple of lashes. But later was arresting and torturing, and afterwards the SS let them out. Months later, the punishment from the SS was to arrest them, and they never came back, or sometimes they beat them up by the gates, and they beat them to death. Most of the time was young boys what they did the smuggling, because they was figuring maybe they can pass by easier than an older man to avoid . . . they usually find places to avoid the SS. Still, later when they found out how they smuggled, so they watched all over. Every day it start to get harder, harder, this life.

ML: I was thinking you might have had more reports about the conditions in the ghetto because your parents were living there, and you occasionally visited them . . .

JF: If you call this how they lived, what kind of living this was, was no living. From the beginning, when it start to get very, very, very bad, everybody said, "Better to die than to live this way." But with the time, you became used to this kind of life.

ML: I read the report of a journalist who was in Lublin in November 1939. He describes that because of transports from all the towns in Poland and from Germany, the Jews were packed into Lublin, from originally 40,000 to over 200,000, and people were living on the streets, in hovels under buildings, where animals were kept, in bombed-out houses, anywhere there was space. He called the ghetto a living grave of orphans and people who had lost their families.

I have the article here: "The congestion, the stench, the poverty, the disease and the chaos which reign in Lublin cannot be paralleled anywhere on earth. . . . Men die like flies on the thoroughfares. . . . At night everything is pitch black. . . . All the wells have become polluted. . . . Cholera and typhus were already rampant when we reached Lublin. . . . Women band together and cook whatever they can gather. . . . Hundreds have not slept for weeks. . . . The devil himself could not have devised such hell. . . . Lublin is giant concentration camp where people spend their days trying to dig their way out of a living grave." [3]

JF: This is what this was . . . you have everything there . . . nothing more what I can tell you about this.

ML: But what do *you* remember the conditions were?

JF: The conditions was you didn't work; you didn't have nothing to do. And money, if you had what you saved from before, a loaf of bread, a kilo of bread, what was before like a *zloty* or seventy-five pennies, became ten or twenty times as much as was before. So this was the conditions. The families start to ration by themselves the amount of food. If you had a meal from soup with a piece of meat, or a couple potatoes, so you start to cut out. Today was only soup, tomorrow you'll eat a potato. A lot of them, you saw people lying on the street, dying from hunger. Do you know what this looks like, a person lying dying from hunger? The eyes, they are looking at something what you cannot see or looking at nothing, and they cannot move their bodies

3. Moldawer, in Apenszlak 1982, 93–95. Frank does not recall cholera, typhus, or polluted wells, but it is possible that Moldawer knew of instances of these that Frank did not.

even to get some food. The bodies stay there on the ground after when they are dead.

If somebody was still alive but was so bad that the other person saw that he or she is dying, they didn't give them anymore food. They couldn't eat anymore. If the situation was so bad that somebody's dying, you couldn't help them anyway.

Electricity, was nothing like this after the Germans bomb, and all the wires was out, and was no coal. Many people was burning their furniture to keep warm . . . especially in the winter. Poland in the wintertime was eight, ten, fifteen below zero. In the beginning you had coal. All the time you prepared yourself in the summertime for the winter, you had to prepare yourself with warm clothing, with high boots. You put up coal, potatoes in the basement for the winter. Not always could you go out to buy food, because of the snow and the icy roads. For instance, Lublin was a very big city, but most of the transportation was in the horse and buggy. From my time, in the twenties, was maybe ten or twelve cars in all Lublin. When the snow starts in December or November, the snow with the ice kept lying till the end of February or the beginning of March when the spring starts. Was supers from the houses, they had special tools what they dig out the ice and they put it on the side to melt.

Was some beggars, especially children. I don't know if parents put them up this way, or they was hungry; they was sitting in the streets and begging. In the beginning, you passed by, you put in some money to the pot what they had nearby, but later you was so used to it, you didn't even look. You passed by, you was in the same position, if not now, the next day or the next couple days.

The *Yiddische Gemeinde,* the Jewish community, had a soup kitchen. I could see the lines when I passed by, when they was standing to get a pot, a plate, of some soup . . . was sometimes fifty, sixty, seventy people waiting.

ML: Do you think those people were eating for themselves, or would they get food and return to their houses to share it with their families?

JF: Before they went to the houses, the pot of soup was finished. Walking they ate up the soup.

I don't remember there should be disease like typhus . . . they tried to keep themselves clean as much they could. Most of the dying was from hunger, not from diseases what they was sick. I think the sicknesses . . . before the war was more diseases and sick people than in that time. People start to think just to be healthy . . . I don't know if the thinking helped them . . . if you had a piece of bread, you didn't die from a disease. You only died from hunger.

Was drinkable water in the ghetto, because there was wells, you could get the water from the ground, many places, except from the water from pipes. The wells was from before—when they made the city water, they left the wells. You had to go a little bit far behind the city, about a half a mile, to carry the water. Was special water carriers what they carried two pails of water on their shoulders, with a wood beam made special to fit their shoulders. He sold the water; you paid for that. The trips he made a day was according to how many customers he had. There was many, many of them. This was lately the business what they could make a dollar or a *zloty* . . . this kind of life.

5

In the Hunters' Lair

The Lipowa Labor Camp

Late 1940–1943

IN LATE '40 THE SHOPS was ready . . . gigantic shops, gigantic buildings . . . tailor shops, shoemakers, carpenters, all kind of crafts-people. The hundred tailors start to work on the Lipowa, it start to be like a regular day of work. In the morning nobody was waiting for you, no SS man came to take you to work . . . you go home to the ghetto after eight hours, to your family. You came freely, you went home freely; so when they said they need two hundred tailors, there was no more problem. The tailors was standing by my house almost in line, to be first to be registered and anxious I should take them . . . the best tailors, I can say, from Poland.

We start to make new uniforms for the Nazis . . . you was busy with working. On the job, your mind was not so occupied what will be the next hour . . . you received the ration cards, so it start to be like a normal way of life. But this didn't keep too long. Every week there was a change for worse.

I used to enter the camp at Lipowa 7. I used the very wide iron gate so the trucks can pass through, or I used the back entrance, the little door from Sklodowsky Street . . . from the back was a guard, a Ukraine high up with a machine gun that no one should go out with-out a pass—the heads from the shops had special passes. Till 1943, I could go out to take measurements for the big Nazis what I made for them the gray leather coats and the uniforms and the jackets.

The camp was four or five blocks the size, machine guns this side, this side, and this side . . . every couple of hours they change the watchpeople . . . was barbed wire on top from the brick walls all around the whole camp, to protect the lot that *Judes* shouldn't go in or to spoil something.[1]

On the right side, I passed by a very modern six-story office what was from the Polish government before the war; there the SS made offices . . . very, very clean, with all conveniences. On the left side from the camp was stables . . . when the circus used to come, horses was stationed there and other animals, tigers, monkeys. I was twice or three times there before the war with my little boys.

About two thousand feet from the gates when I came in from the Lipowa, they dug a hole . . . at the time, we didn't know what the hole is—but later, we found out they dug a hole to conserve water . . . if water will be destroyed or an enemy will bomb or something will go wrong with the street water, so this place, so big was the hole, that they can supply the whole city Lublin with 250,000 people.

A little further from this hole about a half a block, they built the shops. The order was from the Mohwinkel, when six months later he took over the commandantship from Riedel. Mohwinkel was a construction engineer; he designed the layout from the barracks.[2] In normal times, the space from the barracks will be only for 1,500 or 2,000 people, but eventually they put in 7,000 people there.[3] For the Jews to sleep there they made bunk beds, three tiers in the height. In the beginning they supply everybody—that's what the *Judenrat* supply— some blankets, some straw sacks instead of mattresses . . . in the beginning was not so bad . . . but with the time, everything fell apart. You never could change the linen or the blanket because everything became dirty, and was not a laundry there to wash the things.

Outside was some water pipes . . . every five or ten inches was a faucet from the water, what you can get the drips. The water was not

1. There had been horse stables on the lot at Lipowa 7, but from the end of 1939 to early 1940, the lot was fenced in. Guard towers were added by March 1940, and barbed wire by around May 1940 (*SSPF*, 8377). Lublin residents were able to see into the camp, and Mr. Frank recalls instances when non-Jewish Poles watched from outside the gates (see p. 173).

2. According to *SSPF* documents (p. 8377), Mohwinkel also implemented the security system of watchtowers and a two-meter-wide death zone along the back of the camp, which was the longest side.

3. This is a much higher number than the peak number of 3,000 stated in the *SSPF* legal investigation (p. 8376). We can't be sure if Frank's estimate is accurate, and because there were frequently new transports to the camp (not all of which may have been unearthed by the *SSPF* investigation), we don't know if 3,000 is an accurate number either.

really coming out . . . was dripping . . . a little bit . . . whatever is there, then that's how you wash your face. Sometimes the water didn't drip at all; so with the coffee what you received sometimes, I washed myself, my face. For the coffee they used chicory, so was like water.

There around the pipes was not made an enclosure . . . just some wooden poles with a ceiling that the rain shouldn't go on the water pipes with faucets . . . everybody was standing in the line in the morning to wash a little bit their face. On the other side was made the men's room, to urinate or to make the bowel movement. The carpenters, they built a wooden floor with holes, and the one sat next to the other to move his bowels. They dig . . . was a big place . . . was a couple of places even, not just one—they dig a very, very deep hole and from time to time they clean out the hole to tanks, and they use this for fertilizer, the shit.[4] Was a special commando with big cans, heavy, heavy cans with a heavy stick, and two people was carrying this on their shoulders, one on the front, one on the back, and they went about twenty or thirty feet . . . was standing a horse with a wagon and a tank made with an opening. And they filled up the tank, and when the tank was full they went away. A couple of horses stood in the line . . . when the first tank was full and the other took his place, was three or four till the hole was empty . . . every couple of days, they always clean. And they use this on the fields.

I never asked them how they got that job; everybody did their job what they're assigned to do—if they shovel the shit, if they are tailors, if they prepare the food . . . if somebody was working in the kitchen, he was more the luckier guy than the shit guy. Was a job to do—couldn't say this is a dirty job or a cleaner job: they tell him to do it, and that's what he did.

Away in the right side from the sleeping quarters was also a barrack, what they call the *Lazarett* from German, a little hospital. Somebody was beaten up or wounded at work, they took him in there; was maybe a place for twenty-five or thirty people. They had there the Jewish doctors from the prisoners—professors, surgeons, very big people from before the war. When they registered the Jews in the beginning when they took us on the Lipowa, everybody was registered

4. Typhoid fever, hepatitis A, and cholera can be spread through human contact with excrement, so the camp's method of waste disposal was unsafe for the handlers and for the people who ate crops fertilized with excrement.

what they are doing, a tailor or a doctor. Then later, after when the camp and the barracks was finished, they had the list who was a doctor and who was a tailor and who was a carpenter. Many people what I know was taken there when they was beat up from the lashes, when they torture somebody . . . but I saw many what was just beaten and then taken out from the camp and not to the *Lazarett*.

When they used to arrest some people from the ghetto and bring them to the Lipowa to beat them up—they used to bring in some Jewish men or Jewish women, and one time they brought in a pregnant woman. I remember like this will be today. They arrested her husband, and they brought him into the Lipowa to beat him up, and this wife, this pregnant wife, was running from her house to the Lipowa Street . . . Lipowa Street was more on the Gentile side . . . from the Jewish section was about a mile.

The pregnant woman came and was standing by the gates to wait, maybe they'll release her husband. Inside, the SS, the watchpeople, they went out; they caught her and they brought her in. They tell her to take off her panties with everything, and they put her down over a bench and they gave her . . . I don't know how many—we was in the shop, to look out through the window—they gave her some lashes, and they took her away. When we went out, the place what they beat her up was full with blood on the ground.

————

We always went out six o'clock in the morning to stay in the line that they should count us. All seven thousand from us was arranged in companies, like in the military, two hundred or three hundred men and one what he was responsible for this company. Was there the civil prisoners and the Jewish war prisoners, about two thousand war prisoners from the Polish side, what they was fighting against the Germans. After six or seven days from the time when the Nazis invaded, they had the whole Polish Army as war prisoners. Later, they segregate the Jews from the soldiers. Even when a Jewish soldier doesn't want to step out that he is Jewish, the Polish soldier pointed him out: "He is a Jew." So they segregate the Jews from the Poles, and they said, "You have no right to be protected under the international law for war prisoners. You are a Jew, and you belong to the Jewish camps."[5]

For the *appel,* the counting, the Music Professor David came over,

5. This same status is described in Krakowski 1984, 261.

the commandant from the camp from the Jewish population. The Professor David was a very cultured Jew from Germany, very educated in the old way from the '20s, and like most from the Jews what they was from Germany, he was more assimilated. The Professor David received the Iron Cross by the Germans in the First World War, so they respect him a little bit more, they don't want to kill him yet, and they made from him the leader from the Jewish prisoners. So the Professor David count us over, he had a list, he calls us out, and everybody says, *"Jawohl!"* Everything is in order, he brought over the list to the Commandant Mohwinkel, or sometimes is there an assistant from Mohwinkel; Mohwinkel was sometimes not there every morning.

The elder from the Jewish war prisoners, his name was Fisher,[6] he had the same job what the commandant David had, to count the war prisoners and to hand over the list from them. Fisher's duties was to tell all the *gruppen* leaders when they have to go to work, to see that nobody should miss. I never checked on him to see what he was doing; I had to worry about my tailors—I'm sure he didn't sit on the chair to take sunbaths. He was a good guy . . . when it came to the High Holidays, he put two or three guys in front of the shop in case a Nazi would come through when we was doing the prayers. We carried on prayers, had *shabbes* . . . we had an orchestra, actors with producers made plays—where we lived we did everything what was possible, but every week there was a change.

Before the labor camp was sealed, what I am talking in 1940 and 1941, was a canteen . . . was all kind of food you could buy for money what people had from before the war. After March 1942, when they liquidate the Lublin ghetto and make the small ghetto at Majdan-Tatarsky,[7] we could no more go to our houses in the evening. The men what was working stayed in the camp, and their families stayed in this small ghetto.

In this time in '42, after the *appel,* the roll call, we went to the kitchen to get our breakfast . . . in the middle between the sleeping quarters and the shops, was a kitchen made, a very big barrack with very big kitchen stoves. Everything was electric. They received the

6. In February 1941, the Jewish prisoners of war chose Roman Fisher to head a committee they formed to regain their rights as prisoners of war. Krakowski describes him as an excellent organizer who was able to convince the SS to follow a more moderate regime, including increased rations and better beds (1984, 262–63).

7. This is chronicled in detail in the Chapter 19, "Majdan-Tatarsky."

Verpflegung, the raw things, from Majdanek concentration camp,[8] and they cooked there for all the prisoners. We get a dish with soup, mostly of water . . . everybody had on the belt a pot for soup and for coffee . . . coffee, that's all—without milk, without no sugar, no sweet, no other things—and we get about a pound of dark bread, was like clay what you are eating. This ration was for the whole day.

No special way they give out the food . . . just routine, not an order. The waiters, I call them waiters, they were servers . . . they gave out the food from the cook; he was the server, he served everybody . . . was a big spoon, and everybody received so a spoon. Sometimes there was a guy what would say, "Put down the spoon a little bit deeper! *Deeper!*" If the server put the big spoon lower down to the pot, so he caught a potato, and if somebody received the potato in his soup, or half a potato, he was the lucky one; he went out like dancing. "Oh! I have a potato!" he used to yell. But sometimes when some prisoner would say, "Deeper, put it down deeper!" he received a blow with the spoon over his head. The circumstances from this life was so rough . . . sometimes they get into a fight, and he didn't receive the soup at all anymore.

The ration, the *Verpflegung,* was not enough, so the food and bread was traded. Some traded bread for cigarettes, sometimes for a pair of shoes what they was not ripped apart, or boots. They trade, and the next day, the one what he traded something, he died. The next day they found him dead, from not having this piece of bread what he gave away for a pair of shoes, not to walk barefoot or with ripped-apart shoes. Was very, very rough. Not so often was this hap-

8. Majdanek was the central concentration camp in Lublin, which *Reichsführer* Himmler ordered Globocnik to build during his visit to Lublin, July 20–21, 1941. The original order was for a concentration camp for prisoners of war (the SS wanted to take control of them from the *Wehrmacht*), Polish civilians deported from the Lublin region, and other political undesirables. Lublin was chosen because the shops already operating there were productive (such as the one where Frank worked). Also, there were *Volksdeutsche* in the Zamosc region who were to be resettled; railroad lines already existed, and Lublin's location made it a good easternmost base for SS and police units in the General Government (Marszalek 1986, 18–22). Majdanek supplied food to the labor camps in the Lublin region; later, beginning November 1, 1943, these labor camps were declared subcamps under the jurisdiction of Majdanek. Besides Lipowa, other subcamps in the city of Lublin employed native Lubliner Jews: there was a tar-paper factory and shoe-repair shop on Chelmska Street and brush-making and basketry shops at an old airport known as *Plaga Lashkewicz* (Marszalek 1986, 52 and author's conversations with Jacob Frank).

pening, but I remember one case. I came out from the barrack where I finished my soup, to go over to the place with the pipes and water dripping, so I went over to wash my pot. I saw a couple a guys standing around in one place, about ten or twelve talking . . . I went over to see . . . one was lying down, and I ask a guy what happened, and he told me, "This guy, yesterday he gave away the bread." The Nazis took him away to a certain place where they kept the dead bodies for a couple of hours, and then they called the *Judenrat*. They came with a wagon, and they took him out from the camp.

In '43, the condition from the prisoners was much, much, much weaker than 1942 or six months before the liquidation from Lipowa. But most of us what we was there in the labor camp, the physical condition was not so bad because your life didn't wait to end from food. There was some of them, they couldn't trade; they couldn't do anything, and if they didn't have the full rationing, the food, and they gave away for something . . . but this was single incidents. Most of them, they went outside from the camp to work; so being outside, they found food what people threw out in garbage, and they took out and so was maybe not spoiled, and they ate. Some of them was dealing with some Polish people on the outside because they was working on the outside . . . I'm talking more from the Jewish war prisoners, when they went out a couple of thousand every day; so coming back, they smuggle in all kinds of food . . . some bread, maybe an apple, maybe a piece of meat. Most of them could help themselves a little bit, to have a little bit more food than just what they received from the camp.

The other things is, don't forget, 99 percent of us, what we was there, was young people, most of them in their early twenties. So when you are twenty years old, you can survive better than the older man. What I said about this guy what he died, he was an older man . . . in the late forties or fifties. When you was older, when you was weak, the Commandant Mohwinkel and the other SS watched for this, that when you walked a little bit not so straight or quick through the camp from one place to another, they knew that something is wrong with you. If you're too old, they took you out from the camp, and they send you to Majdanek.

But health-wise was not the worst . . . if they wouldn't kill them with the guns and the beatings, the Jews on the Lipowa could have survived another year until the Russians liberated Lublin in 1944. This would be about seven, eight months from November to July.

They could have survived. They could have survived even a little bit longer if they wouldn't have killed them.

———

The SS living quarters was in the six-story building outside the camp, what they had an entrance from the back. Was beautiful, beautiful, a very modern building with general heating and all the nicest facilities. From time to time, I used to come up to Mohwinkel's quarters before he came down to the office. When he need me, he called me to his place where he was living . . . a four- or five-room apartment with fireplaces.

Once I came up in the morning there, he came out in the pajamas to tell me today somebody has to come to take an order in the office. Near the fireplace, between the couch and the chairs was about a hundred glasses on the floor what was broken. After when they finished a drink, they used to throw away the glass on the floor . . . the empty glasses. And later, I heard from a German Jew . . . a short, little fellow . . . the name was Bergman, he was the cleaning maid who cleaned Mohwinkel's apartment. This was their system, when the officers came together, and they was drunk, so after when they finished, they tossed the drink; they throw away the glasses.

Most of the time, when they come back from a hunting—when I say hunting, not animals, but human lives, Jewish human lives—so they made themselves drunk, to enjoy or to forget . . . I don't know. In the shops when they used to beat somebody up or to kill him, when they was getting excited by the killing, they used to yell:

"You Judische schwein! *You Jewish pig! You made me do this hard work to beat you!*"

That was their expression most of the time:

"You made me do this to you!"

I can only describe Mohwinkel as an alcoholic, a drunk, because in the daytime, he was sleeping to ten, eleven o'clock when he came down from his apartment to the office from the labor camp. The German Jew, Bergman, told me that when they came back from a trip from killing, especially in the outskirts from Lublin—there was a town Piaski, in Yiddish *Puisk,* and there was a town Lubartów, *Levertov*[9]—so the

9. These Jew-hunts and ghetto-clearing actions took place between mid-March and mid-April, 1942, as well as those in Izbica, Zamosc, and Krasnik (Browning 1993, 52). Frank also remembers cleaning uniforms and removing blood stains from Moh-

German Jew told me, every night they went out for hunting; before they went or when they came back, the group from Mohwinkel, Offerman and his assistant Klein, and Schramm, so they all was drinking for two, three hours till they fall asleep with their boots on.

What I am telling you is only what I found out from Bergman because he was most of time there, and that's what he told me, because when we saw Mohwinkel, we saw him when he came down with the full-dress uniform, with the pistol. He went around to find something wrong with the prisoners, to take them in to give them some lashes or to kill somebody.

Mohwinkel, Klein, Offerman, Schramm, Lissy, Dorndoff . . . they all was a group. They worked together; they made plans how the killing should be, what town to go . . . because in the beginning of 1940, Lublin didn't have this kind of hunting. They arrest a couple of Jews, and they took them to the Shopena Street 17, they tortured the prisoners, and they let them out almost half dead. The relatives came to take them home and put them in bed or in hospitals . . . who knows? So the beginning was not so bad, but outside Lublin, the killing was worse and went on in the small towns. But later, after two, three months, there starts the same hell in Lublin. This is the things in the beginning what they did. Because of that, they became higher ranking officers because they tried to do a good job. Globocnik, the Police Leader from the SS, he was satisfied from the work what they was doing, and he was the guy to give them the higher ranks.

Jews what they was living outside the Lipowa, in the Lublin ghetto, knew everything, because in that time, '40 and '41, we went to work in the morning . . . eight o'clock we had to be there on Lipowa Street, and after four or five o'clock we still had our homes. When we came home we told the families the stories what we lived through the day, the working day that we was on the Lipowa.

The cleaning maid, Bergman, was a friend from the Music Professor David . . . from the same town from Germany, and Professor David took him in that he should have a better job than the other prisoners. But two months before they liquidate the labor camp, Pro-

---

winkel's uniforms and those of Offerman and Schramm, two officers. One Jewish survivor who worked at Globocnik's house recalled that Globocnik threw Mohwinkel a party after the murder of the fifty-thousandth Jew (Goldhagen 1997, 299; Mohwinkel is referred to as Alfred Dressler, a pseudonym). For Frank's recollection of the first major liquidation of the Lublin ghetto, see Chapter 18.

fessor David with the other German Jew Bergman disappeared,[10] and we didn't know where they went . . . we had an idea they took them out and killed them because they was figuring they know too much, because Bergman, most of the time, fifteen, sixteen hours he was in the apartment with Mohwinkel, and he saw everything—when Mohwinkel's drinking, with the women, with the prostitutes what went on in the apartment before they went out hunting, killing the Jews or when they came back. Bergman, he was not so important for them. They killed him; they took him to Majdanek.

10. In early September 1943.

6

—

The Lipowa Tailor Shop

Shop Operations, Management, and Atmosphere

1940–November 1943

THE SUPERVISOR ABOVE ME, what he was watching us that everything should go smooth, that everybody works and nobody cheats, his
name was Langfeld. He was in the SS but he was not born in Germany.
He was born in Poland, German descent . . . they called him a *Volksdeutsch*.[1] When I had to go out to take a measurement, he used to
get the telephone call to tell me, but sometimes he was out and I receive the telephone call, so I tell him that I have a call, and I have to take
a measurement of somebody in the office connected with the camp.

Langfeld didn't do anything to us, nothing to hurt us. If somebody will do wrong in the shop, he wouldn't do anything, he
wouldn't denounce to Mohwinkel. He was working, especially with
me, like comrades . . . with him I felt he was not like a Nazi, just
somebody in the shop to make sure all work should be done . . . but
with him I know I have a limit not to go over. With the whole time
what I was with him, more than three years, I never said something
what he should have against me, or he should even say something to
have against me or I should have against him . . . because, for three
years—he had a family, a wife with children—he need many things,
clothes for me to make. Always I made for somebody a dress, made a
coat, made children's things, and he was free to take home . . . there
was leftover pieces of material lying in the shop . . . sometimes
Langfeld brought materials. Always was he was bribed from me . . . I
call this bribing, maybe was not bribing, but he was not allowed to

1. An ethnic German.

57

take home material without permission from Mohwinkel, but he never told him, and they never checked an SS man by the gates when he leaves the camp. When we went to our sleeping quarters in the barracks, when the shops closed, he went home, and he went home always with something, packages. He had a good life, he never had so a good life in the three years, what his heart want from clothing, whatever his wife and his children could have.

ML: How do you think the other tailors viewed you and your supervision? Did they think, "Under all the circumstances, this isn't such a terrible place to work at the moment?" What was your way of managing the shop?

JF: My managing the shop was very easy. I didn't even consider myself I am a manager, because was nothing to manage. Everybody was very happy to have me there because when I went up to the office, to take a measurement—not what I want to praise myself . . . I was brought up in a way to be human, not to hurt nobody, and if we was hurt, it was all of us, and there was no reason for me to be different. For instance, the commandant from the concentration camp, if he wants to have something done, he called me in the office, and he told me what has to be done; so many uniforms have to be done every day, or when I need some materials for the uniforms I should tell him in advance, and he'll prepare some bolts with material to cut uniforms. When I had an order, I had a list from Mohwinkel, and from the list I have to tell the tailors what has to be done, how many uniforms this size to cut, how many jackets we need. I came in the tailor shop—I had Klein and Gootmacher, two close friends what they was working with me—I tell them the order, and they told the cutters how many have to be cut from the bolts. That was the management from me.

The shop was a couple hundred people and was divided in groups, and every group, twenty-five men, had a man what he brought this bundle, the material what was cut already, to the operators and to the finishers. Then when they have finished the garment, he took away from them, and he brought it over to the desk where these two assistants was in charge to pack them and to count them, to put in numbers telling the sizes, not to mix up one size with the other. When the amount was ready every day, I went into the office from the commandant, and I gave him the report that I have finished the job for the day, or several days. They took away the transport with a truck what was ready, and they put this in the warehouse. Day in, day out.

But the atmosphere in my shop, I considered it better managed than the others' shops. For instance, in the shoemaker shop was about a hundred shoemakers; there it was more strict from the Jewish leaders. If they gave them an order, the order was very strict. By me, almost was no orders to give; we all worked together. A matter of fact, when they called me up to take a measurement for some Germans, some from the tailors was praying that I should quick be back to the shop, because if I was not there and an SS man came in . . . they used to come in, and some tailors used to be beaten up because they didn't sit right, they didn't stand right . . . always they found something wrong. But when I was there, the first thing, the SS came into the shop, and they was talking to the German supervisor Langfeld, and I was near him, and there was never any incidents . . . and that's why the Jewish workers was pleased that I was always together with him in the shop, that no incidents should occur. Klein and Gootmacher used to always say when I had to leave to take a measurement, "Jack, don't waste too much time there in the office. If you'll be ready, come right away back." Even they was afraid something should happen. You see, if you get used to the devil . . . I was almost ten, fourteen hours a day with the Nazis, so when they called me up or I was there when they came in, I was not so fearful like the other tailors what they was there on the shop.

Once there was an incident . . . Saul Gootmacher, they slapped him in his face because he didn't answer right. He had a swollen face for a couple of days; that's all what happened. He was glad they didn't break his jaw. There used to be a saying:

"A Jew when he breaks one leg, he thanks God that he didn't break both of them."

He was glad they didn't knock out an eye from him or kill him. This life from people in the camp or the prison[2] was like a fly. One minute the fly is flying, and the second minute the fly was dead. Like with the people, life was nothing special; the value from the Jewish slaves in the labor camps or in concentration camps didn't mean anything.

ML: Do you think incidents occurred when you weren't there because the SS always liked to deal with the Jewish leader, and if there was no Jewish leader there they had free reign? Was there something about your presence, your manner?

JF: Maybe this was the point. There was another point. If an SS

---

2. "The prison" refers to a prison in Lublin where Frank was transferred after November 3, 1943. See Chapter 27, "The Lublin Prison."

man came in and I was there, and he start to demand something what has nothing to do with what I should carry out . . . because nobody could give me some orders but Mohwinkel, so when he was making demands what has nothing to do with the tailor shop, I put him over to Langfeld, so this finished the incident when the guy want to start something. Langfeld start to talk with him; this was between them, and then the SS guy left. Ninety-nine percent of the time when I was in the shop, never happened anything to the working tailors, not because I was better or stronger than the other leaders, but because I had Langfeld, so I was with him more on friendly terms, and the friendly terms was—I made some dresses for his wife, some slacks for his son . . . if they will catch me for what I did, maybe they'll kill me. I did it to save the atmosphere from the shop. If I had better conditions with the Nazi guy above me, watching me, something wouldn't happen when I went out for a moment. So that's why there was more order in my place.

But happened a couple times when somebody escaped from the camp, they took out one man, or two or three or four, or sometimes they selected the tenth man from every shop, and they hanged them; always happened something. One time, they took out Dudek Berliner, this was the cousin by my wife—he was the accountant in the tailor shop. A man escaped, so they hanged him in his place. Another time they took out a shoemaker from the line just because somebody escaped. You always was living with fear.

ML: So you couldn't really control the atmosphere of the shop; there was a limit to what you could do. Did you ever feel that the burden of responsibility you had was becoming too great; and that the other tailors mistakenly thought that you were more powerful than you were and that you could protect them when you couldn't?

JF: I didn't feel powerful, I didn't feel that I have any power. But I did what I'm supposed to do; maybe this'll help, and looks like this helped. When I was inside the shop, I was all the time under the pressure to go out to take a measurement. Inside was friends with me: Klein, Gootmacher, they was friends from before the war; we know each other . . . so looks like I was feeling that I have to do something for my friends like I am doing this for me, and they did the same thing.

They tried to do their part to carry out not with fear . . . this is the way what we have to do, to carry out the orders as tailors to make the clothes right . . . because the Nazi was also inside the whole time to watch, to go around, you couldn't sit and not do anything . . . if you should take a couple minutes rest, you should do this that the Nazi shouldn't see you. We also had to talk to the other tailors: if they should do something what this is not proper by the Nazis, they should be very careful that they should not be caught. This was this life in the shop.

ML: We've talked a lot about the different reasons why it was nearly impossible to escape: the Poles would not have been willing to help you; the Nazis hanged people in reprisal when someone escaped. . . . Did anyone from your shop ask you if you could help them in some way to get out?

JF: No. Never. Even in my shop, the ones who escaped never talked with the other ones. Was never an escape from the camp, not more than one person, so he didn't have an organized thing to do with somebody else. Was a time what forty or fifty of them escaped, but this was a whole group what they was working for the *Wehrmacht*, for the regular army. They escaped with the machine guns, with ammunition; they organized everything before. But Jewish prisoners from the Lipowa, if somebody escaped, was only one person at a time. In the four years, from '39 to '43, was about eight or ten escaped.

We never knew how they escape. The length from the camp was maybe about eight or nine blocks, was a wall all around, and the wall had wiring on top; so in the nighttime, the watchmen from the towers, maybe they fall asleep. And sometimes they sent out groups outside the camp to work . . . twenty or thirty groups, forty or fifty people in a group, and sometimes when they came back, and they count and one is missing, they escaped from there. You never knew. Nobody knew from another one if one should escape, because he was afraid to tell somebody.

ML: When someone new began working in the tailor shop at Lipowa, what kind of recommendations would you make to that person to take better care of himself, to get more food? To you, what were the most important things to try to do to get extra food?

JF: I didn't recommend. I never recommend anything, I couldn't recommend anything, and I was afraid to recommend something. My job was only to watch they should do the work what they have to do and not to get beat up for something or get punished for something, to see that they don't suffer because of me that I did wrong, that I didn't carry out the order what I received, so that later they don't take out the whole shop and punish them. The punishment was in the middle of the night to wake them up and to go out in January when it was ten below zero, to go out naked and to stay barefoot on the snow . . . naked for two hours. After when they came in, 50 percent or 60 percent was almost dead, with colds, with pneumonia . . . a lot died, a lot recovered . . . that's what my job was—to watch that this shouldn't happen. And I can be proud of myself to live with a clear conscience that I did everything to help, to do what I could do.

I don't want to talk too much about myself, what good things I did, but I know I never did something wrong—but there was some between us, not too many, when they had the power . . . when the Nazis gave them the power to be a leader or a head from someplace, they used this for their own personal gains to show how powerful they are. And I know I was never powerful; I was powerful when I had all my family. This was my power; this was my strength. But the moment when they took away everybody, I was no more, I had no more power myself.

ML: So you didn't have any personal experiences where someone in one commando wanted to get to another, so he came to you and said, "I can't take this job anymore; I want to come to the tailor shop."

JF: No, was never a refusal. If you told somebody to do something, you never refused that you don't want to do it.

ML: Not a refusal, but someone trying to find a way to get a better job.

JF: Maybe was there was some, I'm sure. There was some what they had ways how to get a better job, but I don't know from this. I never was interested to find out. I'm sure there was some protection, they should recommend somebody for a friend to somebody in the kitchen . . . somebody in the kitchen had to exchange somebody so they could change his friend.[3] I'm sure there was something like that, but I was never interested to ask.

ML: When you were still allowed to go home in the evening after a day at the camp, was food nearly nonexistent at home? Were they trying to strangle the food supply and starve the population?

JF: They tried to starve the population, sure. You didn't have

3. A position was not usually created to accommodate a prisoner who was recommended or who had arranged a bribe. In order to give the new person the job, someone had to be removed, which inevitably became another source of animosity and tension among prisoners.

enough food. But I had a little bit better than the other ones, because when the Nazis came in, when the customers from the *Wehrmacht*, from the regular Army, came in to make for them something, they brought a package with material; they was hiding between the material sometimes a piece of ham, even sometimes was a small bottle of whiskey. All the Nazis, they know me; I didn't have a number like the other ones, and I didn't wear the stripes till 1944 when they took me from Lublin to Radom. So I had a little better . . . better, I mean I had a piece of bread more than other Jews. This was the better things what I had.

ML: Did you see any signs in your shop, or maybe one of the other shop leaders told you about this, that some workers were resentful that the shop leaders could leave at night, in '42 and '43?

JF: No. We all know in the labor camp that if we could leave, it's because the commandant wants us to leave. It's not because we did something that he gave us a privilege and made for us a better life and gave them worse. They all know in the camp that if somebody has to be there, that's what the Nazi wants. It's not up to us. And the moment they liquidate the small ghetto, that's it; it's only up to them. It's not up to us, to make our life easier. You see, the point is, we all knew that we are in the same boat. Was no reason to think that you can do better for yourself—there was some instances that somebody did something against somebody else's life to make his life better, but this was not in the labor camp; this was more in the concentration camp.

ML: What are you thinking about specifically?

JF: For instance, they took out from the Jews thirty or forty people to work by the crematoriums, so they had a little better life. The better life was they received a bigger piece of bread or a potato more in the soup, and they didn't have to go to the crematorium, but they helped to send the others to the crematorium.[4] Was Jews what they carried out orders, even to take the dead bodies out, the ashes out, to clean out the ovens, so there was Jews who did these things to make their lives easier. Not because they want to do this, but when they did this, they treat them a little bit . . . they are their people, they are working for the Nazis, they figure they are carrying out a thing what

4. The groups who worked at the crematoriums were called the *Sonderkommando* (Special Commando), one of many euphemisms used to disguise extermination, like the terms "Special Treatment," "Resettlement," and "Final Solution." For a thorough account of their work at Treblinka, see Willenberg 1989.

they deserve to have a little bit better. When they was working for a longer time, they became people without feeling.

There was some Jews what they took them out to do this kind of work, and they refused, and they got the bullet, and they killed them on the place. When the others saw when he said, "I won't do this," and they gave him the bullet in the back of his head, the others became scared and they went over to the other side, some of them, to do it. That's how this was. What can I tell you?

7

Dialogue on Brutality

ML: YOU TOLD ME THAT AT LIPOWA you remember a man who was given two rations of bread for the day, one for himself and one for his son, but one was an ounce heavier than the other. He couldn't decide whether he or his son should get the bigger piece of bread, and he didn't want to make that choice either. So he put both pieces of bread behind his back and had his son point to a side.

People who haven't been in the camps would either expect that he would have given the larger piece to his son, since if the son was just a boy, the father would be willing to sacrifice his food or his health for him—up to a point—or we expect the opposite, that the son would have wanted his father to have had the larger piece since the father might have been weaker. Those of us with no experience of the camps might think that they could have worked this dilemma out instead of resorting to a random measure. What do you think the Nazis' thinking was behind the camps—how did they expect the prisoners to behave?

JF: They did everything to give the Jewish prisoners conditions that they should fight each other or kill each other. This was their philosophy, because sometimes a Nazi called out:

"It's too expensive to waste our bullets for the Jews. Kill them with something else."

Kill them with something else—with a piece of iron or with another object. To gas them or to burn them—this will be much cheaper. And also, they figured out even with the crematoriums, they used Jewish hands to help; one should kill another.

I have a picture here what I took in Israel at Yad Vashem Museum, the Holocaust museum. I took the picture because I saw this with mine own eyes, when they took a little child by the legs and threw to a brick wall. This I saw with mine own eyes.

ML: Where was that?

JF: In Lublin! Even before they liquidate . . . was in the ghetto!

ML: Do you remember the situation, what had happened before they did that?

JF: No, I don't remember. So a long time, fifty years, I don't remember the situation, but I remember this was a couple of Nazis. They came into the ghetto, and the Jews start to run, and they was after the people, and a woman couldn't hold her child with her when she was running. She put down the child, and she took the child with her, but she was running . . . I don't know if the child was four or five or three years old . . . but the child couldn't run so fast, so the woman with the child was behind the whole runners what they was running away from the Nazis. One from the Nazis ran after her and took out the child from the mother's hands, and he took by the legs, and he threw the child to a building, to a brick wall. I saw with mine own eyes. Similar to this—I took the picture from the museum that a Nazi killed a woman when she had a child on her hand, and he stays with the rifle and killed her.

ML: I wanted to ask you another question . . . about some of your ideas . . .[1]

---

1. This exchange was the first in which I was at a loss for words. It was not that I lacked sympathy or couldn't imagine the scene, but when the brutal force of the story and the photograph hit me, I did not know what would be appropriate to say, nor what I wanted to say. It was the first instance in which I had to stop playing the protected role of interviewer or researcher and did not have a convenient part at my disposal. I would liked to have shown sympathy or empathy, or have made a remark that I understood the severity of a child being smashed against a brick wall, but, truthfully, this was not how I responded at the time. In a very graphic way, Mr. Frank was showing me for the first time that what the victims experienced went far beyond the fact that a child was killed in a particular manner. There was more to this than the brutal way people were killed; there was more to this than his original point that the Nazis would kill in any way possible—and the less expensively, the better. Mr. Frank was pointing out to me that murders like these broke all bounds of what survivors believed people could do to one another. What they experienced was unbelievable, but at the same time, it actually occurred in front of them, during ghetto-clearing actions, deportations, and everyday camp life. I could read all I wanted, listen to all the survivors I could find, but this would not amount to an accurate representation of the magnitude of the event. I was being shocked and told to pay attention, put into the position of realizing that there are tragedies in which one is at a loss to respond. If one experiences them oneself, one responds immediately to these extreme acts of horror; one can cry, tear out one's hair, cover one's naked body, run, scream, or whimper. Being shown the photograph and told the story is obviously more removed and less terrible, but it demonstrated how distant I was from the impact of the original event.

JF: Look at that . . . She is helping her child. Do you see?

ML: It seems to me there's so little you can say.

I imagine that all the other people who saw that were either too terrified or too horrified . . .

JF: Nobody except me is alive, I say, from Lublin. Except there are some alive from Lublin what they was on the Russian side, and after the war, they come back. Not too many, but they was hidden. There was some Poles, they save a couple of Jews, but not too many. These are the people what can say what they saw. But they all are dead, especially from Lublin; nobody is alive.

ML: What was the effect on you of seeing incredibly brutal acts like this over and over again? How did that affect the way, at that time, you saw your own life?

JF: The effect at this moment was very scary, very, very awful, but in a moment later, you was thinking for yourself how to save your body, your life. That's how the feeling was.

ML: Eventually, whom did you see as the ultimate torturer, the ultimate criminal? Did you see Nazis in general, the individual guards wherever you were, or the people responsible for the decisions; did you see the responsible party as the German people as a whole? Or was it really different, depending on where you were?

JF: I see there was some difference. But most of the Germans . . . if you take a nation and you start to hammer some words day in and day out, and every time of the day and every time of the night— twenty-four hours a day—when you start to talk all the time that this kind of element, a Jew or a Gypsy or Russians, that they are your enemies—from 1933 to 1939, six years—even the good Germans start to believe that this is the way to make better their lives. And everybody looks for making their lives better. Even here in the United States, most of the people, they are looking out for themselves, no? We don't live in this kind of country that you can do everything what you want, but if they'll let you, maybe. . . . If we wouldn't have here a constitution and if a leader like Joe McCarthy would be here, or another McCarthy with a different name, God forbid it could be the same thing.

ML: How did you view the commanders on Lipowa Street versus how you viewed the Polish guards at the Lublin prison, for instance? Did you see any difference in how threatening they were or what their power was . . .

JF: There was a difference. The Polish guard was interested to get your money but not your life. The German guard was interested to get your money and then to kill you. This is the difference.

ML: Did you ever wonder what explained these people's behavior, or was this not a relevant question at the time?

JF: It's relevant . . . we knew why this happened, why they are doing this way. You see, you have to know the psychology of a nation. The psychology of the German is: the German always carries out orders. If the leader will tell them to do something, they will do it. They carry out orders here, too, in every country. There are some incidents what the man is carrying out, I wouldn't do this. Even our President Clinton with Vietnam, he said he is not going there. The German is not this way. If you tell him to go, even if he knows he is going to be killed. . . . The American knows there is a possibility he will get killed in the battle, but he is going to live. But the German, if they tell him, "You go there," and he knows he'll be dead, he'll go.

ML: What about in situations where people weren't obeying orders strictly, like this SS man who hurled the child against the brick wall? How do you explain that kind of explosion of brutality?

JF: Like I said before, Hitler told them day and night for six years, or maybe more than six years, he started in the twenties in the Beer Hall there, before he came to power. If you tell a man who doesn't have anything, "Here is your enemy. This little girl is your enemy. If you'll kill her, her father, her mother will run away and will leave the fortune with his gold and diamonds"—what they was always saying the Jew is the rich one—"You'll take away his fortune, and you have to do this. And if you wouldn't do this, then you wouldn't help yourself."

This went on day and night from the radio; in that time they didn't have television. And that's the reason he did this: he saw in this little girl, he saw his enemy. Everything that was Jewish was his enemy. If he saw an enemy, it doesn't matter if this is a little girl or a grown-up man. Even in the Jewish history, in the Jewish books, was a guy his name was Moloch, and he was like a Hitler. He killed Jews from left and right, and the Jews sent out to fight back, and the order was from the Jewish leader: "What you see everything on the road, the cows, the animals, everything—Burn! Kill! The Moloch shouldn't exist anymore in the history. Everything must go. Even the fields what was growing food should be burned." This is in the Jewish history too, the same: "If this is your enemy, liquidate them entirely, with the children, with the cows, with the goats, with the chickens, everything—nothing should be alive. Burn everything to the ground."

That's what the guy did when he threw this little girl to the brick wall. That's what they did with all the Jews. If Hitler wouldn't make the mistake to attack Russia, I don't know if one Jew would be alive except . . . and maybe in the United States, the Jew wouldn't be safe either. You had plenty of Nazis in the United States, even today they are going around yelling "*Heil Hitler.*" So who knows?   .

ML: What kinds of repercussions or selections or checks during work did you see at Lipowa Street, because in the article you translated for me from Yiddish, you made a statement that people were shot; they were beaten; they were horribly tortured.[2] What kinds of things took place there?

JF: For instance, in the tailor shop, after a couple weeks or couple of months, I don't remember exactly, Mohwinkel, he was an engineer. He was a young man in that time also, twenty or twenty-one years old. He came in the shop with a sports-watch, and when you clicked the watch a certain time, like the car races where you give the signal to go or how long the race took. He came in; he was sitting to see how long a sleeve was taking to make. He stopped the stopwatch; it takes about fifteen or twenty minutes. He went to another tailor what he is sitting and working, he made a collar. The collar took about thirty minutes—I give you an example—he knocked off thirty minutes. And that's how long a front to make takes. So he put together all the sections what belongs to a uniform jacket, and he came out with a balance of how long a jacket has to take to make ready. I had 475 tailors, and a jacket has to take a day, so he has to have 475 uniform jackets a day made. And if you didn't deliver—this is an example, this isn't exactly how this was, but you're asking why he came in to torture somebody—if I didn't make the 475 uniform jackets a day, he will take out ten or fifteen tailors from the tailor shop, and he will tell the Ukrainian or the Nazis to give everybody twenty-five lashes with the whip. And if the twenty-five getting lashes will be seen in the presence of the other 455 tailors, and they will have to be in the *Lazarett,* in the hospital for five or six days to be able to go back to sit on their behind, they will see the 475 uniforms should be ready this day. And this happened in other shops; it didn't happen in my shop.

ML: How did you hear about that in other shops?

2. In 1961 during the Eichmann trial, Frank was interviewed in an article called "I Was a Witness," in *The Morning Journal,* a Yiddish newspaper published in New York (June 27, 1961).

JF: I went around to see! What do you mean?—we saw if they took out a couple from another shop, from the shoemaker shop, from the saddlers—they had to make two or three saddles a day—and they beat them; they gave them twenty-five lashes. We saw them taken out. There was a special place where they put them with their heads, with the body; they tell them to let down their pants, and you had to count. *You had to count;* and if you couldn't count anymore, they start from the beginning again. I saw it—what do you mean how? Not only me, at that time there were a lot of us alive, so everybody saw it.

For instance, there was a man, his name was Francis. He knew two or three or four languages. He was speaking perfect German, he was speaking French, and he was speaking perfect English. He was a Polish Jew, a very educated guy. He was a good Jew; he wasn't doing nothing wrong. He didn't *think* he was doing nothing wrong, but he did wrong. He became a supplier to Mohwinkel. Mohwinkel, if he need something, if he need leather, Francis became a mediator between the Nazis and the Jews outside the labor camp. For instance, they gave out an order to wear the King David armband. If they caught some Jewish people taking chances, that you shouldn't know that they are Jewish if they go to certain streets—if they see a Jew, the *Polaks* will denounce them to the Germans. You figure, if you want to go to a Polish section—some Jews at that time was still making a little business with *Polaks* so they had to go to collect money, or to give them money, or to give them some material, so they took off the armband. They caught them, and sometimes they killed them for this, and sometimes they brought them to the labor camp, to us.

So Francis, because he was so very close with Mohwinkel, the commandant from the labor camp, when Mohwinkel needs something—leather or other things . . . first Mohwinkel asked me, "You are from Lublin," he said. "You know the tailors who have materials"—he needs material for his wife or for his friend—"How about to go to your friends to bring me some material?"

I said, "The whole time before now I was working in Warsaw. I don't know too many tailors what they have materials in Lublin." I always knew the Nazis—I knew that if I start with a little thing, then later I'll be involved in other things what I'll not be able to get out from. If I supply them with material for a suit—I knew people who had materials, tailors—I had my shop before I went in to the camp, I had my showroom materials, but I gave them away to Poles to hide them that maybe the war would come to an end, but they didn't give back anyway; they were lost anyway. But you think, your mind works . . . maybe the war wouldn't be forever, maybe tomorrow will be the end, or in a month or two months.

Francis delivered to him all kind of things what he needs. Came a time where if they had something what they was hiding by the Poles, the Jews didn't have any more to give and they couldn't supply what Francis wants. The end was that there was a time that Mohwinkel wants from him something, and he couldn't deliver: "You changed your mind to supply the things what I need."

But Francis couldn't supply, so Mohwinkel killed him. I knew Francis, he was my best friend . . . he was my best friend? What I am I saying? I tried to be with him friends because he was close to Mohwinkel, so I knew him. And Mohwinkel was respecting me a little bit better than the other prisoners, the other slaves, because he need me for his purpose. So I kept up with Francis, but I saw when they took him in the office, and they didn't kill him—they beat him to death. They beat him so long, and then they called in two from the Jewish war prisoners, and they carried him out from the office. They took him in the hospital to help resuscitate him, and he died a couple hours later.

ML: People like this who were beaten and killed, or people who were shot inside the shops for some reason or another, what happened to their bodies?

JF: Like I just said, they called up the *Judenrat* to take out the bodies.

ML: But could the *Judenrat* give those people burial?

JF: Yeah, in the beginning, they gave them. But this was, I am talking, this was in 1940 or in the beginning '41. In the beginning, they could bury them on the Jewish cemetery.

ML: What happened once the ghetto was sealed?

JF: We don't know what happened with the bodies . . . they let them lie on the ground. What happened later with them, who knows? When they start to seal the ghetto, and they start to make some killings, so everybody was afraid to look out and to see. Everybody was for themselves. Still they had families, or they was afraid even to look. And then later, they took some Jews from the ghetto; they went in a house, and they took out a couple of men, and they took the bodies to a certain place, and they let them lay on the ground. What happened with them, nobody looked. We saw . . . we noticed they are dead, that's all.

ML: What was the effect of working and living in this place where there were dead people whom you might have known around you?

JF: The effect was on us—we was sick! We was sick; we start to throw up with the food what we had a couple of hours before. We was crying, to look what happened . . . you couldn't do anything. *You couldn't do anything.* And later you became used to it. If there was a gathering from five or ten Nazis, you knew something will happen; some Jews will be killed. So you almost . . . you expect. And if it didn't happen, you said, "We are lucky."

8

The First Leather Coat

Middle of 1940

THE MIDDLE OF 1940, six or seven months since they open the camp, came out an order that nobody can go out from the barracks. They locked us up; no one could go out till they open the doors, but we gave a peek through the windows. When they start to walk around—I knew when they passed—through the window we could see a bunch of ten or twelve Nazis. What I know them is Globocnik, Höffle[1] . . . above Mohwinkel was a Major—his name was von Alvensleben—I knew him because I saw him from the time I was there, almost every day, passing by . . . not what I saw him I was mingling with him or talking with him . . . and I knew Mohwinkel, Hantke, Schramm, Dolp. So they all was passing by; I could see the bunch but I didn't know what to say. I saw only Himmler when I recognized him from the picture, when he came into the shop with the all *swile*—they call this in Yiddish, the whole group.

Mohwinkel showed them the tailor shop, the biggest from all the shops, because was a couple hundred people with machines, tables, press irons. Langfeld gave a command to stand up, to stay in form like in the army, frozen. The entourage came in and they looked, just had their heads to look at something. For fear, we didn't see no faces . . . we saw shadows.

The same day when Himmler and the group visited the camp, after three hours, about five o'clock in the afternoon, an SS man came in the tailor shop, and he told me to take the tape measure . . . what I

---

1. A *Sturmbannführer* (Major) under Globocnik. In 1942 he was in charge of Jewish deportations from Lublin, Warsaw, and Bialystock en route to the killing centers (Hilberg 1985, 486).

always carried . . . it was like a pass, not my real pass what I had,[2] but I always had this with me for my trade to show what I am doing, that I am a tailor. When there was some job to do, I have to take a measurement, so the guards, they saw my pass, but they also saw the tape measure and know there is some order I must carry out. This time the SS man told me I have to come with him: "You will take a measurement for an officer." He didn't tell me for whom.

I took the tape measure, I went out to the iron gates from the camp, and an SS man escort me. He tells me, "Get in the car," and inside was sitting two SS men with machine guns. They put me in the middle from them, one on this side, on the right side, and the other on the left side. They blindfolded me, and one guy was testing if the blindfold is right that I shouldn't see . . . he corrected it a little bit higher or lower; I know he touched my face, the blindfold on my face. I was not thinking nothing, but to think fear . . . to try to take the fear away, this was impossible, not because you are afraid from your life—you are afraid something should happen; you will never see your family again, or it is something what you don't know to be afraid.

The car start to move, and I was thinking I know where we are going. When they went out from the Lipowa Street, when you was three or four blocks from the Krakow Street, there was a turn, and I felt that the turn is to the left, and this was down to the higher streets. From the Lipowa to the street where we went, they made a right turn, was maybe five or six minutes. So more or less I know how many streets there is from the Lipowa to *Kruel Leszcynskiego*.

In late 1940 the SS moved all the offices to this place named from the *Kruel Leszcynskiego*, a famous king from the Poles, King Leschinsky Street. A new development was there, owned by a Jewish millionaire named Kenisberg. Was not too many Jewish millionaires in Lublin . . . was maybe three or four millionaires, but he was the richest one. He built about fifteen or twenty buildings, a whole community there, and before the Nazis came in, the Polish government had their offices, their tax collection offices and other offices . . . the whole development there was occupied by the Polish government, but the Nazis took this over from them. Once I went to the tax department there,

---

2. The "real pass" was a document signed by Globocnik that Frank was under his protection, and no one had the authority to kill Frank except him.

that's what I know this place. The architecture was very plain—this was the new-style buildings, like boxes, like here—no pictures, no sculptures.

One SS man took me by the arms, to carry me into the building. They took me into a lobby and then into a room, and there they took off the blindfold. They told me to undress completely. I was naked, and they looked me over from head to foot, to see I am not hiding something. I had nothing with me, just in my pocket a handkerchief. In the other corner from the apartment, they had a suit for me . . . didn't fit exactly right, was too big and too loose, but they told me to change the clothes anyway. I put on the suit, and they took me into the office to take a measurement.

I saw for whom I had to take the measurement. I recognize his face from the pictures, with the little eye-glasses, the special glasses. He was wearing a black uniform, just like the other SS officers, but when you saw the emblem, the mark from the rank was different. The face was very, very gentle. I was scared to look at him because the two guys are standing two feet away with machine guns pointing on me . . . this is not the usual way when I do this for an officer.

From the side, I tried to give a look on his face, but I remember, I didn't see a face from a murderer . . . he didn't say anything, no talking, no expression on the face, like a regular guy—not smiling, but not vicious looking. I didn't look on his face directly; the instinct was I was afraid to look at him. Your mind is working that you should have a look, but this takes away a second longer, and my mind, in my brains, was to get over quicker and to finish and to get out from there. I was shivering for fear, shaking.

I take the length, I move around from the back to the front . . . the arms, the waist, the chest . . . usually if I took a measurement in civil life, the customer turned around, but for the Nazis, I turned. I didn't look at his face or see what his figure looked like. I do like I am an automaton. I told an SS man just numbers, not what this is for, the waistline or the length, the length of a sleeve or the width, and he asked me, "Do I have to write for what measurement this is?" and I said, "No, just the numbers."

The next day, they called me to the office from the labor camp. In that time, the commandant was Mohwinkel. Looks like Mohwinkel was a better killer . . . he killed more Jews than before him, the commandant Riedel. Mohwinkel was just a *Rotteführer*—this is like a

Kapo[3]—and they made him for commandant, and they made him for Lieutenant, an *Untersturmführer.* I came in the office and Mohwinkel told me, "You took yesterday the measurement for our *Reichsführer* Himmler. We have gray leather. You will make a leather coat for him."

Mohwinkel took out from the closet a leather coat what he was wearing. It was only one style from all Germans what they was wearing the leather coats.

He showed me: "The one for the *Reichsführer* should look like this. And if this wouldn't fit exactly, you know what you'll get."

I said, *"Jawohl!"* and asked him if I can take the leather coat to the shop.

"Yes, but not for too long. For how long do you need it?"

"For a couple of hours."

"For three hours you can keep it."

Somebody from the tailors in the shop . . . this was in the beginning and we still have cameras . . . he took a photograph from the coat. We looked at the coat; I made a sketch, all kind of measurements, how wide the lapels should be, how wide the collar should be, how wide the flaps from the pockets should be, all the details. I had a picture from the coat, and I had a picture in my head how the coat should look.

In three hours I brought the coat back to the office and hung it up from where Mohwinkel showed me he took out the coat. No more did we have a conversation about this coat.

This was the first leather coat what I made. I was the designer from the patterns; I cut the pattern . . . we didn't keep the patterns because every person had a different measurement. Also I had Klein, he was a very good craftsman, knows his trade very well. In the cutting room, before we start to cut the leather, I mark with the marker where to cut the pieces . . . there was two or three friends, we decide everything is fine; we can cut this. The cutter was cutting the leather; we was standing and watching. Making the coat, just to know for whom the coat would be, we was very scared . . . God forbid if something would happen in the work. We know what this means. It means death.

———•———

There is no special way to work with leather than with material. The difference is only that you take a piece of material, you put away

3. The direct translation of "*Rotteführer*" is "gang leader."

SS-Reichsführer Heinrich Himmler and other Nazis examine a model of the Dachau camp during a visit on January 20, 1941. Anton Mussert, the leader of the Dutch National Socialists, is to Himmler's right. Oswald Pohl, Chief of the SS Economic and Administrative Department wields the pointer. Himmler is wearing a leather coat similar to the style which Frank tailored for him. *Courtesy of the Nederlands Instituut voor Oorlogsdocumentatie, Amsterdam, Netherlands, and the United States Holocaust Memorial Museum Photo Archives.*

on the table, and you have a pattern, and you cut the material. But with leather, you don't have the length what you have from material. Material comes in yards. Leather comes in pieces—when you take off from the animal, there is not a straight piece. So you cut a pattern, and you try to make the top till the waistline; from the shoulders to the waistline you have the length what you can use from the length from the leather. And from the waistline down, another piece of leather. You put together the leather, and you make the seams—the only difference here is with a thinner needle in the machine. Then, you put away the pattern. You cut where the leather is put together, so you try to keep the mark from the waistline on the seam, what you connect from one part to the other. When the leather is cut like the pattern shows you, then to put together the leather is the same thing like material, except you cannot make a mistake. If later the fit will not be right, you cannot take the pieces apart and put back together. The

Himmler during his visit to Dachau. The style of his leather coat is quite evident: full-length and double-breasted, with a wrap-around front and belt. *Courtesy of the Nederlands Instituut voor Oorlogsdocumentatie, Amsterdam.*

rows of holes from the needle from the machine show up and stay in the leather. And if we make a mistake, we cannot ask for more leather; we cannot find somebody in secret to supply us with more.

With material, when the coat is ready, you pass the coat with hot iron or with steam. Leather, you cannot pass with hot iron or to give steam because the leather will shrink. You pass the leather a little bit with a warm iron, but not to keep too long this iron on the leather because you'll spoil the color. That's the way what you make leather . . . there's not a big difference; there's no special scientific technique to do.

The patches and insignias is very easy. The swastikas they gave you ready-made, and you sewed them on the places where they showed you. I used the photograph from the leather coat from Mohwinkel, like when I made a uniform jacket, to see where all the emblems has to be.

The leather coat for Himmler was ready in four or five days, and I brought over the coat to the office from Mohwinkel. He looked it over . . . I don't know in this time what is in his mind, if he is comparing it to his or if he knows what he is looking for. He took out the coat what was his, and he showed me the two together . . . we was staring at his and the one for Himmler.

He looked over and said, "The main thing—if this will fit."

I didn't say anything. I was listening what he is talking, and he gave me an order to leave the office. I never heard about the coat, if Himmler took the coat or if the coat fit him or not, if the coat satisfied him, what he thought from the work what I was doing . . . this last thing was not important for them, only to see what I am doing is what they want me to do, and to get from me the coats.

9

—

The Tailor's Measurements

IN THE TAILOR SHOP, the material was brought in to the cutters, that they should cut the uniforms, and I was telling them what sizes and how many uniforms should be made every day and to go around if somebody was injured to take him to the little hospital there, the *Lazarett*. But a lot of the work what I was doing took me away from the tailor shop—was like a factory, very enormous—to do special work for officers and commandants—because you know there was always two sides to their business: the uniforms, then later the down jackets what we made for the *Wehrmacht* when they was fighting the Russians in Leningrad; and there is the special requests, the special things what the Nazis know they cannot get, the gifts what Mohwinkel gives his superiors. Because maybe the way from Hitler or from Eichmann was, eventually, kill all the Jews but put some from them to work, to use them to serve their purpose for a while—but also the way from the individual Nazi was to get something what he does not have and get it for nothing.

When a Nazi officer came to the Lipowa and wants a leather coat, or a civil suit, or a uniform, I have to go first to take the measurement. The SS calls me up . . . was a telephone in the barrack from the tailor shop that I should come to the office. I had an assistant to my job what when I left to go outside to take a measurement, so he took over the responsibility with the tailors. To get to the office, I used a connection, an entrance to the SS building from the back, from the Lipowa lot.

I came in the room where the customer was, and I went over with the tape measure. He is standing, and I am standing in the back behind him when I take the length from the uniform jacket, then the length from the pants. Then I took the measurement between his legs, to take the measurement from the inside seam. Then I turned

80

from the back to the front, and I take the measurement from the chest
and from the waist and from the hips.

Sometimes they called me up to go to the office, and I had to go
to take measurements for customers from the *Wehrmacht* officers; for
instance, I had a lot of doctors from the German Army. When I took a
measurement for them, they used to talk to you all the time . . . they
was asking me how the prisoners live, if we're getting enough food, if
they beat us. But I never said nothing; I was listening, I never answered, or I said "I don't know." The doctors want only to ask about
the way of life what we had, but I said, "I cannot answer you what you
are asking." He said, "I know what you mean." I cannot trust even
the *Wehrmacht;* we know there is a difference from the *Wehrmacht* to
the SS or from the other parties, the SD, but I never let myself in to
have a conversation with them.

For civil clothes, maybe the officer has some preferences, so he
tells you what kind of style he wants. In a uniform, it's no styling—
one style for all. The army has a style for the jacket, and the jacket
from the ranking officer has a different style. But they give me one
model, a jacket or a pair of riding slacks what they are riding on the
horses with leather on the seats of the pants. They showed me what
they want . . . the same thing with the civil things when they brought
material. An officer wants a civil suit, I ask him, "Do you want single-
breasted or double-breasted?"—not special styles, no big discussion or
big choices. The Nazis never wait for you that you should tell them
what kind from seams, pockets, the cuffs what they could have. They
tell you what they want.

Most of the officers what I met, and I met them in the hundreds,
through the five years and nine months in the camps, from the highest
ranking officers to the lowest, there was some of them what they
know about fashions . . . they came out from richer families; they had
the money, and they was dressed nice . . . but most of them, they
didn't know. It looks to me that they didn't have too much in Germany before the war. When they came in, and you made for them a
civil suit, the officers, they was dreaming . . . when I made for them
one suit, it looks like they never had a suit in their lives: "Make me
this, make me that. Make me another suit." It looks to me like they
never had a suit to wear. There was some of them, more arrogant
dressers what they knew the styles, but most of them, looks like, they
didn't have so good in Germany before the war.

There was times when some officers, they came to have some work for their wives, and they brought some pictures from books, photographs. I was, or I had many tailors, they was artists in their trade. We saw the picture, and we knew how to put it together. Was no problem to copy it, to bring out the same thing what the model in the book shows you. Maybe you are thinking this is incredible: artists, the slaves, they are making the high fashions . . . in private life, they used to tell me that I am an artist in my trade. There was tailors that before they start to cut a jacket or a lady's suit or a man's uniform, they took a pencil, they made a sketch like an artist, exactly like you see in a fashion book. In two or three minutes, you had a sketch where the seams should be—here should be so a collar or so a front, or so patch pockets or inside pockets. They was artists in mine estimation.

I had an officer Offerman, an *Untersturmführer,* a second lieu-tenant, he told me . . . I don't know, he looked to be a little bit nicer than the other ones . . . I made for him a uniform, and then he came, and he said he would like to have a suit for his wife. He brought me the picture, and he brought me the measurement from Germany, when he was on vacation there. I made for him the suit. He treat me a little nicer, looks like he was appreciating the work what I put in his wife's suit. He told me a story that he was working in Germany with Jews. They had a store from yard goods, materials from men's suits. He was working there from when he finished from high school, till he married and had a child; then Hitler came to power, and his father joined the party. Because he was already a grown-up man, his father persuade him to join the Nazi party too. I don't know if he told me the story to make me feel better that he was working for Jews . . . he even told me the name with the street in Berlin when he was there be-fore the war. But he impressed me like he was appreciating the work what I did for him, but most of them, they didn't show you any ap-preciation. This is not just with tailors or with shoemakers or with other craftspeople; they used Jewish doctors in the German hospitals, professors, specialists in all kind of fields. They treat them like dirt. They said to the doctor or to the professor, "If this guy will die, and you can't treat him, you will lose your head; you'll get killed." Every-thing was working for them, not with appreciation, but with orders, to make you for everything fearful.

ML: It strikes me that in these fields like making clothes or shoes or with doctors, professions where the person making something or performing the service shows personal care for the client or the patient, these professions aren't like the industrial situation, where you set up the factory, and you're completely divorced from what goes on there, and you're just interested in quotas and output and product. Nazism is often portrayed as a cold-blooded, bureaucratic machine, but in these trades the relationships were more complex than immediate threats and orders handed down. Human relationships might show absolutely no sensitivity, or there might be some signs of pleasure or appreciation from the officer, but I suppose in the end it didn't matter if the officer revealed his feelings or showed that what you did for him meant something—he could get whatever he wanted out of you.

JF: You are correct that this caring should be this way, but was not. Except like I said before, there was some, even from the SS, what they brought some materials, and they was hiding between the package from the materials a piece of bread, a piece of meat, or some cigarettes. So there was some, but they didn't talk to you; they just gave you the package, and I found it later. They didn't even tell me that something is there.

In civil life, was this way what you is saying. For instance, when I retired from tailoring four years ago, I had customers . . . the first time what I see a woman crying, "What I'll do without you that you are retired, that you wouldn't work for me anymore? Where would I go?" Because there was some customers what they have some special needs—one was a little bit on the heavier side, the figure was a little bit deformed. The appreciation there . . . I was feeling that I was somebody, that somebody need me. But in the camp, even with your artistic talents what you have, this was nothing. If they knew you was an important man, they tortured you more with the words or with the treatment so that you feel more down than a general person. The more they knew you are more intelligent, they put you more down. The first what they went to death was the intelligentsia.

Besides the *Wehrmacht* officers, the Nazis what I made civil clothes for was the higher-ranking officers from around the camp and some from the Gestapo. But talking about Globocnik or Eichmann or Himmler or the Governor from Poland, Hans Frank—his residence was in Krakow—I only made for them leather coats. Leather coats I also made for others . . . they called themselves *Standartenführer*[1] . . . for von Alvensleben, and for *Standartenführer* Gunst, what he came

---

1. The SS rank of Colonel.

Examples of different types of leather coats and dress uniform overcoats worn by high-ranking Nazis. Also note the Nazis' high black leather boots, which Lipowa Labor Camp cobblers made for many officers. This photo was taken during Himmler's visit to Dachau on January 20, 1941. Himmler is second from the right. Karl Wolff, Himmler's chief of staff, is second from the left. Oswald Pohl, Chief of the SS Economic and Administrative Department, is third from the left, turned to the side. *Courtesy of the Nederlands Instituut voor Oorlogsdocumentatie, Amsterdam.*

before *Standartenführer* von Alvensleben.[2] I made a leather coat for Mohwinkel and a lot of leather coats what I don't remember the names . . . the elite from the Nazis, from all the killers. They all was crazy about coats. They could have leather; every officer would like to have a leather coat. Most of them, they had, the higher ranks.

ML: Maybe that was why—it was a sign of their status . . .

JF: I don't know. Always when a smaller, lower-rank officer, when I made for him a leather coat, and he came to pick up the coat from the office—I am talking not from names what they was known—I looked at his face, and he was so happy like he would never own a coat to wear. For a uniform jacket, they didn't make a big thing to be happy or not to be happy, but most of the time they was happy about civil clothes and about a leather coat.

The lower ranking officers, they brought leather . . . they had to. By the big guys, Mohwinkel supplied the leather, through Francis or through Koslow. I didn't ask questions in that time . . . I knew when you ask too many questions what you're not supposed to ask, there is trouble for you. You get educated with them when you was with them for a long time, what to ask and what not to ask.

2. For background on these officers, see notes 2 and 3 in Chapter 20.

ML: In your opinion, since you made several leather coats, for Globocnik, Himmler, and Eichmann, what was your aesthetic opinion of the coats? I know you weren't thinking about aesthetics at the time, but what kind of overall appearance do you think the coat gave to the wearer? Some survivors have described that Göth's coat made him look extremely sinister or powerful.[3]

JF: Very scary. It's not only the coat what they was wearing was scary, but the whole ensemble what they put together: the high hat with the emblems, with the decoration on the hat, all the marks with the ranks on the sleeves and on the collar, and the buckle with the pistol on the waistline, and the high boots . . . the whole look was meant to terrorize you . . . especially with the leather coat, was very scary when you look at them. Even when they didn't have in their mind to kill you, the feeling from everybody was they'll do to you something bad; they'll take away your life. The whole idea from Hitler was to scare the world, that was the idea . . . the uniform, the way they act . . . the whole idea is to put the fear that the whole world should be afraid of you.

ML: And appearance was part of that, not just the fact that they were threatening because of what they'd done previously . . .

JF: Just the appearance. I was not so fearful like the other people because I made the coats and I was used already to them. When you deal with the devil, you think the horns from the devil are supposed to look this way. So for me, being with them for years, from the beginning, I was not afraid—to look at them. I was only afraid when they start to take away every time somebody else from mine family, then the fear came for them, what they'll do to my nearest, but I personally, I was not scared to look at them.

After I made the leather coats, I never saw them later, I never know if they are wearing the coats or if the coats fit them or not. They just took them away. This was a system from Globocnik and the commandant Mohwinkel to show the Jews how, even if they are very good in their trades, what they are doing is only to carry out orders. A man like Mohwinkel wants to bring out that he is doing everything with the power what he has, to show the coat wasn't made from the tailor. With the coat, he is saying, "I had this coat made; I made the coat." The Nazis showed with the power they can do everything, not just

3. Amon Göth was commandant of the Plazow concentration camp outside of Krakow. Mr. Frank relates a story about him in Chapter 16, "The Maven."

with the Jews. They start with the Poles, also with the intelligentsia, to show them that if you wouldn't do, if you wouldn't carry out, that there are some ways. I am not familiar with the Poles, only what I met in concentration camp—politicians what they was arrested and the Nazis took them to camp—they was not together with us, they was in another field. But I met them from time to time in the camp. They took away the leaders from the Polish people, the public; they did also what the Germans want them to do. Was no revolt from the *Polaks* from the time from the war either. On the contrary, the Jews was more fighting against the Germans from time to time in the woods. In the woods, the Poles, instead to kill the Germans, to sabotage German trains, they killed the Jewish partisans. This was also the way from the Germans, to show the Poles: "The Jew is your enemy. You have to help us to kill your enemy." And a lot of Poles, they helped them.[4]

ML: That makes it sound like that was a very successful strategy; they manipulated the Poles by giving them the opportunity to take the pressure off themselves, to change how they thought about their country being invaded and who they perceived the dominators to be. It aimed not only the blame but also the resentment about being dominated towards a different target.

JF: They told the Polish people, "You work with us," because they didn't accomplish what they want in the beginning. They want to put up a Polish government like they did in France with the Vichy government. They couldn't. The Polish were more intelligent guys; they didn't give in to this what the Germans wanted to. Then they start to talk to the general public: "You help us, and you don't have to be

4. The question of resistance, collaboration, and Polish and Jewish partisan relations is more complicated than can be summed up in a few sentences. Hilberg reports that during the last half of 1942, "several thousand Jews were hiding in the woods, joining the partisans and sometimes, banded together in units of their own, shooting it out with German Gendarmerie units. There are reports of such clashes in all five districts of the Generalgouvernement" (Hilberg 1985, 448). In Gruber's Holocaust memoir, he recalls that there was friction and some lack of willingness to cooperate between Jewish partisans and Polish resistance fighters. Krakowski relates two instances where Jewish prisoners of war escaped from Lipowa and made contact with members of Polish armed resistance forces, but were murdered by them (Ressler's group, 266; ten underground members from the tannery workshop, 270). According to Browning's research on "Jew hunts" in the Lublin district, Poles freely gave information to German Reserve Police battalions, who tracked down Jews in hiding and murdered them (1993, 126). Frank recalls rewards for Poles who turned in Jews and generally holds the opinion that Poles offering assistance were the exception.

afraid that something will happen to you. You only have to be afraid when you will be against us. To work with us is to kill your first enemy, and that's the Jew." There was many, many Poles what they was hunting for Jews what they was hiding in certain places.[5] They promised them for every Jewish head, they'll pay them a kilo, two pounds, of sugar. There was many Polish people what they went looking for Jews where they was hiding, and they received two pounds of sugar for every Jewish head. Was many Jews what they was killed because of that—for two pounds of sugar.

ML: Everything had a price, and everything was worthless.

JF: Everything, yes. . . . The Germans, they use all kind of schemes. They used the Poles, they used sometimes single people from the Jewish community—sometimes they found somebody. They tried everything, how to exterminate, how to kill more of us.

ML: So to sweeten their food, it was easy enough to shed blood.

5. Order Police (police battalions that were separate from the regular police, Gestapo, and SS) searched for Jews who had escaped clearing actions and liquidations. They relied on Polish civilians called "forest runners," who ferreted out the Jews' hiding places. Police commanders also acquired information from Poles who reported Jews who stole food from farms and storehouses (Browning 1993, 126).

10

—

Majdanek

June–July 1941 and 1942

AFTER HIMMLER LEFT, the Hell start. The killing start to intensify
. . . till this time, some single incidents was happening that somebody
was killed, but after his being in Lublin, every day you heard somebody else was shot. Sometimes in the Saturday night or Friday night, a
couple of Nazis, they became drunk, and they came into the ghetto,
and to amuse themselves they took out a machine gun and they put
away five, six, or ten Jewish lives, also women and children.

June or July of 1941, the Jewish war prisoners start to leave the
camp to go to an outskirt of Lublin with the name Majdanek. Every
day a couple of hundred from the Jewish-Polish war prisoners, they
used to go out with some SS guys watching them, and they went everyday to Majdanek to build there. In the beginning, they didn't know
and we didn't know what they are building, but later, we found
out.

The elder from the Jewish-Polish war prisoners, Fisher, he became
a very good friend of mine, but I didn't hear from him stories what
this is going on. The way what was set up was not to talk . . . if somebody was a head from a group what the Nazis made him, the first
thing what they told him, what they told us, is "If you'll get an
order, this will be between you and me. If not you get shot." In
the beginning, even the prisoners didn't trust you, because they
know you could have something done to them . . . nobody trusted
the leaders, especially in the camp. Months and months later,
they found out what kind of personality you are . . . so maybe they

88

The barracks at the Majdanek death camp. *Courtesy of the National Museum in Majdanek and the United States Holocaust Memorial Museum Photo Archives.*

trust you more. Fisher never told me what kind of construction there was.[1]

September or October 1941, when you talked with the group what they came back every day, they said that Majdanek is a camp for Russian war prisoners, but they said this not willingly. They are helping the Russians there to build barracks for them. Six months later in '42, again I met from the group what they went out every day to Majdanek to work there. I found out they are building solid build-

1. According to an order of September 22, 1941, from the Main Budget and Building Office, Majdanek was to be a concentration camp for fifty-thousand prisoners. This was expanded when SS authorities, eager to have control of POWs for labor, decided that the facility would house a total of 150,000 POWs and "detainees." By October and November, it was established that Majdanek would be "an SS base which would constitute an economic support system for SS posts in the occupied Soviet territories." To build the compound, barracks, and storehouses, the Jewish POWs were used to level ground, collect sand, transport materials, and build roads, drainage ditches, and buildings (Marszalek 1986, 21–25).

ings—the barracks was already there, but they are constructing other buildings. And then I found out from a Jewish prisoner, in the buildings looks like they are building ovens. One place is already with two doors, closed, with a grill.

I was trying to find out more . . . and I couldn't say this to somebody else, what this guy told me . . . he told me this has to disappear what he is telling me the words, not to mention this to nobody and not to remember this for myself. I remember this, but I didn't tell nobody else because you couldn't . . . the moment that somebody will find out from me and find out from where I took the information—so we both will be liquidated, even if they need me, or they don't need me. Or maybe they torture me, or they let me live later—this I don't know. I know I couldn't say anything.

In late '42 or in the beginning '43, this was no more like a secret, then everybody knew they are digging ditches, trenches, very, very long ones and very deep ones. When the war prisoners ask the Germans why they are digging, they said they are now in war with Russia, and if the Russians will bomb they will have places to hide. Later, we knew this is just a lie . . . we had an idea already that this is prepared for ourselves, for us, because who would go to the trenches? How will the army or the people rush to hide there in the trenches if the Russians will bomb Lublin?

ML: The prisoner who told you he saw these ovens, did he know what they were going to be used for?

JF: I didn't know the war prisoner, he didn't know me . . . just when he is coming back to the camp, we talked. He didn't know. I start to dig, to ask, so he told me that's what he saw but he don't know for what. Looks like an oven; he doesn't know what they'll cook there.[2]

ML: What was the context of what he told you? Was that the only thing he mentioned to you or was it among many things, because the way I understand this, that struck him to such an extent that the oven was the only thing he mentioned.

2. The first crematorium facilities in Majdanek were two oil-fueled furnaces that were brought from the Sachenhausen camp in June 1942. By late August or early September, the Kori firm from Berlin completed five coke-fueled furnaces, the exhaust from which was routed up a twelve-meter-high chimney. As many bodies were forced into a crematorium as could fit; then, at a temperature of seven hundred degrees Celsius, they were completely combusted in ten to fifteen minutes (Marszalek 1986, 30–34).

JF: This is only the one thing what he mentioned. I start to ask him something else; he didn't want to talk anymore. He said, "That's what I know, and if you ask me, I told you everything." He knew me better than I knew him, because I was known better in the camp as the *Schneidermeister,* the head from the tailor shop, but I knew him only because of the group what he went out to work. I even didn't know his name.

11

Crocodiles in the False Walls

1940–mid-1941

YOU ASKED ME ABOUT THE MATERIALS what they came into the tailor shop. They came in from the Germans, and they kept the bolts in a barrack what they called this the warehouse. They supplied the material for the green uniforms for the SD or for the shoemakers for the boots. But besides the regular army uniforms what the material was supplied, some officers from the Nazi party, from the SS or from the Gestapo or also from the regular *Wehrmacht,* they used to bring their own material when they called me up to the office; also Mohwinkel, when he need something for himself or for his wife, civil material, not military . . . sometimes I saw him in a civil suit on a Sunday or another German holiday.

For a year and a half, Mohwinkel had Francis,[1] what he supplied him with the private materials. And the Jew was thinking if he'll supply whatever he needs, he'll be able to save himself or his family. In the meantime, when sometimes they arrest some Jewish men or swomen or girls what they didn't wear the armband, the Jewish David Star, Francis went over to the office from the commandant, and because he was supplying him materials, the commandant did for him sometimes favors—to release Jews what they arrest them. Francis became a hero between the Jewish population, because if a mother or father received back the daughter or the son because Francis intervened to release him . . . the rumor right away spread apart between the Jews.

Mohwinkel needs gray leather to make for the all Nazis leather coats, what I made. Actually in the mind from Mohwinkel, *he* made the leather coats, because whatever I did, it was for him to take credit.

---

1. The reader will recall Francis from pp. 70–71.

This was his way . . . he was thinking this way he'll keep his job as a commandant. Giving the coats for gifts to Himmler, Eichmann, the Governor from Poland Hans Frank, Globocnik, I don't know if this was bribing, but this was in my estimation to have favoritism from the bigger Nazis when they came to inspect, to show them that he is doing a good job. But maybe this is the wrong expression what I said, "bribing." He wants to show them that he is a good manager from the labor camp, to keep up with his management job.

Francis is supplying when Mohwinkel needs something—material for civil clothes, leather for a leather coat, for boots the leather. Where he gets the leather, nobody knew. Nine months later, most of the people from the Lipowa found out where the leather came. Looks like Francis didn't want to tell Mohwinkel, but before they beat him to death, they found out from him.

In Lublin, not far from where I had my shop on the Krakow Street, was a shoe store. This shoe store was for men and ladies, but mostly ladies' shoes, what was imported from the United States or from France or from England. Was very expensive shoes, like a pair of shoes here today, the value like $400 or $500. A man what his name was Koslow owned the shoe store.

Mohwinkel found out from the Francis this name, Koslow. They came to Koslow and they arrest him and bring him to the Lipowa Street.[2] They took him in the office. What he told Mohwinkel, I found out later . . . I knew Koslow, because we was almost neighbors, not far away—I was on top with my shop and about a half a block down he had his shoe store. Mohwinkel wants some leather from Koslow to have one or two leather coats made. Koslow brought the leather; they arrest him, they talk with him, and they let him go.

Later on, Mohwinkel tells him that he needs more leather. The Koslow, he figured out that he'd have the same end what the Francis had, so he stopped it. He said maybe he'll be able to get more from this place from where he is getting the leather. He waits, like he is searching . . . talking to connections, the black market . . . then he came and he said he cannot get more leather.

He had a family also, a wife with children, he has his own house.

2. This point of the account is slightly different in Mr. Frank's deposition of May 23, 1969 to German prosecutors (*SSPF,* 9757–60). At that time, Mr. Frank said that Koslow also worked as a cobbler in the Lipowa shoemaker shop, besides having his own private business in the ghetto.

He was a rich man, leather imported, lizards, crocodiles, other leather, very expensive for people what they have money.

He made a hiding place in his basement. You had to be a scientist or an expert to find because he didn't make it; specialists made this place. Nobody could find this place, because, I found out, the Nazis was there to look for more leather. Twice or three times, they couldn't find.

The fourth time they are ready to rip down the house, and they found there is a blind wall there. Behind the wall there is hidden leather. They took out two big German trucks with leather, piles of leather, the treasure from Koslow, and they brought the leather on the Lipowa, with the Koslow.

They took him into the office, and they took him out dead.[3]

They killed him because he lied. He had leather hidden, and he didn't say. And they took his family, and they shot them there on the place, in their home.

I found out from the Nazi supervisor what he watched me, Langfeld—he told me the story what I am telling you.[4] This was a true story because I saw Koslow taken out dead . . . from the window from the tailor shop I could see the office where a couple of guys from the *Judenrat* took him out from there.

3. In his 1969 deposition, Mr. Frank states that he and other tailors watched Mohwinkel, Hantke, and Schramm beat Koslow to a pulp with whips while Mohwinkel shouted "You lied to me!" in his high-pitched voice. They could see into the camp office through the windows of the tailor shop, which were kept open even in winter because of the heat from the pressing irons. After an interminable hour-and-a-half beating, two or three shoemakers carried Koslow from the office to the *Lazarett*, taking him past the door to the tailor shop. Frank says that he was *"völlig zerschlagen"* (totally beaten) and that his face was no longer recognizable. He heard that Koslow was dead when he arrived at the *Lazarett* (*SSPF*, 9759).

4. Here, Mr. Frank attributes the source of information to Langfeld, but in the 1969 deposition, he states that Fisher, the leader of the Jewish POWs, explained the reason for Koslow's beating to him. The story about having a stash of leather is consistent in both accounts.

12

Hangings, Attitudes, and Suicide

ML: DO YOU REMEMBER ANYONE with a very different point of view than yours? A different point of view could mean: someone who was thinking about escaping from Lipowa, someone who saw a different kind of future for the camp—that could mean either a better future or an even worse future?

JF: There was many what was thinking this way, to do something, to improve their lives what we had on Lipowa so maybe they can do something better for themselves. A lot of people from us what was in camps thought to escape—but nobody knew one from another. I couldn't say that I knew something, but even when somebody had in their mind to do something, they never told somebody else, even their best friends.

ML: Because they didn't want to be discovered if they should attempt a plan.

JF: They didn't want to be discovered, and was a lot of mistrust even between the Jewish prisoners, that to say something, maybe this will hurt them. They escaped from time to time, some, but you could count them on the fingers. In the beginning, when one escaped they took out one man. They used to count in the morning, to take out one man from the group, where the man belonged—there was groups, barracks. If a tailor should escape, they'll take out from the tailor shop a man, and they'll hang him or they shoot him. That's how this was working. Later, if one escaped they took out three to kill them. Good luck was to survive or to die.[1] You didn't know whom they'll choose to take out, or from what group.

---

1. The reader is free to interpret this ambiguous statement. In my mind, it meant that "luck" or fate, in the sense of what happened to the prisoner, could only run one of two courses: life or death. There was no way to mitigate circumstances, influence fate, or find "good luck."

For the hanging, they called you out on the six o'clock on the morning to do the counting, an *appel*. This is to count if the list is correct, that nobody disappeared, that nobody escaped. But the same time when they called us out to wait for the *Kapos* to count us, we didn't know that they have three guys that they are going to hang because one or two escaped from the camp. They was always near the other side of the camp, near the Sklodowsky Street . . . the camp was so long that the other side was a street with name Sklodowsky. In the end from the camp was made the scaffolds to hang the people there.

When they hanged the prisoners, they gave a command, all the *Kapos,* the heads from the groups, to the Jewish war prisoners and to the civil prisoners that everybody should look to the side where they're doing the hanging. And all the time, from the time when the hanging went on, you had to look, everybody had to look, to stay like in the military—you give a command to stay with the head on one side. Many times one didn't so quick raise his head to look in the side where they hang the people . . . they start to beat him up . . . once they took out a man, and they shoot him also on this place because quick he didn't look in the same moment.

ML: So everyone's head is turned, and did they just hang everyone immediately, or did they make some kind of speech?

JF: No speeches, no speeches at all. They just put a bench under the feet, under the hanging person's feet, and then they hang them, and then they kicked back the bench, and that's all.

ML: And did Mohwinkel always oversee these hangings?

JF: No, not always. But later . . . once they hanged three guys . . . this was in the morning when they hanged them, but in the middle of the day, Mohwinkel came down and passed by the camp, he went with a stick and turned around the bodies; he played with them. And they was hanging for twenty-four hours.

ML: Who gave those commands to hang?

JF: We didn't know. We didn't hear no commands. We didn't know who gives them . . . when we came out, everything was prepared, and they came; they took the three guys in handcuffs. I don't remember how this was—chain cuffs or with strings on the hands behind their backs. They hanged them, that's all. There was no speeches, no asking questions, what the man has to say—nothing; just they put on the *petla* . . . what do you call this?

ML: A noose?

JF: The rope, what you put on for hanging . . . the *petla*.

ML: Do you think mistrust developed as soon as prisoners saw they were executing others for escaping, or do you think mistrust developed gradually?

JF: The mistrust developed when they start to punish people for the things what others was doing. Except there was some friends . . . for instance, I used to talk with my associates from the shops, and I was friends with them even before the war, with Gerishon Klein or Saul Gootmacher . . . was also a guy, Yelinevitch, with his sixteen-year-old boy . . . we used to talk about what is our future. Our future is just death; everybody will die. We didn't talk between us; there was not a conversation between us about escaping because we know we have nowhere to escape. Where will we turn? The Germans will catch us, and if the Germans wouldn't catch us, the Poles would give us over to the Germans, so I wouldn't say I know something different from other people what they have in their minds.

ML: Were there people who had the point of view that it would get much worse faster? Or were people not able to foresee how quickly liquidations would take place?

JF: Most of us was looking that this should go faster, to take an end to this life. Even death should go faster than to live this kind of life.

ML: When you say "should go faster," does that mean that you wished the Nazis would speed up the killing process or you wished that your life would shorten; you would welcome a shorter time alive because of the suffering?

JF: We will welcome . . . later, when the war starts with Russia in 1941, life starts to be much, much worse, even in the labor camp, what was not so like in a concentration camp, but still. . . . people was thinking this will be better for them to commit suicide, and a lot of them was praying to go to sleep and not to get up in the morning. It was not a way to think of a revolution, because you couldn't think this way to revolt . . . because you always saw you are under the machine gun or hand grenades, so you didn't think. They prepared you systematically from the beginning—with the rationing with food, to take you from one ghetto to another . . . they prepared you not to be able . . . you felt weak to think; your mind was weakened to think, to fight back. We saw always tanks going through the streets. They showed you always the power—not only us, but also the Poles, how powerful they are, if they want to organize or make some revolution against them to fight back. Was not a time to be able to liberate ourselves against so a tremendous power.

ML: Those people who committed suicide, how did they do that?

JF: They prepared themselves . . . they called this in Polish *chankaly* . . . a poison, a little pill. Some of them, they kept this in a tooth in the mouth. In the beginning, we still had contact with the Polish people, so you was buying it for money. Somebody didn't have money, his wife had an expensive fur coat or a piece of jewelry, so a lot of people could buy their death. But most of them they didn't have time to poison themselves. Even some of them if they have poison they had hidden, they didn't have time to take the poison to kill themselves.

ML: Because anything could happen . . . they could be beat up at work, or suddenly shot.

JF: That's right. A lot of us . . . I don't know . . . I'll talk about myself. Later, when they took away the last from the nearest from my family, I was thinking from taking my life. I don't know if I was a coward, or I didn't have the will, or I was selfish . . . I am thinking till today what was in that time, and I cannot come to a conclusion why I didn't do it.

ML: That seems like a question that could potentially have no answer.

JF: For me, all the years, I'm looking for an answer, and I couldn't find it.

13

———

The Impossible Does Not Exist

Winter 1941

WHEN THE WAR STARTED with Russia, the commandant from the labor camp in this time was already Mohwinkel. He called me in his office, and he told me that now we have work a little bit harder because we have to supply uniforms for the *Wehrmacht,* for the army, what they are fighting in Leningrad. Was, I think, in the winter of '41. Months before, he came into the shop, and he was testing groups of tailors—the operators, the finishers—to see how long a front has to take to make ready, a collar, sleeves, and so on. He came up with a figure that every tailor should be able to make a jacket a day, and this is not too much. Because I have 475 tailors there, he would like to have 475 uniform jackets a day.

But the problem was, on the list was 475 tailors, but I had only about 250 or 260 tailors. The rest, the 220, they was just people what they came from Warsaw, brought to Lublin when the Nazis liquidate there. Some of them was lawyers, doctors. One professor, his name was Borkowski, was a very known professor in Poland; was also a senator . . . Senator Trochenheim. In Poland, for a Jew to be a senator in the Polish Senate was something what he was known from all the Jews from Poland.

A transport was brought to the Lipowa, and we received them. When I say "we," I mean the heads from the shops . . . me and the head shoemaker and all the other heads. We talked between us if this will be possible to save the more intelligent Jews what we heard are coming—doctors, lawyers, and Senator Trochenheim and Professor Borkowski—and if we can take them out from the groups before they send them out from the labor camp and to other camps. When they brought them, they lined them up . . . the Nazis was not standing

around near them, and they left them a little while to have their freedom for a couple of minutes before all the staff from the SS came
down from the offices to count them. We went around, and we called
out if there is a professor with the name Borkowski or a Senator
Trochenheim, and one said, "I am Professor Borkowski." I was talking with him, so happened, and I said, "Where would there be a Senator Trochenheim here, from the Senate?" and he said, "He is
standing the third man." So I said, "We'll try to do something." The
head shoemaker also went around to ask for other names what we
heard a day before are coming on a transport from Warsaw, with the
most intelligent Jews.

I went over to the Commandant Mohwinkel, and I told him,
"There are some tailors here in the group who I know from before the
war. The names in Warsaw are very known, very good tailors, and we
can use them in the tailor shop." The other craftspeople from the
other shops came over to him, and they said they need shoemakers
and other workers. He said, "Pick out the Jews what you need, and
tell me how many you need, and take them in the shop."[1] I took in
four or five of this kind of tailor, and was between them Professor
Borkowski and Senator Trochenheim. Of this kind of people, the tailor shop accumulated about two hundred: they was listed as tailors,
and they was not tailors, because we took them in from transports
from Warsaw, from Lodz, days or weeks before. The tailor shop was
the biggest shop . . . what I mean biggest is the most people was there
occupied; in no other shops was 475 people there. So I had only, like I
said, 250 or 260 or 240 tailors, and to make 475 jackets a day, this
was impossible, because not all of them was tailors.

Mohwinkel called me in his office, and he told me how many jackets he wants to have a day. And I said to him, *"Herr Commandant,* I
don't think this is possible, 475 jackets, because it's too hard to make,
a jacket per man a day."

The answer was in him, he called me in that time, "You *Drecksack,*[2] this word what you said, 'impossible,' is not in the German dic-
tionary! Doesn't exist so a word 'impossible!' Everything is possible!
Get out from here!"

The SS took me out from the office, and instead of taking me

1. Mohwinkel might have agreed to the shop leaders' requests because the camp
had recently come under the DAW, and he was trying to increase its output.
2. "Sack of shit," or "shitbag."

These Buchenwald prisoners were hung by their wrists with their arms behind their backs, a punishment which tears the ligaments and tendons in the arms and shoulders. Frank was subjected to the same punishment at the Lipowa camp in Lublin because he told Commandant Wolfgang Mohwinkel that the tailor shop could not produce 475 uniforms per day. *Courtesy of the Nederlands Instituut voor Oorlogsdocumentatie, Amsterdam.*

back to the shop, looks like the Mohwinkel told the SS what to do, and they took me away to a place where they hung people. This was away from the barracks, where the counting every day or twice a day used to be, not far from the gallows. When somebody escaped or somebody was punished for doing something, they hung prisoners. They took out all the prisoners, the slaves there, and they gave an order that everybody must look to the side where they are hanging the people.

On this place near the gallows, they hung me by my hands, with my arms behind my back. I only remember when they put up the rope on my hands . . . two guys and one from the staff there. I think his name was Dorthoff. He was standing on the side and commanded the ones working on me what to do . . . how high they should pull the ropes. When they let me down, I was unconscious; I didn't know anymore what happened. I only remember when they start to pull me up, in the whole body I feel the pains. But the people from the

Lazarett, from the little hospital what was there, they told me I was almost dead. They told me blood started to run from my nose, from my eyes, from my mouth. They took me down, and they start to revive me with water, and they took me to the hospital. I couldn't move my arms for days . . . but when you're young, you can take more their tortures. Then later, to see what they did to the other ones. . . .

Two days later, I went back to the shop. All the people used to feel sorry for me, but what could they do? They couldn't help anything what they did to me. By the Germans, this was like nothing had happened, and I start again to do my job, my work.

ML: After that, when you returned two days later, I assume the shop still couldn't produce 475 uniforms per day.

JF: Mohwinkel didn't talk anymore about amount. When I came back and the people from the tailor shop knew, all the 475 people, between them they start to rush, to produce more, because of what they did to me. And the amount went up much, much, much more, much more than what we produced before the hanging.[3] So Mohwinkel succeeded. The 250 or 260 had to work for the other half what they was not tailors. They came in earlier, they left a half hour later or an hour sometimes. They work harder and receive less food, because every time, the time became worse, with the food rationing, with the bread.

ML: So rations were slowly being cut?

JF: Cut most of the time, every time.

ML: When you say "every time," what marks those times?

JF: Every time means every month, every two months was a difference in the rationing. You used to receive a little heavier soup; start to be more water. Used to have a pound of bread, then it was an ounce or two ounces less. The whole idea was to take out from you more and to give you less to feed you so that you should die faster . . . because many times they said they didn't even want to use bullets. The bullets was too expensive to waste on Jews—you should die without a bullet, just torturing you or not to feed you. This was the policy we found out later.

3. According to Goldhagen, the peak period of Lipowa's production lasted from summer 1942 until the liquidation in November 1943, during which time the camp was "the DAW's most important enterprise outside of Germany itself" (Goldhagen 1997, 296).

ML: Do you think the other tailors were compelled to work harder because they didn't want you to be tortured again, or they were afraid they themselves would be tortured?

JF: They was afraid because if Mohwinkel could . . . till this time, I was more respected when the Nazis came in the shop. They didn't do with me specially to treat me nicer, but they never hit me. When they came in other shops always, most of the time, they gave a couple of lashes sometimes to the head from the shops, because something was not in order, something was not good. They always find something wrong. And the fault from being wrong was the head from the shop; they made him responsible. I didn't have this kind of treatment when something was wrong, except this time when I was hung.

But you're asking about the people, if they was afraid for them or for me. I don't know . . . they figure if they could do this to me, it was very easy they can do this to all of them, even worse. Sure they was afraid; they was afraid for themselves, because the moment when I went outside to the office or to take a measurement of some Nazi and I didn't come back so quick—because was a couple of miles to go to a private place outside the camp office—the people was counting the minutes that I should be back, especially the couple of friends what they was working closer to me, what they handed out the work to the other tailors. Most of them was more afraid than the other ones, because they was nearer to the leader from the shops.

ML: What work did these other people do that you took on, who weren't actually tailors?

JF: Well, was plenty to do . . . they was always busy, they worked! To take away this bundle, to give it to the men to make the sleeves, to take the sleeves to the tailor who puts on the sleeve; was always like section work. Everybody was busy, even if he was not a tailor. Maybe there was some of them was a little bit older, maybe they was not so fast in working like the younger ones, but everybody was doing something. To clean so a barrack like that, 475 people, after work, in the morning, to oil the machines, to clean the machines, the irons, to sharpen the scissors, everybody was busy. Was not only to sit and to sew with the needle, but if they could sit and to sew, others from outside could do the work to clean or to hand out the pieces—do you follow me? But like I said, not everybody was a tailor, not even everybody was a shoemaker there, or a carpenter, or a painter. Everybody was busy, even if he was not a painter or shoemaker—you follow me? He had work to do.

ML: Do you remember any conversations you had with the Professor or the Senator?

JF: No, no. He was thankful he was appreciated, what I did, that he is in the tailor shop. He and the Senator, I watched them most of the time, that the other tailors shouldn't be mad at me or at them because they are not tailors, but this was not the case. Everybody, most of the time, was willing to do extra work . . . was a discussion sometimes, some of them, they ask me why I am doing this. They have to work for themselves and for somebody else; they have to work harder, because I took in so many "tailors." And the answer in that time was from me: If we'll survive, we can't only survive with tailors and shoemakers: we need doctors; we need professors; we need senators to show us the way how to exist as Jews. In this they understood, and this helped a lot, once, the conversation I had with them.

ML: How did they respond to your argument?

JF: They respond very well. Even was some of them they didn't agree—the majority convinced the minority that this is the right way to do; there's no other way. And this was not only in my shop. We was talking from time to time, the heads from the shops; we tried from between us to make up a way how to speak to the other prisoners that they should agree with the system what we are doing to save what we can. But like I said, we saved them, but not for long. The end came for them the same time, the 3rd of November, 1943. Till that time, they was saved for a year and a couple of months.

ML: Do you see a lot of futility in that—you concocted a story for Mohwinkel about why the shop needed them, but they only lived for another year and seven or nine months?

JF: No, I didn't know when the end will come. I know that we wouldn't survive, but when the end will come, I didn't know.

ML: In hindsight, which maybe has no value for decisions that were already made, do you feel pain from the fact that you made an effort to save them, but because of forces outside your control, they didn't live longer than November 3?

JF: No, I wouldn't say that, because I had there my own wife and my son, so how can I feel bad if I can't save them longer, if I couldn't save my own flesh and blood? In my way, even my life today after from the time what I survived, I live a little bit easier because I feel, all the time—in that time and even till today, fifty years later—that I did everything what a good Jew has to do, to save, even of a moment. There is in the Jewish way, "if you save one life, you save the whole world." And that's what I was trying to do, because I was brought up in this kind of atmosphere in my home.

ML: Ethically, how do you define a good Jew?

JF: Ethically, what I find a good Jew is any kind of help what you can do, what you can help another one what he needs help; that is by me a good Jew.

ML: At the same time, is it fair to recognize that there were times when it was impossible to help someone else?

JF: I don't know of this kind of time. In all the times, I found a way—I risked my life many times to do something for somebody else what I knew that if they'll catch me I'll pay with my life. At that time, I didn't think what the consequences will be when they'll catch me. I did what I had to do, and so happened that I was not caught, and I went on with my life the same way so long as I could.

ML: Do you think with this ethical idea of always trying to help someone else, it's important not to be too aware of the consequences to yourself? Before you said you didn't think about what could have happened to you.

JF: I don't know—I can't answer this question, because the moment when this came to what I did, I didn't think that I am doing something against myself. The moment came to do something, I did it. In that time, I didn't think if I should do or I shouldn't do: I did it. I didn't think that I should be a good ethical man, a good Jew, or a good person to help somebody else; I did it, not because I was thinking about me, what I will be if I will do this kind of thing. For instance, when I say I did it, I did things what I shouldn't do. I took in a tailor, his name was Yelinevitch. He had a son about twelve or thirteen years old . . . this was in the beginning when I could still go home to my family. And Yelinevitch, they took away his wife, and they separate them. He had a daughter hidden with Polish people, and he was only with his son. When he came to me, he wants to go in to work with me, but he has something what he has to tell me . . . what can I do? He cannot go in by himself; he has a son, a young boy, and he can't do anything with him. If I want to take Yelinevitch in, I also have to take in his boy; and if I can do this, he will appreciate it, he will never forget the good thing what I was doing for him. I had an order not to take in boys in this age. He was a skinny little boy but tall, about thirteen years old I think. So I figure—at that time I had two boys of my own—what will I do when I want to save my little boy? So I didn't think too long, and I tell Yelinevitch, "That's OK, we'll do something, maybe in the beginning we'll hide him a little bit when the Nazis come in to check, and when they see him, when they ask me how old he is, I'll say two years older, so we'll find a way."

He came and he brought him in; this was in the beginning of '42 or the end of '41. He was with this little boy till the end when they liquidate the camp, where also my wife and my son was there. That's why I say, when I did something, I didn't think I should do or I shouldn't do—I did it.

ML: But you did reflect a little bit that there was a similarity between his having a son and your having sons.

JF: I was thinking about this. If that was only the one way if I want to save my boy, and somebody will refuse me, how would I feel? This made me to say, "That's OK: you come in with your boy, with your son."

ML: I'm curious about this because I think we do sometimes imagine ourselves in the other person's position, according to the Confucian rule: how we would want to be treated or what we would want done to us or for us. Other times, however, while we might think about that, we can't overcome our own self-interest. For example, I don't want to help that person because I may lose something: I may not get something as a result, or I may endanger myself. But it seems that it's not so much that you thought about those consequences to yourself and overcame them, but they weren't part of your thoughts leading to your decision.

JF: The thinking in that time . . . at the moment, I was thinking about my son if this will happen to me but only for a moment, and then disappeared this thinking, and said, "OK, that's all." I didn't think too much if I should do, if I shouldn't do. Just said, "Bring him in and everything will be OK."

ML: I get the sense that many decisions you made and other people made were very quick, and it's only when we look at them later that we decide, "He did this because he was essentially selfless, he wasn't interested in what he could have had for himself, he only wanted to help someone else;" or, "He only did this because he stood to gain something from it." It seems like many of the decisions were very, very rapid, and whatever moral views I might analyze in them later, they weren't under consideration then; there was no pausing for the freedom to consider them.

JF: There was times when you couldn't take too much time to think. You had to decide on this place to do or not to do. And you didn't think . . . some of them made decisions the wrong way, and some of them made the right way. I was not only the one what I did something sometimes for somebody. There was many, many between us what they tried to do for the next person, for the next Jewish person especially.

There is another thing what I can say about the Yelinevitch. Like I said, he had a daughter what she was with some Polish people hiding, and from time to time, I selected a group every week from the tailor shop to take a bath. There was a city place, a public place, was not a swimming pool there, but just to take showers, a Russian steam room. Because we made the uniforms, the tailors have to be clean. So every week, I send out another group of sixty or seventy to go to this public place to clean themselves. The Yelinevitch, because he had a daughter outside, all the time he was asking me that I should send him with the group every week—not every week are they supposed to go, but once in a month or every two weeks. Because Yelinevitch has a daughter outside, if he goes with the group, the daughter was waiting in the street, and they could see each other. They didn't go near, because God forbid if someone should see they'll be close, they'll see that she is Jewish, then he'll risk her life, but he could see her at least once a week. He came back with many, many thanks that he saw his daughter, that she looks good. That was something again that I shouldn't do this, but I did it—not thinking if I am doing the right thing or the wrong thing. I knew he wants to see his daughter, and he had a chance to see his daughter in the street. What the leaders from the shops could do for their people what they was working for them, everybody did the same thing.

ML: You mention the other shop leaders also made decisions that would have caused them grave repercussions. Do you think an atmosphere or a climate was established where several leaders' actions reinforced others to act in a similar way,[4] or do you feel that they made these decisions independently and to different degrees?

JF: They did independently; we never talked between us what I did or the other told me what he did . . . we never knew this, what somebody was doing. We knew if there was a possibility to do some-

---

4. In the first part of my question, I intended to distinguish a situation that developed in the camps specifically, rather than a general ethos of goodwill and urgency to give assistance when under duress, which existed in the Jewish tradition prior to the camps.

thing, everybody what he was working with somebody else, even in the time when they was working outside the camp, one was helping another one. One Jew was feeling very weak, and he fell down; he couldn't work anymore. The other what was near him, he picked him up when the Nazi wouldn't see them. He tells him, "Try! Try! If they'll see this they'll kill you." This was also a help. So everybody in the camp, especially where I was—I can't talk about other camps, but I am talking from the Lipowa—everybody was helping the other one.

14
—

The Photographer

Summer 1941

ON THE LIPOWA, I knew a Jewish young gentleman, eighteen or nineteen years old, he was a photographer before the war. Even before the war I knew him. I had my quarters on the Cziwulniche Street, and he used to live in the same building. In that time before the war, I had no interest to talk with him . . . he was living on the third or the fourth floor, and I was living on the second floor. I was a little bit older than he was; I had a wife with two children already, and he was single. So before the war, I really knew him only to go down the stairs or to pass by the building.

Every day an SS watchman took the young gentleman to the SS headquarters at *Kruel Leszcynskriego* to work in the morning, and they brought him back to the Lipowa camp to eat dinner every night.

I don't know what kind of work he is doing there, but looks like he had an order from *Rasenführer* Höffle that if he mentions what kind of work he is doing there—his father died, but he has a mother, and he has one sister—so they tell him, I'm sure they tell him the same way they tell the other ones, that if he'll mention something, he's not sure with his life or with his mother's or with his sister's life.

When he came back in the evening or the afternoon about six o'clock, in the summertime was still early, light, he took his ration of soup with his bread, the supper. He was sitting in the side, eating his meal, but he never talked. Around him we was sitting around a table, a dining room for the leaders from the other shops, separate where you could sit down with a table and a chair. We was sitting, talking one to another, but he never communicated with us. We was figuring maybe he can't, he's afraid of saying something, or maybe he's one from them, from the Germans, because sometimes single Jews, when they had the power, they start to act like the Nazis . . . but you could count them on the fingers. From a thousand there was sometimes one or two.

He knew that we was living in the same building from before the war. So I moved over to his side to start to talk to him, not from what he is doing—but in general, to ask him how his mother is, how his sister is, since at that time we was still living in our apartments, not in the camp. After the supper what we ate there, we went home.

This took me maybe a couple weeks. Finally I ask him, "What are you doing there?" Everyday I was at SS headquarters to pick up from Globocnik his uniforms or uniforms from Höffle or from other Nazis to clean or to press them. I came over with another guy; they brought us with a car, we took home the uniforms to clean. I saw this young gentleman from time to time sometimes there, too, when he went out from a strange room. I found out this is a photograph development room, because there was a sign that nobody is allowed to go in.

I tell him once—after a long time we was talking, and he became a little bit looser, you could talk to him, so I asked him—"What is the sign there that hangs on the door? There is no Jews there, so what is this? A sign for the Nazis not to go in?"

"Yeah," he said, "This is very, very private . . . nobody can come in because I am developing some pictures, what the Nazis take."

He didn't tell me anything else. But after a certain time, I ask him, "If there is a possibility, I am very anxious to see the pictures what you are developing."

One day when I came over in the morning and nobody was on the hall where the developing room was, he took me in, and he showed me. He developed a picture—the Nazis went out five or six days before to an outskirt of Lublin, to Belzcs, a little town, more there was farmers, but about thirty families was living there, sixty or seventy people . . . thirty kilometers from Lublin.

The Nazis took out all the Jews with the women and children, and they killed them with machine guns. When they killed them, I didn't see it, but I saw the picture what the photographer developed for my eyes. They lay out all the people in a line, and they was all lying near one another dead, with the faces up.[1] The leader, Höffle, was in

1. On November 11, 1965, Mr. Frank deposed that Mohwinkel, Riedel, Schramm, Maubach, and Hantke were in the picture. They were holding shovels and standing by the corpses. He recalls seeing the photo in summer 1941 (*SSPF,* 7382).

charge to make pictures, films, from the dead Jews after when they killed them, after the atrocities what they did, and he used this photographer to develop the pictures.

I didn't tell anyone what I saw this, because the photographer told me if I'll mention—he had the confidence to me that I wouldn't—he said if I'll mention this, we both'll be dead, and with our families. And what was the use to say to somebody? The only reason to tell somebody is if you can organize to fight back. If only you tell and cannot fight back, the rumors will spread apart, then this will come to Nazi officials, and they ask you from whom did you hear this, and that's how this will go. So I didn't mention.

You couldn't organize resistance in the beginning, because they did everything so secretly that you shouldn't know. And even if they know that you'll know, if you'll do something, they shut your mouth; they killed you not to have witnesses. So you never . . . we at the Lipowa didn't know what they are doing in Belzcs or in Lubartov, when they killed later all the Jews or the fifty families what was in Piaski. Nobody knew from another. We found out when everything was liquidated, and there was no more Jews. Some of them from the all towns what I am mentioning . . . they didn't kill everybody . . . they took out the very healthy young men, eighteen or twenty-one years, and they brought them on the Lipowa,[2] and they didn't know either what the Nazis did, because when they took their families away, they was still alive. So the Nazis was always trying not to have witnesses.

The pictures what they made, this was for their propaganda, for the Germans in Germany. I don't know why they need this, but we couldn't try to find out why. I saw this one time, but a couple weeks later I asked the young gentleman, "If you have something new, I would like to see some pictures."

He said, "Mr. Frank, that's it . . . I never want you to come here again. You was after me all the time, so I was figuring I can trust you, but I cannot do this, I cannot show you more pictures."

---

2. Jews were assigned to Lipowa shops, to other small labor camps in Lublin, or to separate work brigades that did cleaning and construction work. Until the all-encompassing *Erntefest* (Harvest Festival) exterminations on November 3, 1943, in the Lublin district it was routine practice for the Nazis to select some of the men for work before they marched their families to the forests to shoot them.

15

The Steam Bath

I DID NOT SEE GLOBOCNIK everyday . . . I went over to his office on the *Kruel Leszcyinskiego* everyday, but I didn't see him everyday. The maid, the other Nazi, what he was taking care of his things, he prepared the uniforms to pick up. In the three years when I was in Lipowa, I saw him maybe five or six times when he came with a bunch of Nazis to inspect the labor camp. I never had no contact, no talking with him . . . with what would he discuss between us, with a Jew? Only once was I close to him, when I took the measurement to make for him a uniform. He didn't talk to me, he didn't even see nothing.

But I had a pass, signed from him, because when I went out I didn't wear mine armband. Globocnik wants me to go out from Lipowa to pick up his things, but so as not to have some incidents in the street.[1] So they let me go without the armband—and in the beginning I didn't go with a watchman. But later, they escort me. The pass from him said that nobody should touch me, nobody could kill me, except Globocnik's name what is signed.

I had an order to go every week to go to a place where they had there steam baths, to clean myself, to wash myself. Was also Russian steam baths and saunas there. I had to go with this pass—not that I could go, but I had to go—always to be clean; I had clean underwear

---

1. With the Gentile sections of Lublin free of Jews, it would have caused a distur-bance were Frank to be seen wearing an armband since it was illegal for Jews to be out-side the ghetto. This type of protection was not privilege but served Globocnik's purpose of having a prisoner who could move freely and without being "accidentally" killed.

. . . always to be clean, so when I came to the SS headquarters not to contaminate, so that I shouldn't have lice, to spread typhus fever.[2]

At the steam bath, was there everything . . . tools to make exercise, lockers, dressing rooms, saunas . . . this was for the Poles and for the Germans; a Jew was not allowed to go in there. Every Friday I was going to the bath "Labensky," and this steam place was off the Kapuchinksy Street.

I came in; I had a locker. I undressed myself, and all men what they are nude, you didn't know if they was a German or a *Polak,* but they can see that I am a Jew. All the time what I used to go I never felt comfortable, but what could I do? This was the order from Globocnik and through Globocnik to Mohwinkel and through Mohwinkel to me. Sometimes through the Professor David, the Jewish commandant, and he reminded me, "Did you wash yesterday, to take a bath, to take a shower?" I said, "Yes, I did."

When I was inside in the steam room, sitting on the second tier on the benches, on top, to have the steam, a guy was sitting not far from me, also on the same bench. He gave a look on the lower part of me, and he said, "A *Jude!* Here?!"

He told me to go down and to go out in the other room where the lockers was. I told him, "Yes, I am a *Jude,* but I have an order from the *Obergruppenführer* Globocnik that every week I have to be here. When I take a measurement from him, I have to be clean. And I have a pass"—this was another paper special for the "Labensky" place that I am allowed to visit there.

I am nude; he is suspicious. He says, "So let me see the pass what you have. Come out, come out." I went out with him. I opened my locker, and I showed him the paper what I had, the sign from Globocnik . . . and he told me, "Even with the sign, I don't want to be in the same place with a *Jude!* Get dressed and get out from here!"

That's what I did. I didn't finish my washing; I dressed myself, I hurry out.

2. Frank doesn't specify if he was able to visit the bathhouse more frequently than the tailors in his shop, who went either once every two weeks or once a month. Receiving clean underwear was a considerable privilege, and the other prisoners were not entitled to this.

16

—

The Maven

Late 1941

THE FOLLOWING IS A STORY that Mr. Frank told me during a
break for lunch. Usually, after talking for several hours in the early
part of the afternoon, we sat at the dining room table, near his
sewing machine and dressmaker's mannequin. Usually my tape
recorder was off during the meal, because I assumed we needed a
brief respite from the world of Lipowa. At first, we did not talk about
it while we ate, but then, it turned out that we could not keep away
from the subject. Mr. Frank would either spontaneously begin a story
that contained new and vivid details, or he would remember an incident or a person he had forgotten for years. It was as if our discussion
and excavation of the past could not stop. Before the meal, I almost
always had to initiate the conversation with a series of questions and
hope that I would hit upon something that would evoke a new
episode or a new insight. After the meal, in a new setting, Mr. Frank
spoke more freely, telling me stories on his own initiative. He told me
this story as if it were a puzzle, except he did not express pleasure in
its solution.

Seven or eight months after the Lipowa camp opened (the latter
third of 1941, when the shops were fully operational), Langfeld, the
shop supervisor, told Mr. Frank that he was needed in the office to
take a measurement. Mr. Frank hurried to the office, and was faced
with a young officer, an *Untersturmführer* who wanted a leather coat.
Mohwinkel had promised the officer one of the imposing outfits, and
the young Turk had brought his own bundle of leather. According to
Mr. Frank, Mohwinkel made presents of these coats to high-ranking
officers to secure preferential treatment and demonstrate that his camp
was efficient (and could produce artful work); Mohwinkel supplied the

material for these coats.[1] Because the *Untersturmführer* was neither in a position to grant Mohwinkel favors nor was he his commanding officer, all Mohwinkel provided was the use of the *Schneidermeister.*

Eight or ten days later, Mr. Frank gave him the first fitting, and the coat fit without any problems. He promised him the finished mantle in a week, and the officer seemed satisfied with the progress of the work. When the officer returned, he brought a maven with him, an SS who had been a tailor before the invasion, before the camps. The officer tried on the coat and, though Mr. Frank couldn't compliment himself out loud, he thought it fit well. The *Untersturmführer,* obviously on a higher plane of power, didn't voice his opinion.

But the maven believed the coat was too tight in the waist.

Mr. Frank interrupted his story with a short discourse on Nazi fashion. The SS wore their leather coats very tightly, with their pistols and holsters on the outside, and they liked the coat to bundle in pleats over their ribs and sides of their chests. If the coat was too tight, these pleats would cut into the flesh, making it uncomfortable, so Mr. Frank always measured the waistline precisely, with an eye to accommodate the fashion.

"I can fix it; I can make it larger," Mr. Frank promised without hesitation.

"He's a *gonif,*" the inspecting tailor told the officer.

("What he actually was saying in Yiddish was that I am a thief," Mr. Frank told me," but he meant that I was a liar, because this leather, if you take it apart, then the needle marks show up. I knew this, but I didn't know what to say.")

The expert drew his gun and pointed it at Mr. Frank's face, with the barrel under Mr. Frank's nose. "Do you smell something?" he said.

"Yes."

"What do you smell?"

"I smell death."

"Ohhhh, it's good that you know. What'll you do now with the coat? You'll spoil the leather. What'll you do now?"

"I'll make the coat wider."

"This is impossible. You cannot make a leather coat wider, because when you let out the seams, you'll see the holes from the needle."

When Mr. Frank made these shiny SS carapaces, he could never

---

1. See pp. 84, 92–93, and 139–40.

make a mistake cutting the leather, so he and his assistants were always extremely careful with the pattern and the shears.

"I can fix this," repeated Mr. Frank, knowing that he wouldn't be able to obtain enough new leather to make a whole coat again.

"He cannot fix this," advanced the other tailor in a stalemate.

Commandant Mohwinkel arrived to investigate the disagreement. I don't know whether he ultimately wanted to see the *Untersturm-führer* satisfied or only wanted to convince him to not follow the expert's advice so closely, but since it was his camp, and Mr. Frank his slave, he intervened:

"When can you have it ready?"

"In forty-eight hours," Mr. Frank said immediately, knowing he would at least have forty-eight hours to live.

The *Untersturmführer* closed the deal with precision. "You have the forty-eight hours, and we'll be here in forty-eight hours. If the coat will not be exactly as it should be, you know what will be with you."

"*Jawohl!*" said Mr. Frank, mechanically asserting that he took the impossible order as an imperative.

The maven measured the waist with a tape measure so he would know just how much Mr. Frank would claim to have widened the coat when he would try to deceive him in two days. He knew it was not possible; these Jews were all liars who would say anything to protect themselves.

The unrepairable coat was taken to the tailor shop in the labor camp and spread out on a table under bright lights. The most accomplished tailors gathered, fine clothiers from Warsaw, from Lublin, the artists I had heard about who could design a whole garment just by looking at a photograph. The group of five or six sat down and discussed the situation. Mr. Frank listened to "the suggestions what one said from this way and from the other way, but this shouldn't work out the way what they said."

I imagined myself as one of the tailors staring at the front and back sections taken apart, gaping at the minuscule punctures and cutting the pieces topologically in my mind to recombine them, seams hidden. My first reaction was to believe that it was all a matter of superior intelligence to outwit the opponents, mind pitted against mind, and that it was possible to combine trial and error with savvy craft until an answer was found. Couldn't one of the front pieces be used as the back, since maybe it was wider, and the back could be remade into the front piece that goes underneath the wraparound front? Couldn't all of this be sewn using the same seams as before? If not, couldn't the back have a nicely finished overlapping seam down the middle, with a part from the wider front piece sewn into the back? Couldn't a scrap piece be found somewhere?

But this wasn't a problem where any possible solution would be a correct one; the solution had to be accepted by the *Untersturmführer* and his expert. While in some measure this depended on whether the coat looked exactly like every other leather coat (my solution would be judged botched—you can't have a strange seam down the back; the coat would look as if it had been made of scraps), the Nazi was free to find the smallest flaw or to invent one. A task might be technically impossible, the prisoner might have to dig ditches all day without proper tools or carry metal on awkward pallets with a partner who hadn't eaten a full meal in two years, but that didn't mean that the prisoner couldn't be punished for being unable to accomplish the task. In this case, superior intelligence on the part of these tailors wouldn't be sufficient to outwit their captors. The two sides weren't opponents on equal footing; the Nazi practice of immediately killing the "indolent," the incapable, or anyone who could be blamed was stronger than any of the prisoners' clever maneuvers.

One of the tailors said, "There's only one thing what we can do, and that is only the one thing. The thing is to take apart the coat and to nail the parts to a board, like you do with fur, and to stretch the coat apart a couple of inches, and then we'll cut away the holes from the nails what we nailed down the parts, the fronts with the back. We don't need too much . . . an inch or inch and a half will be enough."

The tailors worked the whole night. They took apart the coat, wet down the leather, and tacked the individual pieces to a board. Overnight the leather dried out under the tension, and in the morning the tailors took the coat off the board and trimmed where the nail holes had been. They resewed the coat, and it was about two-and-a-quarter inches wider in the waist. On the day that the *Untersturmführer* and his maven returned, Mr. Frank brought the coat to the camp office. The *Untersturmführer* tried it on; the Nazis advanced no criticism. Under the questioning eyes of the two SS men, he refused to tell how he had changed a coat that could positively not have been changed. The Nazi tailor measured the coat, and finding that it had expanded more than two inches, he was suspicious of foul play. Some deception had been in the works, that was the way of this race: sly, underhanded, always involved in machinations to their own advantage.

Commandant Amon Göth riding a horse at the Plazow concentration camp, which he ran between February 1943 and 1944. Frank made him a leather coat in late 1941 when Göth was still an *Untersturmführer.* He and his advisor claimed the coat was too small, and Frank and the other Lipowa tailors had to find a way to fix it. Photo by Raimund Titch. *Courtesy of the United States Holocaust Memorial Museum.*

It was impossible this was the same coat. "The Jew must have stolen more leather and made another one!"

"So then it was another thing," said Mr. Frank, throwing up his hands. When Mohwinkel saw these new dissatisfactions smoldering, he took command. The *Untersturmführer* was endangering the reputation of his house and was beginning to infringe on his rights as master and proprietor. Such a lesser officer could not glide into the camp, have a coat made, and usurp the privilege of killing Mohwinkel's tailor, if that was what he intended. "You have your coat; it fits. It's what you wanted; now take it and go."

At the end of his story, Mr. Frank informed me that the *Untersturmführer* was Amon Göth, who later became commandant of Plazow and was infamous for shooting prisoners from his balcony for amusement.

17

Eichmann

1942

IN 1942 A NAZI CAME for an inspection to the labor camp.[1] The whole staff from the Nazis—Globocnik, Höffle, Maubach, Mohwinkel, Schramm, Klein, Hantke, the *Standartenführer* von Alvensleben—they all went around to show the guest the shops, how the Jews are working, what they accomplish with the Jews in the camp. The Nazis running the concentration camps or the labor camps want to show the higher-rank leaders that they are doing something very important because they want to keep their jobs, to keep from going to the front to fight the Russians. All the time they brought some big Nazis, some generals and others, but this time the guest was Eichmann. Later they called me to go over to Shopena 17 to take a measurement for him for a leather coat, to make the same leather coat what I made for the *Reichsführer* Himmler. So I found out that this was the Eichmann they later tried in Israel and executed him. In Israel he said he didn't do anything; he only carried out orders what they gave, but I know what he did. Matter of fact, he was very knowledgeable with the Jewish way of life. He spoke Hebrew; he spoke Yiddish . . . I don't know how he was educated, but this is why he said he knows very much about the Jews. That's why they made him in charge of liquidating them.[2]

1. This chapter resumes with Mr. Frank's account.
2. Eichmann was practically the paradigm of the criminal who acknowledges his crimes and their quantitative significance, claims responsibility for them (probably to earn fame), and self-importantly exhorts historians to take note of his actions. At the same time, he was sociopathically divorced from the murderous character of his actions; Hannah Arendt remarked that he was a self-inflated and self-effacing "clown" once he took his place on the witness stand. He was an *Obersturmbannführer* (Lieutenant Colonel) in the Reich Security Main Office (Jewish Division), where he was re-

In that time, we could still go to our homes what they gave us outside the ghetto. When I came home, my wife told me Kestenberg[3] had been there and told her that when I would come home from work, I should see him. The *Judenrat* was across the street from where my living quarters was so I didn't have to go very far. I had a bite to eat, and I went over to the office from Mr. Kestenberg.

"Mr. Frank," he told me, "something happened. I had a telephone call from the *Standartenführer* von Alvensleben, and he told me that he has a guest what he wants to come and inspect the orphanage here." In the same building as the *Judenrat,* there was an orphanage with Jewish kids.

"Eichmann wants to visit to see the conditions how the children are living. I know that Eichmann is not interested in the conditions, but I think something will happen. Because you took a measurement to make a leather coat for this guest, when he'll come if you'll be here, maybe you can help out with something."

This was about five-thirty, and about six-thirty, two cars with the SS came in, and Eichmann was between them. They walked in . . . I saw through the window on the first floor when both cars parked, and they went out from the car. The way they walked was like heroes, so stiff and laughing and talking. We didn't hear from inside what they are talking about, but we could see the faces there, the mood, how they walked, and how they laughed, and how they talked to each other with a smile on their lips.

Kestenberg was waiting when they came in from the corridor. The orphanage rooms was on the second floor, but in the front was the offices. When they came in, was a very big office with three or four desks. Mohwinkel brought Eichmann with the whole group—he was walking side by side with Eichmann and the others behind him, but

---

sponsible for working out deportation plans for Jews outside of Germany, initiating anti-Jewish laws, and working out the smooth operations of the train system (Hilberg 1985, 408). In his first position in the Vienna office of the SD, he "acquired a smattering of Hebrew, which enabled him to read haltingly a Yiddish newspaper. . . . [H]e studied the organizational method of the Zionist movement, with all its parties, youth groups, and different programs. This did not yet make him an 'authority,' but it was enough to earn him an assignment as official spy on the Zionist offices and on their meetings; it is worth noting that his schooling in Jewish affairs was almost entirely concerned with Zionism" (Arendt 1976, 41). For insights into his personality, and lack of one, see "An Expert on the Jewish Question" in Arendt (1976, 33–56).

3. The head of the *Judenrat.* See the Chapter 3, "Invasion, Escape, Entrapment."

Mohwinkel was in the front with Eichmann. Mohwinkel yelled out the name "Kestenberg!" He was standing not far away, and he stood very, very stiff. They talk . . . I couldn't hear exactly, I was standing far away from the group on the other side of the room. Eichmann started to talk to Kestenberg—how many are working in the offices, and later, how many children there are.

Eichmann told Kestenberg he'd like to see the children in the rooms, and they started to walk, Kestenberg with them. The others from the *Judenrat* and me, we was left standing in the room while they went around through the buildings. They came to a large room what was there twenty kids, and they inspect all the rooms where the kids are. Then Eichmann asked Kestenberg, "Who is responsible for the welfare from the kids?"

So was a man there on the first floor, and Kestenberg showed him the man . . . his name was Schmul Wollmann, a very prominent citizen from Lublin. Wollmann's parents used to import and export things—they was dealing with the Polish government in the iron business, rails for railroad tracks—so the father, Saul Wollmann, was a very rich man. Eichmann said all the kids should come down, and he told Wollmann that he should take all the kids together, and they should be concentrated in one place. They all came from all the floors, from all the rooms—children from three years to eight or nine years old. He asked him how many children there are, and he said there are 118; he counts the 118. Eichmann said, "They have no place to be here. The Germans don't have milk to feed Jewish children." The tone was always to give orders—very harsh. All their voices when they talked to Jews was very strong, to put you in fear.

ML: I read he had a kind of split personality where sometimes he would be very severe, then other times he would act very friendly and convivial, and he would make a certain promise to you, and then within seconds, he would completely change . . .

JF: Well, that's right, I'm just coming to this split personality!

When Eichmann asked Wollman all the questions, how many children, the children don't have a place here, that there is a special children's camp for Jewish children, and they should go there, his voice was very harsh. I was standing twenty-five feet from the group, from Eichmann and Mohwinkel and the other Nazis, with Wollman and Kestenberg, and a minute later he was very, very mild, his voice changed . . . his voice was changing into a human being, like a regular person.

He said to Wollmann, "If you would like to stay here, you don't have to go with the children. We'll take care of them." We all heard Wollmann, he thanked him very much, and he said, "I took care of them all the years, and I'll go with them where they'll go."

This was the change in the voice from Eichmann. He said, "OK . . . if you want to." With a very mild voice, he told him, "You should dress the children warm," because in that time it was October, and was a little bit chilly. Eichmann wants to give them more food for the journey, so he tells Wollmann, "Give every child a half-ration of bread." The other Nazis was standing around, Mohwinkel was there, other high-ranking officers . . . you can imagine how everybody was feeling this moment. They start to dress the children and to put them in warm clothes.

The whole bunch with the Nazis went out, and they called up the office to the Lipowa camp that they should send two trucks, and in twenty minutes there come two trucks. Wollmann with the help of Ukraine Nazis start to put up the children on the trucks.

In the end, there was two kids left, and I was standing watching how they load them up on the truck. In that time, I was outside by the side from the building with Kestenberg, and Wollmann was near the truck to help put up the children. A Nazi came over to me and he said, "You go help the last two children get up on the truck."

I took them in my hands and put them in the truck and he said, "You can go together with them." With the machine gun he pointed on me, and what could I do? I went into the truck, and I was sitting near Mr. Wollmann with the children.

In the truck, all the children was crying . . . we start to calm them down, and we couldn't calm them down. The trucks slowly moved out from Lublin about ten kilometers, then drove into the woods. I knew the places around Lublin . . . this place on the outskirts was with the name Trawnik.

They ordered Mr. Wollmann and me to take down the children, take the bread from them what we had given them before, and to line them up . . . that's what we did, and we was the last ones. They gave an order to march.

A half-kilometer into the woods, very isolated, I saw two black SS cars waiting for us, with Eichmann, Mohwinkel, and the whole gang standing very straight when the line of children was coming closer. Mohwinkel saw me. He shouted out to me, furious—

"You *Drecksack!* You sack of shit! What are you doing here?"

"The SS man told me to go with the children. He pointed to me with the gun, and what could I do? I had to carry out his order."

Mohwinkel moved over to Eichmann and spoke to his ear. Maybe he told him I was the tailor what was making the leather coat for him, but I don't know if the Mohwinkel would want to say that this was his mistake that I should be there. But so important was this that Mohwinkel should make sure that his guest received the leather coat, he shouldn't want me killed in that time. I was saved, but I don't think I can say Mohwinkel saved me. To use me and the other ones, they have to keep us alive, but at the same time, they are making more killings . . . I cannot give him this treatment when I say this, that he would do such a thing *for me*.

Mohwinkel ordered an SS man to take me away in one from the cars. A minute later from the car I heard shots, machine gun shots, and I figure what they did with the children . . . they finished off Wollmann and the 118 children.[4]

4. Stanislaw Mikolajczyk, Vice Premier of the Polish Government-in-Exile in London, reported at a July 9, 1942, press conference that "108 children from two to nine years old were taken from a Jewish orphanage, led to the outskirts of the town [Lublin], and murdered with their nurses" (Apenszlak 1982, 95–96). This is probably the same event at which Frank was present, although there is a discrepancy in the number of children. Mikolajczyk reported the date as the same as the liquidation of the large Lublin ghetto, the night of March 23–24, 1942, and while Frank, in this chapter, dates the killing of the children in October, he stated in his deposition of November 29, 1965, that the event was in conjunction with the liquidation of the ghetto (*SSPF*, 7384). It is therefore likely that the date is correct.

Regarding a separate issue, researchers who examine Mr. Frank's first deposition (June 3, 1964; *SSPF*, 5693–97) will see that when he related the story about the orphans, Mohwinkel, rather than Eichmann, was the central actor and decision-maker, and Mohwinkel was the one who had the conversation with Wollmann about the children (with Mohwinkel's speech coming across as more insulting than the Eichmann version in this chapter). However, when Mr. Frank told his story to the Yiddish newspaper the *Morning Journal* three years earlier (June 28, 1961), Eichmann was the central figure. When I asked Mr. Frank why he didn't mention Eichmann at the 1964 deposition, he said it was because the prosecutors were only interested in Mohwinkel. Mr. Frank also reaffirmed that he is certain that Eichmann (along with a large group of Nazis including Mohwinkel) visited the orphanage, that Eichmann was the one who spoke to Wollmann, and that Eichmann was in the woods outside Trawnik where the children were rounded up.

18
—

The Liquidation of the Lublin Ghetto

March 23–Early April 1942

IN LUBLIN, there was a Jewish family, a Jewish butcher what he had a butcher shop in the Gentile market. He was selling meat, but not Kosher meat. He had a daughter, her name was Helen, in Yiddish, *Chaiyah*. She fell in love with a boy from next door, from a Polish butcher shop, the next one over. She converted to Catholicism, and she married him. In that time, the Jews, if somebody went over to another nationality, it was like he was dead. They sat *shivah* for her; she was dead.

That happened about twenty-five years before, we didn't know anymore about her, and people forgot about this. She had two boys with the Polish guy—one was a lawyer, and the other son was a doctor. When the Nazis opened the labor office they made the lawyer for the head, that he should send away the people to work, what places they should go. But instead to send them to work, he send the people what they was supposed to go to work to the woods to fight the Germans with guns and with hand grenades, and this went on for a lot of months, and nobody knew about this. I don't know how the Germans found out about this, but before they liquidate the ghetto, about two days before, they took the family to the synagogue, to the *Marschal schul,* with the Helen Tupper, what she convert herself to Catholicism, with the two boys, the doctor with the lawyer, and they killed the whole family—except the *Polak,* her husband, the father from the boys. Him they didn't touch.

During the years 1940 and 1941, all the craftspeople on the Lipowa was living in the large ghetto what was the Jewish section from

124

Lublin.[1] On March 23, 1942, just before *Pesach,* the Nazis came out with an order that all the husbands or sons what they used to be able to go home to the ghetto after working on the Lipowa couldn't go home anymore. They need them to work there more, so the Nazis said.

Two days later, they took all the Jews from the ghetto, and they concentrate them on the streets . . . all the Jews in the ghetto and the families, parents, wives, and children of the workers on the Lipowa— everybody except those hiding somewhere what the Germans didn't know about. This took a couple of days and a couple of nights. They took all the Jews, and they sent them away. We didn't know where . . . they say they sent them to labor camps, but in that time it was 1942, and we didn't, we couldn't imagine that they are sending them to the gas chambers or to shoot them.[2]

Only the shop leaders from the Lipowa had the right to keep their immediate families because we was living already away from the ghetto, a couple of thousand feet.

In the same time, they took also my family. My father, my mother with the six sisters, with the sisters' children, they all want to keep together, and this was on the first day in the evening. My wife and I was living a couple of blocks outside the ghetto, and they gave an order that all the leaders from the shops have to come down with their families also, so we came down, and I saw my family standing in the line. They put us away near the wall of the building, on the sidewalk, and they was on the middle of the road, thousands and thousands of people. I saw my father with my mother, with the sisters with the children, and I want to go over to say good-bye to them. A Nazi with a machine gun put his gun to my shoulder, to my back, and he said, "If you don't go back, you'll get shot; you'll get killed right away, with your wife, with the two little boys." He clubbed me with the end from the gun over the shoulders; he pushed me back, and I couldn't say good-bye. We was standing for two hours . . . was about ten in the evening, in the night. I remember Mohwinkel came over to the group, the families from the leaders from the shops, and he said, "You go back to your apartments or to your rooms or to your houses." Also like an order: "Get back to your places!"

1. The native Jewish population was between 38,000 and 42,000, and with transports and deportations to the ghetto, it is estimated the population rose to as high as 250,000.

2. In fact, they were gassed at Belzec (Arad 1987, 383; Browning 1993, 52).

When my wife and I went back to the upstairs to our apartment, through the window I could see when the Nazis start to yell. "March! *Schnell! Schnell! Schnell!* March! *Schnell!*" and some of them start to give lashes over their heads to some people, not to march, but to run, and they took them away from the Grodzka Street to the side where the gates was between Kowalsky and Shiroka Streets, and from there . . . I don't know, I couldn't see anymore.

They had no possessions; some of them had in their hands a jacket, a blanket, or a coat, almost nothing with them.

The moment when I saw this picture from all the hundred of thousands of people, including my whole family except my wife with two kids, I saw in my mind in that moment, not just in that moment, but all the time forward, that I didn't believe that someone from us will survive. Sooner or later we'll all go the same way—still, they need me, or they need the other ones, so they are keeping us with our families not to disturb the way of work what they want us to do. But my mind was made up that this was the end from everything.

The children was crying, but me and my wife, looks like we both lost our voices. We couldn't speak. We looked at each other, and we couldn't say anything . . . we fall to each other's arms, and we start to cry, and I said, "Dora, what happened? What happened?"

She said, "I don't know, Jack . . . I want to ask you what happened. . . ." That was the word, just to talk out. We was sitting and looking at each other, crying; we didn't talk too much. I said, "I think that's the end from all of us." It was very bad before, at least my family was alive, and now I don't have nobody except my wife with the two little kids, but the all family from fifty or sixty people are gone. Sitting so for an hour or more than an hour, we fall asleep sitting, we start to like dream and daytime start to come up, and I had to go again, to get ready to go to work to Lipowa Street . . . so I have to go again to do the same routine, the same things to do because maybe they will come again, or maybe they won't have time to finish us off . . . and this was what I could think in that time.

I had to leave at half-past six to be eight o'clock in the shop to carry on with my work. In that time already, I had about 450 tailors what I had to manage. The war with the Russians went on, and we was working for the army to make down jackets for the soldiers for Leningrad, where it was cold, so we had to work very hard.

When I came to the Lipowa, a lot of the people was waiting for us, the heads from the shops, to come to find out what really happened

. . . the workers knew that something happened there, but they didn't know the liquidation came so quick from all the people from the ghetto. So we tell them like this was. We didn't keep back—before you used to keep back secrets because when they took away one or two, we kept secrets, because maybe if you say something, maybe they'll take away my family or somebody else's family. If they took away all of us, all of our families, was no more secrets, so we told them like this was. And everybody was crying; everybody had the same feeling what we had even when we was there. All the leaders from the shop, we went home together, we want to say something, but we didn't know what to say to each other, and we didn't even talk about what happened. I was the most hurt guy, because I had the most people from my family there, but the other ones didn't have so many. Some of them, maybe they had their parents or one parent, but I had maybe about forty people together, with the children, with the brothers-in-law. So I was more hurt . . . they looked at me, and I cannot talk.

Five o'clock in the afternoon when I came home, my wife gave me a piece a bread there, to have a little bite, and to look at her face, how she looked . . . we start to talk about what was twelve or fifteen hours before, and we couldn't come to a conclusion what to do, really to decide anything, to find in ourselves what we can do and if we can do something to avoid another liquidation like this, but we couldn't come to an answer. Sitting and talking so, I said to my wife—and even now when I start to remind myself this conversation, I can never forget this kind of conversation—I said to her, "Dora, what we saw what happened yesterday, this can happen again: today or tomorrow or next week. We don't know. I don't know when this will happen. But God forbid if this will happen, and they take away somebody, not all of us, but somebody from us, what should we do? Go together like all my family went together, or should we hide somebody from us? Or I should hide? If they should take away one little boy, we should stay with the other little boy? Or should we go with this little boy what they'll take away?" We was sitting and talking for maybe five or six hours, and we couldn't come to a conclusion, we couldn't decide really what to do . . . and we left this hanging in the air.

ML: What were some of the feelings that your wife had?

JF: I can say she had the same feeling what I had. What kind of feeling could she have!

ML: You didn't disagree about plans—together you were talking about the plans and couldn't come to any decision . . .

JF: No, no disagreement at all. She used to say, "What you'll do, whatever you'll decide, I'll be with you what you'll decide." I told her the same thing—"Dora, you tell me what you'd like to do, and I'll do what you want me to do." Back and forth and we couldn't come to a conclusion. The feeling was the same thing. We had two other rooms; the kids was in the rooms playing. They was little kids, and we didn't want them to listen to hear everything . . . but the feeling was a mutual feeling. The feeling was we didn't know what we should do.

ML: Do you also think you each wanted to know securely that one person would agree to whatever the other person wanted . . . that no one in such a situation as this, where there was no definite decision, could simply impose a selfish decision?

JF: Most of the time, in the Jewish house, the man decides very important things, not all the time, but most of the time. But in this case, when lives was involved, lives from the children and the life from my wife, I couldn't take the responsibility to say we'll do this way or do another way. In the same way, I feel she had the same feeling. I gave her the opportunity to decide. Like I said before, the man from the house used to decide, but in this moment, I gave her the right that she should decide what I should do, and I'll do what she wants me to do. Maybe from my way of thinking . . . maybe I want to release myself a little bit from 100 percent to be responsible for that. Maybe I want that she should make the decision. I don't know if this is the case, but that's how this was: we could not come to an answer.

ML: To release yourself from responsibility seems very natural to me . . . "natural" isn't the right word—plausible . . . I can imagine doing that myself because who can decide in life and death—and not only that—who can decide about a whole number of situations where you don't know the outcome?

JF: That's right.

ML: What do you think about this inability to decide as compared to the Nazi philosophy, which had very clear directives—systematically kill, kill and punish as the individual sees fit—it seems like exactly the opposite situation?

JF: It's nothing for me to think about this, because later, in that time, you didn't have time to think about the difference between you and the German Nazi, because you felt you are the victim, and the other carries out to victimize you. That's how this is, that's the way they are, that's what they will do, and that's what they are doing. It was no time for me to think, to think about them. I was thinking only about what I could do—*if* I can do something—and I knew I could not do anything.

19

—

Majdan-Tatarsky

Middle of 1942–June 1942

WHEN THE NAZIS LIQUIDATED Lublin in March 1942, Kenisberg, the Jewish millionaire,[1] he hid in the Jewish hospital on Lubartovska Street. Before the war, he was a philanthropist, and so it was that he financed this hospital, and then came there because he thought this would be a safe house . . . many of the prominent Lubliners thought this way. The SS killed all the nurses and patients from this hospital, but for some reason what I am not sure, they didn't look for him.

Near this hospital was the *Jesziwa Chachmy Lublin,* the Lublin Yeshiva, what inside was a replica made of the old Temple of Jerusalem, made by architects from all over the world. All the books and *torahs* from the *yeshiva* was destroyed by the Nazis, but this replica was not . . . even the Germans came to see this replica.

But this was not true for all the places what was important for the Jewish way of life. Before the end from the ghetto, the Nazis was using the synagogues for places to make killings. Most of the transports what the Nazis took away from Lublin, they took them first to the synagogue there, and they concentrate them in the synagogue . . . was very huge, about a thousand or fifteen-hundred people could go in. What I am talking was the *Marschal schul* or the *Maran schul,* with balconies like an opera, on the street between the Grodzka Street and the big ghetto. In the beginning, they didn't destroy the buildings, they just took in the Jews there, and a lot of them was killed in the synagogues. From there, the Nazis would take them away, except one

---

1. See Chapter Eight, "The First Leather Coat."

130

time when they send away a couple of thousand at once, what they called this in German the *Aussiedlung*.[2]

When they liquidated the big ghetto in 1942 and there was no more Jews, they took apart the houses. They hired Polish workers, and they took apart the buildings, with the synagogues, with the mind that the Jews was hiding their gold and jewelry and diamonds in the walls. They took apart every brick, every stone there to check, and the SS was standing and watching if something they'll find. If they didn't find anything, they put the whole Jewish community what was before the ghetto on fire. After they took away the people to Majdan-Tatarsky, then they start to finish off every sign from the houses what was Jewish. If this was a house or this was a store, this was a synagogue, everything what was Jewish they straightened out with the ground.[3]

The people in the labor camp who lost families what they was sent away when they liquidate the ghetto, they were locked up and couldn't leave the labor camp—except the twenty or twenty-five shop leaders what we was still living outside the ghetto, what we still had our homes. In the beginning of 1943, they took out the shop leaders and about two thousand or eighteen-hundred people—the families from the workers in the labor camp. They put all of us together into a small ghetto on the outskirts from Lublin, with the name of Majdan-Tatarsky.

Over there was farms—where Polish farmers was living before, and they had to move . . . the Nazis gave them the houses where we lived in the large ghetto, and they put us in their little farm houses, with roofs made from straw. Was a distance maybe a quarter of a mile on both sides, and in the middle was a road, not asphalt or a road like here a car can drive . . . the width from the road was so one horse with a wagon can go through.

From that time, they closed up this small ghetto so nobody could leave, and we couldn't go home anymore by ourselves from the labor camp. The shop leaders was escorted under the gun from the SS in the

2. A forced evacuation.

3. The destruction of the physical premises of the ghetto and the subsequent cleanup also included the complete demolition of uninhabitable buildings, the cleaning out of latrines, and the sealing of habitable structures so that they could be fumigated with poison gas (to kill vermin and pests). Separate crews were used for each task; in Lublin, the cleanup extended into June 1942 (Hilberg 1985, 490).

morning from the small ghetto to the camp, and in the evening they brought us home on a truck to the ghetto. Because the craftspeople, the men from the families, was locked up on the Lipowa, they couldn't go home anymore to their families for the night. In the small ghetto, women used to come visit my place . . . "How's my husband there in the camp?" This was only the way they had to make contact.

ML: What were the means of getting extra food or extra clothing or anything you might need? Was there organizing with outside contacts, a black market?

JF: Not too much, no. You couldn't make too much contact with the Polish population, because the anti-Semitism was so big. What I remember, the Polish people, they was standing outside the houses, on the sidewalks, when they took us from the big ghetto to the small ghetto when we was marching. Was about two or three miles . . . the whole three miles you stayed in the line, and they watched like a parade. You was marching as prisoners, and most of them they was laughing, to feel they was liberated from the Jews. They didn't think that they'll get the same life later when we was gone. But later the Nazis killed a lot from them . . . especially the intelligentsia, also a lot of priests; they took them to Majdanek the same way, not in the quantity like the Jews, but also thousands of Poles was killed. I'm sure at that time they was not laughing. But they was laughing before, when they took us to Majdan-Tatarsky, not even to the concentration camps. All Jews what they took them to the small ghetto, we all saw how our neighbors was looking at us and to laugh and to have pleasure how the SS are treating us. How could you have contact with this kind of people? You're talking about smuggling, clothes; we didn't have in our mind that we need clothes. We was satisfied with this what we had to wear when they took us. Some of us had little valises in our hands what we could take with us, some clothes or some food, but the thinking was only to have water and a piece of bread or some potatoes . . . to feed the children.

When they move the big ghetto to the small ghetto, the Nazis came out with an order, a good order for the Jewish population in the small ghetto. They came out with posters hanging on the walls saying that the children don't receive enough milk, enough nourishment, and they say they'll check the next time they visit to see if the children are receiving enough nourishment, milk. Especially the heads from the shops, we was surprised. What an order—are they really worrying that our children don't receive enough milk? We was walking to the ghetto after work, so we could talk a little bit freely, to look around if nobody from the SS was near, and I said to Moishe or to Yanke, to the friends what we came home together, "Something is cooking. Something they are preparing. If not, they wouldn't come out just to ask about our children."

In the next three or four days—not right away, two or three days—they called out that there would be a counting outside the ghetto. Outside the ghetto, they called out that they had something to say, that we don't keep the ghetto clean. They took out one or two, and they killed them; they shoot them. And then after two hours they open the gates to go back. It was like a comedy play; they had fun to do something like this. Without reason, to do something that you should suffer after you was thinking that they try to do something good, to confuse you.

———

When I came home one evening from work, I had a bite, and I start again to have a talk with my wife. We saw already that they took away our parents, with our brothers and sisters, and all the Jews— what should we do if something should happen, if they'll take away one boy from us, what should we do? Should we go all together, or should we save what is left over? Before in the discussions, we left this open. When something will happen, we'll act the way how we think to act. This was a very hard discussion, but we didn't have no other choice. Before this time, we was thinking maybe we'll survive; maybe they wouldn't do what they did, but then being with them, I saw that there is no other way than to decide something what to do. But what could you do under the circumstances, against machine guns, against tanks? Nothing.

I know they wouldn't let us live there too long. They'll liquidate us—all of us. I decide what I would like to do. I talk over with my wife, "How's about to make in the basement a hiding place?"—so if something will happen, my wife with one boy should go down there. We'll prepare some food, some water, we'll camouflage the place. Outside the building was a door to the basement, and on the floor from the kitchen, we made an opening to be able to go down and to put in a table with some carpeting. In the meanwhile if something will happen and I will be in the labor camp, maybe I can do something for them through the Nazis what I work for them there, maybe from the commandant. If you know the devil for a long time, you get used to him already, what he is thinking is not so strange, and everything with him will show out . . . maybe you will not know when he will do something exactly, but I always had an idea when something might happen, and maybe I could do something to save them. Better they should be alive so that I could maybe do something for them—I did not know what I could do or if I could do—but to know the devil is not to have the power over him.

I decide that if something will happen, my wife would go down with the little boy Nunyek, and I'll take the older boy Monyek with me to hide him in the labor camp on the Lipowa. Working for four months, we made a false wall in the basement; I had some help from a shoemaker with the name Blank, who also decide to do something like this . . . he had a wife with two kids too. His hiding place was different from the one I built—his house was a smaller place, but he made from the basement. He made a wall from wood, with a sliding door; the door was made from plywood. On one side was clean, straight, and inside was rough . . . with a table and a chair there. I don't know in the end how this looked; I was only helping him when he made the wall with the door to slide. He's only the one what he knows about me, and I knew about him, but we was afraid that somebody else should know, because if they found out, they'd do what they did with other Jews.

We prepared some food and some water, and I took mine older boy, from six years, to the camp, and he was with me in the labor camp. And I think this was in June of '42. I would come home to my wife and the younger boy, and the older boy slept by himself in the labor camp, and I came the next day in the morning to work.

20

Officers

FROM ALL THE NAZIS what I met in the five years and nine months, from the lowest rank to the highest rank except Hitler, I met them in the offices. Like I said, Lublin was the SS headquarters, and they all used to come there. What I found out most of the time by the Nazis was: even between the big ones and the middle ones, there was *some* from them, they used to talk to you like one person to another, and *others* from them, when they talked to you they didn't see your face, and you couldn't see their face for fear; you saw a shadow.

From time to time, I met some very big ranking Nazis, Gestapo people, from the SS or the SD, and when they talked to you, you was thinking you was dealing with a human being. But the moment when you turned around, somebody else behind him was taking over the conversation about uniforms . . . special conversations, they never had with me, only things I should make for them what they was interested for themselves. When the other type turned around and he talked to you, right away you felt that some devil is talking to you—not a human man, but a devil with horns. And that's what I want to say: they had all kind of systems. One was doing the killing in a way you didn't expect—till they killed you they kept you a little bit; they fed you a little bit better; they didn't hit you like the other ones, but when the end came they liquidate you in the same way. But the other ones, before they killed you, they tortured you; they gave you lashes—was made special tables what they screw you in the middle with your hands, with your arms,[1] and you had to count. You had to count. If they tell you twenty-five lashes, you have to count the twenty-five

---

1. Goldhagen describes that "virtually all of Lipowa's personnel carried whips or some functional equivalent," and he also mentions the special whipping table to which Frank refers (Goldhagen 1997, 297).

lashes. If you skip one from the beating, you lost your consciousness; they revived you with water, and if you felt better they put you back, and again and again; they finish you off. This was what I want to bring out about the big ones and the low-ranking officers.

I was a young man, but I think my mind was working much more than a twenty-five or twenty-four year-old man. My thinking was like a thirty-five year-old man. When I talked to many high-ranking officers, majors, colonels, captains, lieutenants, I found out when I talked with them—not I talked with them, they talked to me—I found out before the war they was butchers, clerks, was a lot of criminals what they let out from the prisons, and they was good killers, and they made them for high-ranking officers.

I remember the *Standartenführer* Gunst, this was like a major, the first leader before Mohwinkel.[2] He was living on Shopena 17, and he called me that I should come in his house, eight o'clock in the morning. I came in his apartment; he took me in a room, and the room was like a Frigidaire—the whole room was like a freezer. On top was hanging pigs, whole pigs, and a lot of baloneys, liverwursts, hanging like in a delicatessen store. The whole ceiling was covered with so many meats, prepared, smoked. I saw he was a butcher—he didn't have to tell me! He gave me a whole wurst to take home . . . this was in the beginning, in 1940, when a Nazi might offer something like this, not like later when the killing is coming down harder with them. So pigs, half-pigs was hanging on the ceiling special-made with the hooks, like in a regular slaughterhouse! A room, was before maybe a bedroom, a living room, was made a freezer! And you opened the door . . . that's why I said my mind was working a little bit more ahead than the age what I was.

ML: That reminds me of a diary I read by a German count named Reck-Malleczewen. While living in Bavaria on his farmland, he wrote a secret journal from about 1936 to 1944, and he kept this journal hidden on his land. He was from the old guard and the old nobility whose land and status and culture was threatened when the Nazis

2. Readers will recall Walter Gunst as the Nazi who registered the Jews in Lublin shortly after the invasion (p. 23). Gunst held the post of *SS-Standartenführer* beginning April 20, 1935, and served as the first commandant of Lipowa for a brief time from the end of 1939 to 1940. German court documents describe him as an active commandant who took part in day-to-day operations of the camp. Due to his corruption (his biography in the court documents doesn't give details), he was replaced by Ludolf von Alvensleben (*SSPF*, 8404).

took power. The journal contains incisive portraits of Hitler, dissections of the new German mass-culture as shallow and gluttonous, and also what aggrandizing wheeler-dealers the Nazi leaders were. He wrote about rumors circulating in Berlin, what was happening to the old, more cultured nobility at the time. Several times he remarks very sarcastically that the Nazi party was a party full of second-class clerks, high school teachers, nobodies, postal workers, tradesmen who failed in their crafts, and the SS was nothing but a pack of thieves, burglars, gangsters, and he discusses something similar to your observation about this butcher.

JF: That's how this was. The difference from one to another, the same rank, the Gunst what I am telling you with the pigs and lambs hanging in his freezer room. . . . After when he left, another came in his place. The other was entirely different. This was von Alvensleben. *Von* is like *Sir* in England. He was maybe thirty years old, but his life was entirely different. Every day in the morning, he never came down seven o'clock in the morning like Gunst used to come down to the camp. He came down eleven o'clock. He had every day in the morning a bath, because Bergman, the Jewish maid who used to clean the apartment, used to tell about this. Always it used to become a little bit colder in October, and von Alvensleben's nose was always dripping; he couldn't take the cold. He was more delicate, his walk, the talking from him, a very intelligent face. The difference from him to the Gunst was like from day to night; he was more from the intelligentsia, but he was the same killer. When it came to killing, he did it, or he gave the orders, but his manners was . . . you could see the education.[3] The Germans took the intelligentsia and involved in . . . what do you call this when people eat people?

ML: Cannibalism?

JF: Cannibalism. They made their culture into this. The manners, his was different from the Gunst. Between his colleagues, von Al-

3. According to his German court biography, von Alvensleben wasn't interested in running Lipowa and distanced himself from the camp; perhaps his education or temperament had something to do with this, or perhaps he was more interested in other duties. Because of his apathy, he entrusted the day-to-day administration of camp to *SS-Obersturmführer* Dolp, described in court records as "especially brutal, gruesome, and without any initiative to meet the needs of the camp," while *SS-Oberscharführer* Franz Bartetzko took charge of the camp's workforce. Both men were accused of shootings and beatings, but were never tried because they were killed in the war (*SSPF*, 8401–2, 8442–45).

vensleben was very pleasant, but kept himself distanced; maybe he didn't feel at ease. You could see even between the all staff from the camp—was Riedel, Schramm, Dorndoff—you could see who was really a gangster from before and who is more an educated killer, who finished college or high school.

ML: I read that a lot of the camp commandants went to Dachau first and studied there, as if in a school, and they learned the system from there.[4]

JF: Possible, sure, because in many instances, they had the same system in many camps, the system for killing was almost the same. Oh sure, this was a special schooling. The schooling was that people shouldn't find out what will happen an hour later, because through a word, there will be disturbances from riots or to throw Molotov cocktails or to have guns to shoot or stones. Everything to make with a plan, and they made this systematically, not at first outright killing. First they made rationing a little bit less, and then later how to live a little more dirty, not so clean, not to supply you with soap or detergents . . . always with a system, always with a system. Sure they went through a special school. In the beginning they took out the gangsters, the criminals what they was in the jails, and they taught them— the same way what they did to other people before they was in jail, they should do to Jews or to the intelligentsia or to intelligent Poles or to priests or to other nationalities.[5] That was the way they could ac-

4. Yahil (1990, 135) states that guards and commanders were trained in Dachau, "hence the uniform style of contempt and cruelty" among personnel in separate camps. Marszalek reports that Rudolph Höss, the commandant of Auschwitz, claimed that the intense discipline of Theodor Eicke, the commandant of Dachau and Inspector of Concentration Camps, permeated all the concentration camps and influenced the SS men stationed within them (Marszalek 1986, 12). Yet Marszalek grants that personnel, local authorities, and the purpose assigned to a camp gave it an individual character (Marszalek 1986, 37). An educational system was not the only common element; not every *Kapo*, block leader, guard, and commanding officer was trained with the same methods. Criminal inmates, Hiwis (Ukrainians trained at Trawnik), and officers who had no training prior to supervising in labor camps came from different backgrounds and behaved differently. Frank's description of the different tastes in clothing and levels of education also indicate this idea. Frank affirms the idea of "special schooling" to express his view that the heinous treatment of Jewish prisoners was the kind of common practice that only an institution could create and to stress that exterminations were organized operations, not the fiat of a few individuals.

5. With an agreement between Himmler and Minister of Justice Thierack (September 18, 1942), the Ministry of Justice arrogated the jurisdiction of German criminals (as well as Jews, Gypsies, Poles, Ukrainians, and Russians) to the SS (Hilberg,

complish what they did. And not only this, they received help to carry out their work from the nations what they occupied. In some countries they put up governments to carry out; in France with the Vichy government, they carry out the work what the Nazis told them to do. They carry out in other countries. So happened in Poland they didn't succeed . . . they tried in Poland many times to put up a Polish government to work for them like a puppet government, but they didn't succeed with the *Polaks*.

ML: But the Nazis instituted their own government instead of indirectly influencing the Poles and controlling them with a Polish puppet government—Hans Frank, the Governor of the Government-General, and Globocnik, the Higher SS and Police Leader . . .

JF: You have everything about them in the tapes.[6]

ML: But this is also from my reading of the history. The Polish government in exile in London was fairly ineffectual. I don't know if there was any news about that while you were at Lipowa Street.

JF: I don't know too much . . . when I am talking about to you what you have, even what you was reading, my knowledge was not taken from there. You see, I was face to face to Hans Frank or Globocnik, so I am talking what my life was with them, not what the historians is writing about Poland or about the names from them. I'm sure they know more about it than I do, but I am giving you what they was in that time.

I can tell you, for Hans Frank, I made a leather coat. I don't know if he was wearing . . . you see, the thing was, when I mentioned before that my mind worked in that time when I was in the twenties like a man from thirty, in that time I was thinking about what Mohwinkel was offering Hans Frank. If Hans Frank needs a coat from me, a coat from the Lipowa Street—Hans Frank has so much, the whole Europe is his, but Mohwinkel wants to show what he is doing. They promote Mohwinkel to commandant,[7] and he brings out something like a

---

454). The transfer of criminals to concentration camps was completed by November 16, 1944 (Hilberg 1985, 1002). Because criminals had free reign over protective-custody prisoners and could supervise them at work and in barracks, they were a constant means of repression and violence against "political prisoners, Social Democrats, Communists, Christian and liberal politicians" (Distel and Jakusch 1978, 58).

6. Frank is referring to recordings of our conversations in which we discussed these figures.

7. Mohwinkel's promotion to commandant was during Lipowa's third regime of command. As an *SS-Oberscharführer*, he began under *SS-Untersturmführer* Horst

leather coat, so beautiful a work—was really beautiful—so he wants to show the big shots. That was my way what I was thinking what the leather coats are. Eichmann knew he needed my coat. But the first thing when a big Nazi came into the Lipowa, not only to me he comes for a coat, he comes into the shoemaker to make a pair of shoes. The Polish shoemakers was very known, not only in Poland . . . that's what I heard, even outside Poland. In France, they was very known for their boots what they was making . . . special, they had heels to up here, special stiff boots. You have to look in a museum, and maybe you can see a Polish boot; looked different than an American boot, what a rider of a horse wears. Even the riding pants what the Poles was wearing when they was hunting was different than the Germans, so there was some difference what they liked. And Mohwinkel knew the differences between what they liked most, so he liked to have these gifts made to show the big Nazis what kind of nice things he is carrying out with the slaves, because he was the manager; he was the commandant.

You asked me if there was a conversation between me and the General-Governor Frank from Poland. You can never have the conversations with them. Sometimes I was listening what they are saying and standing like a soldier to a general and to listen, but you couldn't talk to them. After Eichmann visited, Hans Frank was the next guest to inspect the slaves . . . he came from Krakow. When Mohwinkel brought him in with the whole group to inspect the tailor shop, I was standing by the office table, and Mohwinkel called me by name . . . I don't know, he just wants to say something, to do something; I don't know why he did this. He called out, "Frank!" He meant me, and the General-Governor turned around, and he was thinking Mohwinkel called him!

Mohwinkel knew right away he made a mistake to address the

Riedel; Riedel was in charge of the business and administration of the camp, while Mohwinkel, his adjutant, supervised the work operation. Riedel had come to power around August 1940 because of a report he wrote stating that his predecessor von Alvensleben and his underlings had mishandled Lipowa's finances (*SSPF*, 8366). In November 1941, Riedel lost his post to Mohwinkel because Globocnik found him too arrogant. According to his court biography, Mohwinkel also had an arrogant demeanor, but his main personality trait was his brutality toward Jews, driven by his ambition to fulfill his goals for the camp (*SSPF*, 8408). This made him far more violent than a mere taskmaster. While at Lipowa, he was promoted to *Untersturmführer* (Second Lieutenant) in January 1942 (*SSPF*, 8408).

highest officer in such a way as this. He apologized, he said, "The *Jude,* the *Schneidermeister,* the tailor, his name is Frank."

When he said, "The *Jude,* his name is Frank," Hans Frank was ten feet from me from the desk where I was standing. Everybody was standing like soldiers; he came over a little bit nearer to the table.

"What is your name?"

I said, "Frank." What else was I going to say?

"How do you sign your name?"

So I felt, that's it; that's my end. I remembered that time I was between the crowd, and I saw the incident with Sturm a year ago there in Majdan-Tatarsky, and I figure that is me . . . if I have the same name and I am a Jew, I have to go.[8]

I signed my name, and he didn't say anything. After an hour, I looked up, and I see myself alive—I didn't know if I *am* alive even.

So that's the story if you had conversations with them . . . you never had conversations with them . . . sometimes they want to have conversations with you, they want to find out what this is in your mind, or from where do you know some rumor . . . so they talked with you. But when they talked to me, I said "I don't know"—I always find a way not to answer. I met one Nazi what he asked me some questions, and I said to everything what he asked me, "I don't know." He said, "You don't know anything?"

I said, "I know something what this is in my trade; I know a lot of things, but out of my trade, I don't know. I'm not so educated"—what this was really true too. I didn't finish college, I didn't finish even high school, so I didn't know. They took me as an honest Jew. I knew that I couldn't say anything, because from the experience, I know a lot of Jews was killed for talking . . . they would be killed anyway, but right now they would live a year later or a year more, but they ask them, and they want to know from them more.

The Schramm what I was mentioning from before, he was an electrical engineer. Like I said, every shop had a Nazi what he was above the Jewish head from the shop, so the Schramm was the head from the electrical shop, from the electricians. In the beginning, he was the quietest guy from all the staff from the labor camp. I never saw him to hit somebody or to punish somebody from his shop or like the other

8. Frank is alluding to an earlier situation in which a Jew named Sturm had the same name as the Nazi in charge of liquidating the Majdan-Tatarsky ghetto. The Nazi Sturm shot the Jew Sturm for this reason. See p. 161.

Nazis from the staff from the Lipowa used to do. He never became commandant; for a long time, he was only an *Unterscharführer* [corporal]. As the time progressed, Schramm became all of a sudden more violent—I don't know why. Maybe Mohwinkel was complaining about his way that he is conducting himself so quietly; maybe he made him change, or maybe Schramm was a split personality. He looks like a quiet guy, and what he did in the nighttime or when he was not in the camp, I don't know, but all of a sudden, in one day, Mohwinkel was away and Schramm substituted for Mohwinkel this day to do the counting, to take over the list from all the laborers from the camp, if someone's missing. One from a group, he didn't stand straight or he said something—I really don't know because we all stood on the counting six o'clock in the morning, and this was a couple hundred yards away from me and I don't know what was there. But I saw from far away when Schramm took out his pistol from his holster from his side he was wearing, and he gave him the bullet in the back of his head from this guy, and he fell down dead.

Before, the people used to pass by and to raise their hats to greet him—this was the way what you had to do if you wore a hat. People used to pass by and to see him in the labor camp when he went in from the office to the electrical shop—they was feeling comfortable. From that time on, they start to fear him. After the one man what he killed, he killed a couple of guys—I don't know for what. Schramm start to rise in the ranks, from *Unterscharführer* to *Oberscharführer* and then to *Untersturmführer*, and the last distinction I put on his collar was *Obersturmführer*.[9]

———

I remember they asked me to take a measurement for a Nazi. I don't remember his name, but he was an older man in the sixties in that time, but he was from the SS party. A Nazi watchman took me with a car to his home. He was living about a mile from the labor camp. I took him the measurement for a uniform jacket with a pair of britches, pants what you ride on a horse with leather on the seat. When I had ready the uniform ensemble, they took me back to his home to deliver this. He tried it on, and he was very pleased. How he talked to me was not like a Nazi, but like a human being . . . he was so

9. Beginning as a Corporal, he subsequently became a Sergeant, Second Lieutenant, and finally a First Lieutenant.

pleased, he gave me a drink, a fruit juice. That a Nazi from the rank of colonel should give a Jew something to drink, to offer him something, this was for me something new.

The colonel has a wife, an older woman about fifty-eight, and also little children, his grandchildren living there. When I start to leave, his wife asked me if I can fix something for a little girl, a dress, to make smaller or to make shorter, and I said, "Yes, sure." I took this with me to the labor camp, and I fixed this little dress. The next day the SS man took me with his car to deliver this little dress for the granddaughter.

The SS colonel was not home, but his wife, she was home, and she start to talk to me all kind of things. I was listening, and she asked me something, to answer her questions what she asked me, and I was playing the part like I don't know or I don't understand, because I knew that if I'll say something what I shouldn't say, something they don't like, later this will come out to her husband or to another Nazi. I was thinking, maybe she wants to trap me, maybe she wants to get what I am thinking out from my mind, and then they'll use this against me.

I was sitting at the table there, and she served me on the table lunch . . . in years I didn't have so a lunch what she prepared for me, by the table, like a human being. I couldn't believe I am in a Nazi home to be treated like this from his wife. The time what I was eating, she was sitting across from me by the table, and she was talking and I was listening.

She told me, "I cannot understand what the SS people are doing to the Jews. I know my husband doesn't do this kind of thing. I re- member when I met my husband the first time when I was eighteen or nineteen years old . . . we was almost the same age. We had a picnic on a field. Near the blanket where we was lying down on the ground and eating, a worm was crawling near the blanket. I told him to kill the worm, and he said, 'Oh, no! God brought these kind of things into the world, so why should I kill it?' He took the blanket, and he moved to another place, and the worm went his own way . . . not to kill the worm. I can't understand: in that time he doesn't want to kill the worm, and after the years passed by, now all the other ones—not my husband—" that's what she says—"they are killing people."

She asked me what I am saying to this, and I say, "I have nothing to say. I don't know." She saw that I am afraid to talk, to answer the question what she asked me.

And nine months later, I found out that they made her husband for a commandant from another labor camp. I found out that her husband, what she says he doesn't kill—that he doesn't want to kill the worm when he is young—that he is the worst henchman from the whole staff from the camp there. He kills from left and right; he kills the Jewish prisoners there. That's what I found out from the Jewish war prisoners on the Lipowa. They went sometimes to this camp to bring some food or to deliver something, because all camps received rations from Majdanek concentration camp, so the Jewish war prisoners went to Majdanek to bring the big kettles and carry them to the other camps.

I was thinking the story what his wife told me was true, but times changed, and he belonged to the party, and this way, maybe in his view, maybe if he'll kill the Jews, maybe he'll get some money, gold, diamonds. Maybe he'll get a bigger name; they'll advance him in his rank—who knows? That's what this is: they made from him a commandant, looks like he started killing before he became commandant, because they only made commandants what they was good killers, what they can kill a lot of Jews at once.

———

ML: We've talked about several different types of Nazi leaders and officers, for example, this one whose house you visited and whose wife served you lunch, whom you described as being more of the old school, not outwardly following a doctrine of violence. You saw people who were lower in the ranks but wanted to climb much higher and probably realized that violence was one way to achieve that. You saw people who were without question extremely brutal, like Mohwinkel. And you saw a man like Schramm, quiet, but who suddenly became a murderer. It seems there were so many psychological types of these SS members who ran camps or had high positions in the camps.

JF: Well . . . that's how this was.

ML: Do you think you can always expect that where people are committing horrendous crimes they'll each have a different way of approaching them? Some will commit murders for status, to get a higher rank, some because they experience something from killing, an enormous sense of power, or . . .

JF: My answer to this is you could never figure them out, what their purpose is from killing, to get a higher rank or to show that he has power, that he could do everything what he wants, or to show the higher ranking officer that he carries out his orders even more than what the order calls for. Nobody could figure out . . . I never could figure out their motives. There was times I was taking a measurement for a Nazi officer . . . by the measurement he was very polite, he told me how he liked to have his trousers made, his riding britches, he was a horse rider . . . it was very polite . . . and with a moment later he raised his voice, and he became like the Nazis like I know what they are. But you can never figure out what they'll be the next, how their mood is, what they'll do the next moment, the next minute. You never could figure out.

21

—

The Airport Rebellion

Middle of 1942

ML: SINCE YOU MADE a lot of SS men uniforms and coats, and often you sewed on their decorations or new ranks, what did you think about the idea that you were creating clothing, which people wear not only to keep themselves warm or so they won't be naked, but because it's part of their status, it's a uniform, and they're trying to appear a certain way, important or powerful? Was that a very strange position for you to be in: to make clothing for a person's appearance in this world where everything was upside down?

JF: No, I didn't think at all. I think I said this—we didn't have time to think; they didn't let us think. We was always under the gun or under the stick. You couldn't think straight, but they didn't start right away to be the way that I am telling you, the killing with everything. They didn't start right away. They systematically had a plan how to carry out what they want, the final solution, how to carry out this without casualties.

First, to take you out from your house or your apartment outside the ghetto where most of the Jews was living before. They took you out from there, and they put you with all the Jews. When you was living between the Gentiles, you had a nice apartment and nice furniture and mirrors and paintings, like a human being. They took you out from there, and they put you in the Jewish community, what even before the war was very poor people living there; they didn't have this life like Jews living outside from the Krakowsky Street or Bernadinsky Street or other streets had. They start to take you out from the luxury, to live a simple life. Then later they start to take away the freedom to buy open-market food; they gave you rationing cards. Later after this, they made a closed ghetto, with gates, and you couldn't go out. First

146

the Jewish police was watching the gates from the ghetto, and then the SS was watching the ghetto. Before the ghetto, they tell you to wear an armband with the Jewish star, so they know that you are a Jew. From the ghetto, they liquidate the big ghetto, and they make a small ghetto—and the small ghetto; they liquidate the small ghetto to take them later to Majdanek, to the gas chambers.

There was a plan from the beginning, systematically, not all at one time. This way, they prepared you not to be hasty, not to fight back. If they took away one thing, you figure maybe they'll let you have the poorer life, so maybe you'll survive, maybe the war will not be forever. You couldn't think. You took everything that this is the way what it should be. Till the Warsaw ghetto . . . when they start to fight back.

It came to my mind what I didn't remember for years.

In Lublin they had another labor camp with shops, and they had there women, only women. The camp was in a place what before this was an airport. When the Germans bombed, they destroyed the aeroplanes there, so they made there a women's labor camp.[1] From one day in the week, a Sunday, they brought some women from the labor camp from the *Plaga Lashkewicz*, this means from the airport, to us, to the Lipowa Street. The war prisoners and the other slaves from us, when we saw Jewish women, we start to talk to them. After that day, they took them back.

The next week, they took a group from men from the Lipowa Street to visit the women. And to tell you like this was, they made a whorehouse. The Nazi mind had it that the boys should have intercourse with the women. There was even times what the Nazis was standing and watching and telling them to have intercourse—to degrade you. Why I'm telling you this is to show you they didn't make this one time so bad, but to prepare you systematically, little by little.[2]

The main thing what I want to tell you now . . . before they liquidate the Warsaw ghetto,[3] they made some selections; they brought some Jews from Warsaw to Lublin. Lipowa was in the beginning a

1. While Mr. Frank recalls exclusively women, Goldhagen reports that of the 3,500 to 5,500 prisoners in the Main Supply Camp of *Plaga Lashkewicz*, 2,000 to 3,000 were women. For more information about this Globocnik-controlled camp, see p. xvi, note 15 in the Introduction.

2. Other types of violence at this camp included regular beatings and shootings (with little pretext or no provocation on the part of prisoners), experimental gassings in the barracks, and rape (Goldhagen 1997, 306–7).

3. April 1943.

transport camp; they transfer slaves, the Jews, to other camps from
there. A train could go into this airport camp; there was rails. The
trains from Warsaw came through Lublin to the airport, and from
there, they took them out from the cattle cars, and they brought them
over to the Lipowa, to our camp. From there, some of them they left
on Lipowa Street, and some they send away to other camps.

My wife's cousin was taken from the labor camp to the airport
camp. In that time, not all the women was on the *Plaga Lashkewicz*—
some Jews was at Majdan-Tatarsky, like my wife was there hidden with
one little boy. I found out that her cousin was on the *Plaga
Lashkewicz;* her name was Adja, in Yiddish, Esther. At that time, I
could go out from Lipowa because I was still wearing my civil clothes,
to go with a group to the women's labor camp to visit her. In the
same time when I came with a group to work, there came a transport,
a train, with twenty or thirty cattle cars, with maybe a thousand Jews
they brought from Warsaw.

When the train came, we was standing five-hundred feet from the
rails what the train stopped by the station. In that time, they didn't let
out nobody from the women's barracks or from the group what we
was there, but we looked out from little openings, little windows, to
see what the Nazis would do when the train stopped. Thirty or forty
Nazis with dogs and with machine guns, they opened the doors from
the cattle trains, and they let out the Jews what they brought over.
And everybody—"*Schnell! Schnell! Schnell!*" and they start to beat
them. Was a very long train. I didn't see what was going on at the
end, but I hear some shots; I didn't know if they killed some of the
people.

Not far from where I was standing and looking out from the window from the barrack, I saw that all the Jews was emptying from the
cars. They went out already, and they was lining up to march to Majdanek concentration camp, about two miles. All the Nazis was standing in packs watching with the dogs. I saw a young man standing on
the edge from the opening of a cattle car. He maybe was eighteen
years old, so looked to me from far away. I remember like it was
today—half from his body, you could see, and half was still in the cattle car. You couldn't see him whole; his half head was in this open
place.

The Nazis always used to yell, so we could hear one yelling:
"Don't you want to go out from the car?" . . . in this type of way,

that's what we figure from his lips what he was talking to him. "Won't you go out from the car?"

The same moment the boy moved out a little further. He had a machine gun and he start to spray bullets where the Nazis was standing, and five or six was falling down dead . . . these rounds, these shots, they just drop down . . . it was a whole mess there . . . I start to hide myself, and we all go away from the window.

In five minutes there came a wagon with a big machine gun, and they start to shoot into the car deep . . . throwing in hand grenades . . . I remember the whole train was falling apart from the shooting, breaking up like crackers.

When everything was to an end, and they took us back to Lipowa Street, I hear later that the body from the boy what he was shooting with his machine gun was found in pieces, maybe a mile away from there. He was shot all apart all over . . . they shred up the train in pieces with him. We discussed between us, but was nothing new for us. We knew that every minute, every day, we will have something like this, so we was already used to that.

ML: But you were even used to the idea that someone single-handedly would undertake a wild rebellion like that?

JF: It was something what we admired that some had the courage. We couldn't do; we was locked up. Matter of fact, we did something on the Lipowa, not me, but the Jewish soldiers. In the beginning of 1943, Fisher, the commandant from the war prisoners, he escaped when he took a group to work, from an outside job for the *Wehrmacht* . . . he escaped with twenty or twenty-five Jewish war prisoners.[4] Later, after the war, I found out he is in Israel.

Nobody knew how he planned the escape. You couldn't know, because for the security, your plan had to be left secret . . . if it should be let out, the word might go around from one to another, and you will be caught. Since Fisher was the leader from the two thousand prisoners, he had contacts from the outside . . . when I said they escaped about twenty or twenty-five, it was only the closest what he can trust them. It was an organized group. They escaped to the woods, and they fight till the end of the war.

---

4. Fisher escaped on March 30, 1943, and tried to contact the Polish Home Army, but didn't succeed. For an account of acts of resistance and escapes by Jewish prisoners of war in Lipowa, see Krakowski (1984, 262–71).

Usually was some revenge by the Nazis for this, to show what would happen again if there should be an escape or just to find another reason to punish us. Till that time, they always took out a couple of guys and hanged them. But after the escape from Fisher, nobody knew that they escaped. You see, the twenty or the twenty-five men, they was not from the Lipowa. He went to them; they organized a long time before, and they let him know when they was ready, and he could go out without a watchman.

ML: But were there some people in Lipowa Street who thought that what that eighteen-year-old did wasn't admirable because there would be severe reprisals by the Nazis, that they would then liquidate everyone, even people who were working, who weren't going to Majdanek?

JF: At that time, we couldn't think about this, because every Jew was under the lock and under the gun, locked up in the small ghetto or in the concentration camp, so the Nazis could do anything without this or with this. Without this rebellion, they did the same thing. The killing, the gas chamber was working day and night before the young man came and killed a couple of Germans, so what's the difference?

22

Schama Grajer

1939–June 1942

I WANT TO TALK a little bit about Schama Grajer. He was a barber when he was young . . . a matter of fact, he cut my hair most of the time, but he was associating with the wrong crowd, and when he became older, about eighteen or nineteen years, he came a pimp, and he had a couple girls. From being a pimp, he married one from them. They had a whorehouse, and his wife was the madam.

When the Nazis occupied Lublin, they gave out ration cards for *Verpflegung*[1] for everybody, and we used to stay in the line for a loaf of bread for a whole night, so in the morning we should be first in the line when they open the store to get this loaf of bread . . . the Poles was also getting the *Verpflegung* cards there. If you was the twentieth or the twenty-fifth person, you come to the door, to the window where they gave out the bread, and they said, "No bread anymore."

Across the street from where I was born was a bakery, and one evening, people start to line up to be in line to get the bread and stay there a whole night. One *Polak,* what he was a superintendent in a Jewish house on the same street, he was standing and watching the line, and he saw a Polish woman standing in the line where she is almost the last from the line. He took out a Jewish woman, she was first, near the door from the bakery, and he changed the place with the Polish woman. He put her in the first of the line, and the Jewish woman, he put her to be the last one, and she couldn't say nothing because she was afraid if she would not go out from the first of the line, he'll beat her up.

Schama Grajer was standing and watching this, and because he

1. Food rations.

151

was from the underworld, he went over, and he took out the Polish woman, and he put her back in the line where she stood before and put back the Jewish woman in the first place. And there start to be an exchange of words with the Polish super.

A word to a word . . . Schama Grajer start to have an exchange with this guy . . . very, very hot, a very high exchange, and they start to fight, both of them.

Schama Grajer beat up the super, and a couple of minutes later, two Nazis, SS soldiers, they come over and saw something is going on near the store. Schama Grajer escaped, he run away from this . . . and the SS people, they found out what happened, that a Jew beat up a Polish guy. They start to look for him. Then later, shows out that the super was from German descent—they called him a *Volksdeutsch*—he had German parents; they was born in Germany, but he was born in Poland. When the SS heard a Jew beat up a *Volksdeutsch*—already he is considered a German—they start to look for Schama Grajer, and they couldn't find him.

Schama Grajer had a mother and two sisters. One sister had a candy store on the same street about two blocks from where the incident happened, and another sister and her husband had a dance studio.

The two Nazis found out from the Polish guy because he was a super in the same street, so he knew Schama Grajer; he knew his family. He told the two Nazis, "He has a family here," so they went and they picked up his mother with two sisters and two brother-in-laws, and they arrest them. They put out a note, a poster . . . they gave out a time, a couple of days . . . if he wouldn't show up by this time, they'll kill all his family.

Schama Grajer, looks like, he was a good son and a good brother, so he went to the Nazis, and he said that he is Schama Grajer, and they let free the family. The Jewish community, they figure the SS, the Nazis, will kill him—they wouldn't make a big thing with him. But after a certain time, the Jewish community forgot about this whole thing what happened, and we didn't hear no more about Schama Grajer. He's gone.

Three or four months later, all of a sudden, we saw Schama Grajer walking on the street. He is wearing a very beautiful new suit with high boots, and he is free. We couldn't understand what happened. The Nazis let him free after so an incident that he beat up a German? But Jews begin to talk between them that there's something not kosher. Must be something with the Schama Grajer.

And then later we found out that he became a spy for the Nazis, and looks like they persuade him if he'll tell all the secrets from the Jews—he'll tell what they want to know about Jews, whether somebody is rich, where they live and where they are—so if he'll do the work that they'll tell him to do, they'll let him free. Looks like he accepted, and they let him out.

Schama Grajer start to do his work, what he promised the Nazis what he'll do, and he start to mingle around between the Jewish ghetto. To the Jews, he showed some things that he can do . . . some women or girls was arrested for not wearing the armband, and he freed them. The Jewish people, when they saw he can do something to save their lives, they start to turn to him. They say he should do this and he should do that, and he became a hero between the Jewish community.

Much later than all this what I am talking, in November 1942, he came out. He called a conference from the Jewish community to the synagogue—there was there the *Maran schul* and *Marschal schul*.[2] In that time, there came a couple hundred people, and he had a speech for them, that every Jew, what they have gold, diamonds, jewelry, they all should bring the jewelry with the gold pieces, with the diamonds what they have, to the synagogue, and he'll bring this to the Germans, and he'll save the ghetto, because there are rumors the Germans would liquidate the ghetto.

The Jews when they are in trouble, they don't know what to believe, so they figure, their lives are in danger, what do they need the diamonds, what do they need the jewelry? They brought a lot of jewelry and a lot of gold pieces and all kind of expensive things. And he brought everything over to the Germans, and after five or six days, when the Germans felt that the Jews wouldn't bring any more, or they don't have any more to bring, they decide to liquidate the ghetto.

2. Kestenberg, who had been the head of the *Judenrat,* was killed when the large Lublin ghetto was liquidated in March 1942. Grajer then became the main liaison between the Nazis and the remaining Jewish community.

23

Schama Grajer's Wedding

March–November 1942

JF: I TOLD YOU ABOUT SCHAMA GRAJER. You remember what I told you about Schama Grajer?

ML: Well, we talked about him maybe two days ago . . .

JF: So you should remember.

ML: I remember all of it.

JF: What do you remember?

ML: What do you want me to tell you?

JF: The beginning and the end. What do you remember of the beginning and the end, so I know what I have to . . .

ML: I won't tell it, I'll just tell you certain things that I remember to give an idea of what you already told me. You told me he used to cut your hair, he was originally a barber . . .

JF: Yes!

ML: You told me that he got involved in the underworld, and he started prostituting some women, and he formed a whorehouse, and he married one of them who became the madam. Then you told me the story of the switching of the Jewish and Polish women in the bread line and the fight, his escape, his turning himself in, his disappearance for several months, and then appearing in the new suit and the new boots and the rumors in the community about what happened to him, then his becoming a spy and eventually head of the *Judenrat*. You finished the story by telling about the Germans commanding all the Jews to bring all of their gold and valuable and jewels.

JF: That's good, that's correct. So I have a new thing what I remind myself. Like you just said, he married the madam from the prostitutes, and he was living with her for a year by the time of the occupation.

He went over to a Jewish girl, eighteen or nineteen-years-old . . . a beauty. *Really* beautiful. He said, "I love you and I want to marry you." Just like that. It's an interesting story, no?

She knows already who he is because everybody knew him. He made himself, and when he went out from the prison, he was known. He was wearing a new jacket with a pair of high boots, very elegant. I used to see him when I came home from the labor camp. From the time when he went into prison and came out from prison, I never talk with him, but our eyes was meeting once, and we both was smiling, because he knew me, and I knew him when he was a barber and he cut my hair. For years we knew each other, for years. We was living on the same street. In that time, I was not married, I was single. He was older than I was, some years . . . three, four. I was already seventeen years old when he cut my hair. Most of the time I was in Warsaw; when I came back from Warsaw to the community where I was born, he was a labor-man working as a barber in a barber shop—was not his shop—so he cut my hair for a couple of years.

He was an elegant guy, to make this money from prostitutes . . . and nobody knew in the Jewish neighborhood what he did. This whorehouse was also on the Grodzka Street between the Jewish community and the Gentile community. Most Jews didn't go much there to know him. But I came back from Warsaw in that time, and there was a slang expression, a *ganser macher*, a big shot. I was so elegantly dressed; I was making a lot of money, I was very young . . . I made so much money that a married man didn't make so much, and I knew my trade very good, and they paid me for my work. I knew my way in my business.

After when the war broke out and he came out from prison and became a *ganser knacher*, a *ganser macher*, I was head from the tailor shop, so we met each other, our eyes met, and we smiled at each other. So the smile was, "Look! You are a big shot this way, and I am a big shot this way." But was a big difference.

So he went over to this girl, and he said, "I love you and I want to marry you." He was still with his wife, with the madam. This girl was very scared, and she start to run from the street to her house . . . was not so far; everybody was living in the same neighborhood. He found out where she lives, he went after her, and he went in to see her parents. Her father, he was in Germany for twenty years and then he was sent back from Germany when Hitler sent back thousands of Jews to Poland. A lot of Lubliner citizens took in somebody from the German Jews; some of them had families in Lublin, and some had no families.

The father from this girl, in Yiddish, he was *chazen*, a cantor in a synagogue in Germany, but he didn't have a job in Lublin at that time, but looks like he had money so it was not such a bad situation. He had two or three children, and I knew the father—and how do I know the whole story? My friend, Gerishon Klein, my assistant from the tailor shop, and the cantor, they was cousins. Klein told me the story of what Schama Grajer did.

Schama Grajer talked to the father. "I went over to your daughter . . . I'm a Jewish guy; I wouldn't harm your girl. She start to run away; she was very afraid of me. Tell her that she shouldn't be afraid of me; I wouldn't hurt her. I help *Yiden;* I help Jewish people—not, God forbid, to hurt them." He was playing like an angel Jewish man.

A year later, nobody knew . . . Schama Grajer told this girl's father that he shouldn't spread stories about him through the neighborhood because he is not a man who tries to hurt somebody.

"My Jewish mother lives here, my whole family lives here, I am here to help people. Don't spread false rumors about me."

The father said, "I'm sure you are gentleman. I wouldn't say anything."

Before they liquidate the big ghetto a year later in March 1942, Schama Grajer went back to the girl's family, and he said to the family, "I want you to give me the blessing to be your son-in-law. I want to marry your daughter." I don't know the right expression in English, but in Yiddish sounds different; sometimes you can't translate exactly. Was a tremendous comedy! A tragic comedy!

"I want to marry your daughter, and I want you to give us the blessing!"

The father start to beg and cry and to talk with him.

Schama Grajer said, "This will nothing help you. If you want to survive, if you want to survive the war, and if you want to be alive with your other two or three kids and your friends and your family and everybody, you need me like I need you. I love your daughter; I'll respect her, and I'll treat her nice. You'll have a nice son-in-law."

The father said, "No."

He told him, "If you say no, then I'll have another way to have your daughter for a wife."

The father said, "No. You can kill me; you can do whatever you want, but she is the lens from my eye." Like I said, there are some Jewish words what you can't translate . . . the apple of my eye.

"She is my life. If you take away my oldest daughter, you take away my life, everything, all the life from my family."

The father hid his daughter, and she was not seen anymore.

At the same time, Schama Grajer went over to his wife, to the madam, and he told her this story, that she should leave him, or he is leaving her. He already made the preparations, even when the father said no, to marry this girl . . . he figured he'll find a way. He told his wife that he's marrying a decent girl, a decent Jewish girl, not a whore to have for a wife. The madam start to cry. "*Schamaladen!* My sweetheart! What are you saying? So many years!"

"This will nothing help you. I have another wife, and if you'll talk too much, you'll be arrested." I'm sure she knew what he is doing, what kind of work he is doing. Some other Jews maybe had an idea, but they couldn't say—but she knew.

A couple of weeks later, they liquidate this big ghetto. The madam, his real wife, went with the whole crowd away to Majdanek concentration camp, to be liquidated. The whole family from the girl what he wants to marry her, the whole family was saved to go to the small ghetto to Majdan-Tatarsky.

He came in to the new father-in-law, who received the nicest house in the Majdan-Tatarsky, from a big farmer. The roof of his house was not from straw, was from shingles. Schama Grajer asked him, "How do you like your new home? I told you, you have a good son-in-law."

They was still in pains, the family . . . a big house, a small house, a nice house, not a nice house. . . .

What the conversation was between them I don't know, but in a week, the Chief from the Gestapo, Worthoff, he came to the father from this girl, and he said, "Your daughter is to become Schama Grajer's wife. The wedding will be in three days. The best man will be the assistant from the Chief from the Gestapo; his name is Sturm. The Gestapo will pay for the wedding."

ML: A Jewish wedding?

JF: Didn't say a Jewish wedding or a Gentile wedding.

"The wedding will be an outside wedding. The whole ghetto, the neighborhood, the whole city, the whole Majdan-Tatarsky is invited to the wedding."

And so it was. There was an orchestra, and it was a Jewish wedding. There was wine and champagne . . . food . . . dancing . . . a Jewish rabbi . . . the Nazis said he is a rabbi, I can't remember if I knew him or not . . . he gave them *chuppa gedishen*[1], the ceremony he prepared, with the rings . . . and she became his wife. If you would have made a movie from this what I am telling you, this would be a first-class picture. I can't describe how this really looked, the wedding. Fifty or sixty Nazis, high-rank officers, was drinking and saluting this couple to wish them luck. The whiskey, the vodka, the wines, the champagne, was thousands of bottles they brought into the ghetto. The wedding took from ten o'clock in the morning till ten o'clock in the evening, the whole day. The people had an order not to be in their houses; they had an order to participate in the wedding. There was no more *Judenrat,* Schama Grajer was the *Judenrat,* he was the leader, and he invited the ghetto, with the kids! The kids had a special place not to interfere with the dancing. From the Jewish families, they watched the children, there was baby-sitters . . . there was not in that time babies, there was orphans. The wedding was organized exactly, the order was exactly in the military way what the Germans want this to look. They made a stage, thirty, forty feet high with stairs, so the whole city should not miss anything, with a *chuppa,* with everything, all Jewish customs.

After a couple days it was quiet. Nobody was talking when they went home, not even the same day, because they was afraid to talk one to another.

"Now we have the spy in the ghetto! Before we didn't see him! Now we have him and his wife, his family: we didn't know if we can trust them. Before it was a nice, Jewish, intelligent family, now you don't know. The best man was Sturm, and the leader was the Gestapo chief Worthoff."

Schama Grajer and his wife had a house, the nicest bungalow in the ghetto. He was riding around the ghetto on a German motorcycle, a big motorcycle, with a pair of boots and a leather jacket with glasses. After a couple of months, we see his wife wearing some motorcycle trousers, leather trousers, with a pair of boots with a black leather uniform, a necklace, with a leather hat . . . she was sitting on the back, holding on to him. We saw a beautiful couple . . . he was a

---

1. The *chuppa* is the marriage canopy in a Jewish wedding, and *gedishen* is Yiddish for rings; this is the part of the wedding ceremony when the rabbi instructs the groom to take out the ring and place it on the bride's finger.

handsome guy, too, and she was a beauty, and in this uniform, she looks like a million dollars.

In five or six months, we saw her belly, she was pregnant. Pregnant with a big belly on the bike. Nice story, eh?

We never saw anymore the Nazis what they went to the wedding. The Nazis promised Schama Grajer that when everything will be finished, he'll have a house. They took him out and showed him a beautiful house with all conveniences, outside the ghetto, where a Polish family used to live.

"The house is empty. You can choose any furniture you like; we'll decorate your house to your specification, to your taste."

When they will liquidate the Majdan-Tatarsky ghetto, they tell him he will be able go out with his wife and to live free outside, free from the ghetto, outside in his house what they showed him.

The Nazis told to them both, he with his wife, that no one would be allowed to live in Majdan-Tatarsky, in the small ghetto. All the Jews was taken to Majdanek concentration camp.[2] It was three miles away, and everybody knew it was a concentration camp, but we didn't know what was in there, what they're doing there. It was so discreet, the whole work there was to keep a secret that nobody should know. We knew that it was a concentration camp, but how many they are killing, if they are killing, or if this was worse working conditions than a labor camp or than a ghetto, we didn't know exactly. In the beginning, you didn't know that there are gas chambers. People came to tell us, but we didn't want to believe . . . it's impossible that this should be true. Unfortunately, it was true.

They tell Schama Grajer he can go out from the ghetto, and he and his wife start to walk, and they tell him, "Don't walk, but run! Run! *Schnell! Schnell* to your apartment!"

They both start to run, and running they fall down with the bullets in their heads. They both was lying on the ground dead, she with a big belly.

2. See Chapter 24, "The Liquidation of Majdan-Tatarsky."

24

—

The Liquidation of Majdan-Tatarsky

November 1943

ON THE LIPOWA was still thousands of Jews, and all the workers was sleeping in the camp and didn't know what is going on in the small ghetto. The Nazis was liquidating people what they had jobs by Germans, cleaning up outside the camp, other craftspeople not in the camp, all the families from the workers on the Lipowa, and all the Jews what was left from Lublin.

About two o'clock in the morning, they set up machine guns with other *waffen,* and they surrounded the whole ghetto. I heard noise about half-past two in the morning. I looked out through the window, I couldn't see anything, but at five o'clock in the morning, the megaphones start to yell that everybody should go out from the houses, and I figure I know already how they are working in this kind of time, so I told my wife to dress the little boy Nunyek and to get ready to go down to the basement, to the hiding place, what we prepared from before. She'll be there with this little boy, and I figure if something should happen to me and the other leaders from the shops, they'll take me out from the crowd with the other leaders, and they'll take us back to the labor camp. From there maybe I can do something to save her life and the life from this little boy. And that's how this was . . . about five o'clock in the morning, we went out. I dressed myself, and I prepared everything. I covered the entrance to the hiding place from the floor with a piece of carpet and a table on the top, and also outside, the door was planted with grass that they shouldn't see that there is an opening.

I went out with the whole crowd, with all the Jews, through the gates of a big lot, and they was already waiting, thirty or forty Nazis from the Gestapo, from the SS, from the SA, all kind of colors in the

160

uniforms . . . yellow, green . . . they was waiting for us already. This took about two-and-a-half hours before they have everybody out from the ghetto.

One of the heads from the Gestapo was a man with the name Sturm, and the Sturm called out that they are making a selection from the small ghetto from everybody who is not working, and whoever doesn't have working cards can't get rationing. Too much food the ghetto needs—the Germans don't have so much food for Jews. So the Sturm, he was standing on a *bimah*,[1] and he called out, "Anybody here Sturm, with his name Sturm?"

A Jew, he was thinking that he will say he has the same name, maybe he'll give him a job, something to do, and he'll be saved! And he came over, he raised his hand, one from about 1,900 people on this lot.

Sturm said, "Come over here . . ."

He came over there, and he said, "Your name is Sturm?" and the Jew said, "*Jawohl!*"

He took out his pistol, and he said, "Ohhhh, two Sturms, one a *Jude* and one a German officer, this cannot be."

And he gave him right away, here, like this was now, right now I see this with my eyes, I was standing not far away from him . . . he gave him the bullet in the back of the neck.

We heard sounds from the megaphones that they announce in the ghetto, everybody left over there, if they are hidden, or they don't want to come out, the ghetto will be set on fire, and everybody will perish. About nine o'clock, they took all the people, women with children, and men, to the concentration camp Majdanek.

This was the first time what I went to Majdanek, and I couldn't observe too much . . . they managed so you couldn't see anything. They took us in to a big gate and kept us in a place . . . the crematorium was maybe a half a mile away, and everything was electrically wired. There was a couple of fields, one separate from another. If you want to escape, you have to escape through three, four rows of electrical wiring.

We was not too long at Majdanek, a couple of hours. Like I said, I had learned about Majdanek while on the Lipowa because there was some Polish war prisoners from Majdanek, and when they were on the

---

1. A platform. A *bimah* is also used to denote the platform at the head of a synagogue, where rabbis and cantors stand, and where the *torah* is read.

Lipowa, the Jewish prisoners was talking with them. I heard the Red Cross came to look at the concentration camps, but they didn't find Jews there, only other nationalities' prisoners. They killed them too, some of them; they hang them, they shoot them, the same, but not in the quantity what they did to the Jews. But when the Red Cross came to inspect how the prisoners was living, in the front with the barracks was flowers, with blankets, with pillows, the kitchen was with food with beautiful soups what they taste, so everything was done to fool the world. They had a plan how to do it.

When we came there, men from the SS and from the Gestapo was waiting, and they start to segregate us, to take away the women with the children and to put the men on a different side . . . I think I would never forget the scenes what I lived through this moment . . . unforgettable scenes . . . to take away the women with the children from the men—and the crying . . . and the women start to beat themselves on their heads. With one hand they kept a child and with the other hand they beat themselves. A lot of them fall down on the ground, and the Nazis was surrounding them with dogs, and the dogs, they start to want to bite them. The Nazis kept them back with the chains, and they stood up from their hind legs; the gnashing from the teeth was like they are hungry for them, and the Nazis kept them back just enough so they are almost on top of them . . . scenes unforgettable. And this didn't take too long, takes maybe about fifteen, twenty minutes, and they took away all the women and children from us to the right side. We didn't know where they are marching, but we had an idea that they are taking them to kill them, and next we'll go.

I saw Mohwinkel, the commandant from the labor camp. He start to look around the crowd, was about a thousand or twelve-hundred men, and he picked out all the leaders from the shops, and he put us on the side. He took me out from the line; he took out Blank, the leader from the shoemaker shop. They took us away from the crowd, about ten or fifteen feet. We was not surprised . . . we knew, we had the feeling that they'll take us out because there was unfinished business in the shops, unfinished uniforms, unfinished boots. Was hundreds of uniforms in the middle of the work, so we know they wouldn't sacrifice the workmanship.

A truck came, and they took about sixteen or seventeen from us away to the Lipowa, to the labor camp. The other men, hundreds, they took them near the crematorium—who knows? I didn't see anymore; I don't know where they took them. I know this was the last place to be alive.

They brought us back to the labor camp. The work went on normal like nothing happened. The workers didn't know what happened; they only knew that the leaders from all the shops were not there, but they figure something must have happened. But when we came in, my little boy was waiting, and he said, "Daddy, what happened? Daddy, you are so late, what happened?"

I couldn't tell him what happened; I don't know what to tell him where Mommy is, and where Nunyek is, that they are hiding. "Don't worry; I cannot tell you where they are, but right now they are safe." He was six years old, but his mind was already working like a fifteen or sixteen-year-old boy, because the time taught him to be mature, to understand what is going on.

In the evening we had to go for an *appel,* for the counting if somebody escaped. If somebody was missing, it happened sometimes somebody escaped, they took out from the line, from all kind of shops, one or two or sometimes three people, and they hang them. We had to stay in formation, and they gave the order that we should look to the side where they are hanging the people. After the hanging, we were standing about a half hour or three-quarters of an hour, and we have to go in the shops and do our work. Every couple of days was the same thing.

ML: Did your older son have questions about this? Did he ever see anyone who was punished or was killed there?

JF: Sure he saw. When they hang somebody they took everybody out from the barracks, and we stood in the line, and they gave a command that everybody should look to the side where the hanging comes, and he had to turn his head like me, like the other ones.

ML: Did he talk to you about that?

JF: He talked to me like . . . he was crying . . . was nothing, just asked me "Why?" So I explain him why . . . he knew why they hung the prisoner.

ML: Did he have any reaction when you told him why a prisoner was hung?

JF: The first time when they hung somebody—most of the time the hanging came in the morning by the *appel* when they count . . . you went to take the breakfast: the coffee, chicory, and a piece of bread. The first time after the hanging he threw up, I remember, he threw up what he ate, this piece of bread. After, we went in the shop, we had our pots on our knees, and that's how we eat. He act the same way like a grown-up; there was no difference.

———

Now I had to think what can I do to save this life from my wife and this little boy hiding in the ghetto. When my wife went down to the hiding place, I gave her a secret sign. "If somebody will come to take you out, he'll tell you these words what we made up between us, then you'll know that you can go out. If not, don't go out." Thinking about what to do, I had an idea. The liquidation from the small ghetto—the Gestapo was the power responsible for this. In the rear from the labor camp was an office from the Gestapo, on the Sklodowsky Street. And I figure . . . I knew there an *Obersturmbann-führer,* in the rank a colonel, what he was in charge from the Gestapo, and I used to make for him uniforms and things for his wife and for his children. If I can go to him, I'll tell him this story that I know they'll start to burn up the houses from the ghetto, so they'll be dead anyway. Maybe to save them for a couple of days or a couple of months, maybe he'll do for me this thing.

While I was working on the Lipowa with my older boy, Blank also had a little boy the same age hidden on the Lipowa Street. His wife with a little girl lived in the small ghetto at Majdan-Tatarsky, like my wife and younger boy. When we used to go home to the small ghetto before they liquidate, both of the older boys, my boy and Blank's boy, was in the labor camp sleeping by themselves, and we went home to our wives with the other little kids.

The day after they brought us back from Majdanek, in the morning we had to go out to be counted, and also my older boy and Blank's boy used to be on the line every day to be counted. All the time, when it happened there was a killing or some action, to be involved in death, I had something in my mind . . . I really can't understand even today . . . always came to my mind to do something. So came to my mind to take my older boy to the little hospital that he should stay there for the time from the counting. When the Professor David came over to my line what I was standing to be counted, he said, "Where is Monyek?"

"That's what I want to tell you, Professor. Monyek is in the *Lazarett,* and he didn't feel so good." So long that you gave him the name, you tell him where he is, was acceptable for the rules—so long as he in on the list that he is in camp. David made the counting, and Mohwinkel was standing about forty feet away from the line. David gave him the list, and Mohwinkel came over near the line. David gave a command to stand out at attention, and Mohwinkel took out Blank's little boy and put him out from the line from the right side. Blank went over to Mohwinkel and said, "*Herr Obersturmbannführer,* why are you taking out my little boy? He didn't do nothing wrong; he was standing still in the line."

"I have an order from Globocnik that no small children can be in this camp."

Blank said, "*Herr Obersturmbannführer,* I would like to go together with my little boy. He can't be by himself, he's just six years old."

"Fine, if you want to go with him, go."

He went over to the right side. He was standing separate from all of us, and they took him away; I never saw him again. That was the end from this day, and my son survived this selection.

ML: What did Monyek do during the day while you were working, while at the camp?

JF: I was all day busy, what do you mean? What? In the shop?

ML: What did *Monyek* do?

JF: What he was doing! He was in shop helping to move things around . . . he always made himself busy, because if a Nazi came in— the Nazi Langfeld what he was the supervisor in shop, he liked him very much, he was a very, very good kid. He was very busy; he took away the bundles from the tailors. He brought over to them some threads, or what they need, or needles . . . a guy broke the needle to the machine; he went over to the desk to say this man needs a needle to his machine. He was running around a whole day busy; he was more busy than somebody else, and even Mohwinkel knew this because the watchman said, "This little kid, he is very, very busy; he is a very good helper, and he has a very good reputation." Even Mohwinkel liked him. He didn't talk to him, but I could see when he passed by he saw him. And I was glad, thank God, that I could have him with me, and he is safe, safer than in the ghetto.

But not, like I said, for a very long time . . . was very short.

ML: What happened to Blank's family once the ghetto was set on fire?

JF: He had a wife; he had also the two children. Before he was taken out from the line with his boy by Mohwinkel, this is what he told me before he went away. A couple of hours before they put guards around the ghetto with machine guns with the Nazis all around, a couple of hours before the liquidation, his wife went out from the hiding place with this little girl. She went into this place what the people from outside used to shit there.

ML: Was it an open place or was it an outhouse?

JF: It was half-closed and half-open. On top was a desk with holes what you can sit and move your bowels, and on the outside was a wall to cover, not to see that you are shitting there. Was half-open, half-closed. You couldn't see the people from outside. She hid herself with this little girl. That's what he told me. And this little girl start to cry . . . she choked this little girl—to death. She left this little girl there; this girl was like an infant, eight months or nine months. His wife came out from the lavatory . . . the shithouse was almost on the end from the ghetto. How she came out I don't know . . . when nobody was there, looks like the gates was open or something. She came out from there when she didn't have the baby anymore, by herself, and she survived. She left for Israel; she survived the war.

ML: When did Blank tell you the story about his wife hiding in the shithouse and choking her daughter?

JF: He heard from the Jewish war prisoners, from the next day they came to clean up the mess there. That's what he told me before they took him away.

ML: Did Blank . . . comment on what his wife had done?

JF: No, no, no. Never. Never talked about this. I was only listening to what he is telling me—that's it. I couldn't say anything, comment if it's right or wrong. That's the way what she did. There was some facts like this, but not too many.

ML: From what I've read, it was not an irregular occurrence that people would have to take the life of someone . . .

JF: Wellohhhh, I'm telling you exactly like this was, exactly what this was . . . not what this was, what I saw. There are many things what I didn't see, who knows, but I am talking what I saw or what I heard directly from this person or from the other person. Sure was facts like this, but not too many. Most of the Jews, they didn't have time. They rushed them so quick to death, they didn't have time to hurt one another. "*Schnell! Schnell! Schnell!*" With dogs, with lashes, that's how this was.

We knew, we heard, when the ghetto start to burn . . . it was about half a mile the length, the width a quarter of a mile . . . they put all around with gasoline, and they set fire so the whole ghetto should burn. Some of Jews made hiding places like I did for my wife and my little boy . . . some of them start to run out because out of the fire. There was more dead Jews from the ghetto, dead lying on the ground. They escaped from the fire, and then they got the bullets from the Gestapo.

The war prisoners cleaned the houses, to give back the territory, the properties, where the Polish farmers used to live. The Jews' possessions . . . the Nazis gave the war prisoners orders that they should make bundles with fires, and they burned everything, even the furniture. They made clean from all what was left over from the Jews, what they couldn't take with them to Majdanek.

The ghetto was burning for two or three days. We didn't know details, but with the bodies we find out, when the Jewish war prisoners came back from a day's work to the camp, they told us how the ghetto looks. You just see fires. In the middle of the ghetto, in the middle of the fire, there was a lot of Jewish people, women, children. They are lying in the middle; also the bodies from Schama Grajer and his wife. The war prisoners didn't even touch them.

The war prisoners saw also what happened with other Jews. There was a tailor also, a very good friend of mine, a young gentleman in the twenties, with a wife with two small kids. He was working under the Gestapo. His name was Majer in Yiddish, in Polish Mark. He was working three years for the Gestapo, and before the day they liquidate—they already took out the people to go to Majdanek—the Gestapo promised him that they'll save him with the family. Before they killed Schama Grajer, the Nazis went into the house from Majer, the tailor, and they made him dig his own grave. He was working for a day or two days; this was a big grave. They told him to go into the grave with the two kids, with the family, and they killed them. The four of them. The war prisoners used to cover the graves, to make straight with the earth, and they left him there. So there was more death to clean up than Schama Grajer and his wife.

ML: When you found out about your friend and his family being killed, how did that affect you?

JF: It affect me like the effect when they took away every person from my family. You couldn't react . . . to sit and to cry and to mourn, that's all you could do. You couldn't do anything. Your mind—what I remember—your mind didn't work at all, to do something, because it was nothing to do. It was nothing. Your mind's work, if you want to think something, there was nothing.

ML: Do you think that happened in stages? Do you think, for example, at a later time your mind was even more closed off from doing something? Were there different stages of this "nothing"?

JF: I know what you're asking me, but the mind didn't work in stages. The mind was working with one stage, that we will all be dead. That's what I remember my mind was working: we all will be dead, and with whom I was talking, I heard the same thing: "Jack, it's nothing to worry about the others, what your wife or my wife was killed, because the next day this will be our lives—or the next week or the next month, if we'll survive a month. There's nothing we can do." That's how the mind was working for most of us.

25

Dora and Nunyek

November 1942–October 1943

I WAS ONLY THINKING to save my wife with the little boy in the hiding place, and there is only one thing what there is left for me to do. If I would be able to go out from the labor camp, to the office where the Major from the Gestapo is there . . . for years I am thinking to remind myself of his name, and I forgot. His picture lies all the time on my eyes; I can see him even. Every couple weeks I saw him, I talk with him, and every couple of months I made clothes for him or his wife or children. The only the one thing I was figuring I could do was maybe, *maybe*, he can help me. There is no reason now to keep even a secret that they will burn the ghetto the next day;[1] they will be dead anyway. So maybe I can try, maybe I'll succeed with something if I'll try.

By the other side from the labor camp was standing a watchman, a Ukraine, with a machine gun watching by the door, a small door what you could open and go out from the camp to the free world, to the offices. He understood a little bit of German, and I show him that I want to talk to him. At that time, I was still wearing a watch. I show with my hands on the watch that I want to give him the watch. I was a couple hundred feet from him, on the ground, and he was higher. When he saw the watch he came down, and I said to him in German, "I want to talk to you."

He said, "Come nearer."

I said, "I am the *Schneidermeister*, I am the head tailor from the tailor shop, and I want to talk with you. I'll give you the watch. Let me through. I want to go to the Major"—at that time I said the name.

---

1. Chronologically, the trip to the Major's office takes place before the burning of the Majdan-Tatarsky ghetto, which was described in Chapter 24.

"I'll be there for five minutes." I had always with me the tape measure. "I have to take a measurement."

I don't know if I bribed him and I gave him the watch, if he took the watch and let me out, or he took my word that I have to take a measurement . . . he let me out.

I came into the Gestapo office. I was without an armband, and all the time I was dressed in my civil clothes with a jacket, like I was always dressed decent. I tell them I want to see the Major, and they announced me . . . I was waiting there. Another guy brought me up to the second floor, they let me into the Major, and he told me to sit down . . . he treated me like a human being, all the time.

I said to him, "I came not about business, but I have something to say." I know I am taking the risk to get killed, but I have no way. I have a secret what I have to tell him, and I made up my mind before. I was figuring a whole night what to say and what to do, and I decide to say the way like this is, and what will be will be. I told him the whole story, that I heard they will go to burn the ghetto, and I made a hiding place for my wife and my little boy, and I tell him one boy I have with me in the labor camp here. When I tell him the story, he said, "I have one woman working for me, and if I can get your wife out, she'll be with this woman."

I told him my wife wouldn't come out till they'll say this word, what I told her the sign, and this is the sign I told him to say. Before I left her in the hiding place, I told her, "I'm taking a chance. Maybe I'll try to do something, maybe I'll come here by myself or somebody else will tell you the words what I'll tell him, and then you'll come out. But not before—if you come out before, you'll be dead this way or another way. This is only the way what I can try to save you." I told the Major the secret words—the names from my boy and from my wife—and he went to the ghetto and found the place.

He called out through the door made in the floor: "I know you are there with your little boy. Nunyek is his name; the Jewish name is *Noah*. Your name is Dora; your Jewish name is *D'vorah*. You have a husband; he is the leader from the tailor shop. He has a son there, your son, his Jewish name is *Moshe,* the Polish name is Monyek. You call him Moyetchku. Come out! I came here from your husband's side, what he told me the whole story. You come out, and I'll take you—I have special facilities where one Jewish woman and a man, a barber, are working there. You come out, and you'll be with them."

They came out. Was waiting there a truck, and they took her to his house where there was the Jewish servants . . . and the one woman was Adja, the cousin of my wife who I visited at the *Plaga Lashkewicz,* the airport camp.[2] She was saved from this camp a year ago . . . somebody who knew the Major took her out to be his cleaning woman. So Dora and she was together at the Major's house. This was not really in his house; he had there like a little camp. Every big Nazi made something like a labor camp . . . if he needs a couple of Jews, so he took from here, from there, so he had Adja Fried, he had a barber, and he had my wife. They had two rooms, separate in the backyard. The barber had one room, and the Adja and my wife had one room.

ML: I was wondering if the Gestapo or the SS came through the ghetto after they had taken everyone out, and they were searching for people who were hiding. Wasn't it possible they could have had a list of every person, and they could have gone into the houses and yelled out their names? They could have yelled out, "Dora Frank! Nunyek Frank!" Since the code words were these names, how did she know if the person saying them was trustworthy?

JF: They didn't have no list. Was no list in the small ghetto. Not in the small ghetto, not in the big ghetto. They just put up megaphones, and they called out: "Everybody should go out. The gates are open." They gave a time, and if somebody will hide in the ghetto at that time, they'll perish there. They'll burn up; they'll put fire to the whole ghetto, all the houses. I don't know how this sounds in English what I say, but in German they announced in the megaphone that all the ghetto will be on fire, burned up. But there was no list that they should call out somebody. And another thing, why should they bother? They didn't bother with us to waste time to call out names! Why should they? They didn't need us! They need us dead! So what's the difference if they kill them in Majdanek, or they'll burn the houses in the ghetto?

ML: So you considered the names to be a safe code.

JF: Oh, sure. And this was the code what I tell her: I told her that when I come, I'll tell you that Monyek is with me, and you should come out with Nunyek. If I wouldn't be able to come, this is the code that they'll give you, and they'll have to know where Monyek is. Even

2. The reader may recall Mr. Frank's visit to this camp, when he saw the young man on the transport from Warsaw spray the Nazis with bullets. See pp. 147–49.

if they have a list like you said, they wouldn't know that Monyek is in the labor camp.[3] This would only be a half-a-code, so she wouldn't come out anyway. There was no list. Why should they bother with us to liquidate this way or another way? They have a quick way to get rid of the Jews.

She came out, and he took her to his place there, this little camp, and she met there her cousin. Everything was fine, and I knew when the Gestapo guy, the *Obersturmbannführer*, if he said that he'll do it, that he did it. I didn't have a way to find out or not, but I figure that he'll do it. I didn't have nothing to lose. I couldn't go in there to take her out, even if she'll die with the slaughter.

I didn't know this, but the same day, the *Obersturmbannführer* had to leave Lublin. I don't know if they ordered him to come to Berlin, or he had plans to go to Berlin . . . he never told me this, and I didn't know. Another Gestapo guy took over to manage his house. In the morning, the system went on the same way—if this is a labor camp from three people, or from three thousand—they had to go out in the morning to count them. This was the system, and the substitute from the *Obersturmbannführer* did the same thing. He called them out at six o'clock in the morning, or half-past six, and my wife came out with this little boy. And the bandit, the *Obersturmbannführer* what he left, he didn't tell the other Gestapo man that there was a little child there with my wife. He knew a woman has to come there, but he didn't know about the little boy.

The substitute asked my wife, "What is this little boy doing here? Who is this?"

"This is my little boy, and the *Obersturmbannführer* brought us here."

"I have no orders to keep a Jewish child here. You have to give this little boy to me, and I'll put him in a children's camp."

My wife already knew what the children's camp was . . . the children's camp means that they're put to death.

"I can't give you my boy. I'll go with my little boy to the camp where you want to send him."

He took her in a little open truck to Majdanek. On the way was

3. Lipowa camp officials would have known that Monyek was in the camp, because he was being counted on the roster every day. However, it is unlikely that if a party of Nazis searched the Majdan-Tatarsky ghetto, they would call out names of persons they knew were in the camp.

maybe about four or five miles, so looks like we always knew what we have to have with us . . . I don't know how . . . she had a piece of paper with a pencil, and she wrote sitting on the truck, she wrote a few words in Polish:

Please, whoever will find this note, please give this to Jacob Frank. He is on the Lipowa 7 in the labor camp. His wife is being taken to Majdanek.

A Polish man found this piece of paper.

ML: She folded it up and threw it off the truck?

JF: How she did this, I don't know. I'm sure that's what she did . . . I wasn't there, I don't know. The Polish guy took this piece of paper, and he delivered. Every morning the Jewish war prisoners went to work in the Majdanek concentration camp, fifty or forty or sixty, a big group, and then they came back in the evening to Lipowa from Majdanek. So the Polish guy was waiting near the Lipowa labor camp. A lot of Polish people used to go there . . . some Polish people enjoyed to go there to look, how the Jewish prisoners are suffering, and some Polish people, maybe they feel sorry for us, but not too many. This guy looks like he was a human being, more human than other ones; he managed to stick this piece of paper to a Jewish war prisoner what he was in the line to go in the camp. He came into the shop, and he gave me the note, so then I found out she was in Majdanek.

I went in to Professor David, and I tell him the story that maybe he could help somehow in this situation. He told me, "If you want me to talk with Mohwinkel, if I'll see him, we cannot tell him the story what you are telling me. I cannot tell him that somebody took out your wife from the ghetto and took her to his place, and they took her from his place to Majdanek. Let's not mention this what happened between them. I'll say that your wife with your little boy is in Majdanek, and if he can do something to save them."

I said, "I agree that is the right idea."

In the same time, a couple of hours later, we had a counting, an *appel,* when the groups from the Jewish war prisoners came back from Majdanek to Lipowa. They count everybody . . . even the civil workers from the shops, to count if anybody is absent, if the list is in order. Every group had a leader, from the war prisoners and from the civil prisoners. The head from the group had a list, he counts, and they all came and gave all the lists from the all groups to the Professor David. The Professor David checks that everything is correct, that nobody is missing or escaped, he signed, he gave the list to Mohwinkel, and Mohwinkel took the list to the office. After when David gave him the list, Mohwinkel walked nearby me, near my line. When Mohwinkel passed by I stepped out from the line. I tell him the story that my wife with my little boy, they took them to Majdanek, and they are there . . . they took only me out with the other leaders. They brought me here, but she is there. I fall to his knees; I fall on my knees and kiss his boots, and I beg him in a crying voice:

"*Herr Obersturmbannführer,* please help me, maybe you can save the life from my wife and my child! I worked, I carried out all the orders what you gave me before, and I will carry out further, but please, please, let me not lose my wife with my little boy!"

He kicked me in my face, and he knocked out from my mouth three teeth. He said to me in German, "Get up you *Drecksack!* Get back in the line—because if not, if you don't go back right away, you'll get shot in your head! You'll be killed, so you'll not have to ask for somebody else."

I stood up, the blood was running from my face, and I went back to the line.

ML: Do you think if you had asked him that in private, he would have treated you differently? Did it have something to do with being in front of all the other prisoners?

JF: I wouldn't ask him in private things like that. I never went to him in private except when I came up to his house to pick up a uniform to clean blood off it or to press his clothes. This was my private connection with him. I could never ask him in private something like this.

ML: I'm considering that since it's a full camp roll call, that must have sent a powerful message of discipline if he kicked the head tailor in the face—one of the most respected people.

JF: This was not the case. I was not respected. We didn't feel that we are respected. From time to time, we feel that they need us a little bit more, because the Nazis couldn't speak to ten or twenty or fifty people to give the orders; they needed one to do this. This could happen to anybody, was the same what happened to me. We shop leaders didn't consider ourselves that the Germans think we are better. To the other prisoners, maybe we had more respect, but between us, we didn't think so.

ML: But I was asking if you thought Mohwinkel was doing that especially to you because you were the shop head, or he would have kicked anyone in the face like that?

JF: He would have kicked anyone. Many times, I was the lucky one that I was never beaten up, but all the leaders, they was beaten up many times in the presence of other prisoners. This didn't mean nothing for him.

ML: You did tell me in another discussion that it was humiliating and degrading for a shop leader to be beaten up.

JF: Oh, sure, sure. That was the policy from them. "Don't think that because he is the head that he is better than you." If he is doing something wrong, he'll get the same treatment as the other ones. Mohwinkel only kept them, like I said, because he needs something: he needs one to talk to the men. But the moment when he didn't need, when he wants to punish him, he didn't think about if he'll be degraded. It didn't mean anything.

ML: So this one man, the Jewish leader, whether it was the elder from the prisoners or the shop head, it was just the man to give the orders to. The rest of the time, he was scum, he could be beaten like anyone else.

JF: That's right. And I felt this. In my inside, I never felt that I am better than the other ones. On the contrary, I can be many times more punished than the other ones, because I saw Mohwinkel more times. The other ones didn't have business with him. I had the business with him—to take the orders, or to listen what he had to say to me, and I was more on fire than the other ones. And I never felt that I am better than the other ones—on the contrary.

———————

I stood up, and I went back to my line. After two hours, the Professor David came into my shop, to the tailor shop, and he called me to his office . . . was not far away; the office was maybe thirty feet. He told me that he was in the office by Mohwinkel, and Mohwinkel told him, "Tell the *Jude* Frank that I'll try to see what I can do for his wife." He didn't mention my younger boy. I was a little bit relieved, but I ask David, "You told me about my wife, what about this little boy, my little boy Nunyek?"

"I am repeating what he told me. I don't know."

I never talked to Mohwinkel again about this, but most of the time, I talked everyday with the Professor David; maybe he knows something. With this I was a little bit relieved, and I figure maybe, maybe Mohwinkel will do something. I know that most of the time, 99 percent, they was lying, maybe 100 percent. They always lied to tell you stories so you should be confused, to carry out the work what you have to do, but I didn't have no other choice.

A couple days later Professor David told me that Mohwinkel already called up Majdanek. Mohwinkel talked with the commandant from Majdanek and asked him to do him the favor. David tells me that Mohwinkel said the commandant from Majdanek will take Dora out from the barrack what from there they are going to their death, and that he'll tell the elders from the other barracks what they was living and working there that she should be transferred to another barrack. Dora is saved with her life, because instead of taking her to the crematorium, the Gestapo commandant ordered that she should go to be a helper to clean the barrack—was women Nazis also in Majdanek what they took care of the barrack where the Jewish women are located. She was safe in the meanwhile—for how long, I didn't know in that time.

When I found out she is there, I try to find a way to go out and to see her in Majdanek. Before, I could go out to take measurements without the armband, but in this time, nobody in civilian clothes could go out.[4] When the Nazis came for measurements, they were always inside the office, in the big building connected with the camp, so I couldn't go out. But I am sure she is already in a barrack, because I had communication through the Jewish war prisoners. They was working near the crematorium in Majdanek, sorting the clothing what the Jews undressed themselves before they put them to the ovens or before they shot them to go to the ditch. They put aside the shoes and the dresses, maybe to find hidden some gold or diamonds or money.[5]

I went over to the commandant from the Jewish war prisoners, Fisher. He knows me and I know him, he respects me, so I said, "I have something to ask you if this is possible."

"Go ahead, Mr. Frank."

I tell him the story, if there is a possibility to go out with this group what is going out to Majdanek, so I could see my wife. Maybe I'll take with me a little package, a piece of bread or something, but how can I go out? I'm a civilian.

"Don't worry about this. We'll give you a uniform what fits you, and you'll go out with the group."

He gave me a Polish war prisoner uniform and I went out with

---

4. After the Majdan-Tatarsky ghetto was liquidated, the only Jews remaining in Lublin were those in the SS camps, such as Lipowa and *Plaga Lashkewicz,* and tradespeople who were the private "servants" for individual Nazis.

5. This was the *Sonderkommando,* to whom Frank referred earlier as the "people who became without feeling."

this group. The night before, somebody from the war prisoners let my wife know there's a possibility—they are not sure—that I'll come out to visit her in the morning, and she should come out in that time from the barrack. I went out with the group, and I came over to Majdanek. Was there electrical wiring . . . some from the group was doing work on one side nearer the barracks, and some from the group was nearer to the crematorium. I was standing on the side further away from the barracks.

When I came there, I was standing not far from the wire, what separates the two sides. Dora came out; she knew I was coming, and I look at her, but I didn't recognize her. Her face was all with blood, beaten up, looks like she couldn't wash off the blood from her face. When they took her to Majdanek, they want to take away the little boy Nunyek from her. She didn't let him go . . . she didn't let him loose, so they start to beat her. They beat her so long that she lost consciousness, and she doesn't even know what happened with this little boy. She start to yell to me that Nunyek is not there, this little boy is not there. And I hear her . . . to comfort her, because what else could I do?—I lied to her and I said, "Don't worry about Nunyek. Nunyek is with me"—but this was not true.

I had a little package, maybe a pound of bread, with two apples, with two pieces of sugar, and I throw this over the wire fence. In that time, I was young: I could throw a little package further than today. I don't know if she received; in that time, this package was important, this little bread, but I was more interested to see her than to find out about this package.

But in the meantime, there was the watchtower, with a Ukraine sitting there on top with a machine gun, and he saw me throwing over this little package. They also used Ukraines to kill the Jews; they was very tough too, the same like the Nazis; they trained them how to kill . . . fast.[6]

---

6. Ukrainians, Lithuanians, and Latvians who had been war prisoners were recruited as guards in the labor and death camps. The Nazis offered them freedom instead of the starvation, brutality, and probable death that they would have likely encountered in a POW camp. Known as *Hilfswillige* (Volunteers) and trained at Trawnik, they were an important source of manpower for liquidating ghettos (Browning 1993, 52). Ukrainian guards had a reputation of being equally brutal, or even more sadistic, than their German overseers. Some survivors have related that the Ukrainian and Baltic guards killed more readily and with less provocation because of their long-standing anti-Semitism. However, it has also been reported that Ukrainian

He start to yell, *"Halte! Halte! Halte!"* I want to go away when I throw over this package, to go a little bit nearer where the group is, because I was almost by myself there, about five, six feet from the group. He points at me with the machine gun. I raised my hand, but he didn't shoot—if he will shoot from the top he will kill me. He came down from the tower, and he shoot me through the arm, and the bullet went through mine arm.

When he came near me, there was an SS man from the Lipowa, and he saw the incident that the Ukraine is trying to kill me, one shot went out from the gun—maybe this was not a machine gun, maybe this was a regular gun, because a machine gun would be a lot of bullets—and the SS man start to yell, "Don't shoot! Don't shoot! This is the *Schneidermeister!* This is the tailor from the Lipowa, from the labor camp!" Since he was an SS man, and the other was a Ukraine watchman, the Ukraine listened to the SS man and stopped shooting.

The Nazi man saved my life from the Ukraine watchman, and he took me away from there, to the Jewish war prisoners. Was there a little room where a couple of them used to stay, ones what they didn't work by the crematorium. He took me in there, and he said, "Take care of his wound . . . they shot him. He is the *Schneidermeister* from your camp. Take him home."

They took a towel or a piece of white rag, and they put on mine arm. They kept it so my blood shouldn't run, and they took me right away with a horse and buggy to Lipowa street.

They took me in the *Lazarett,* the little hospital, and they start to treat me for my wound. Over there was big doctors, professors, surgeons . . . German professors, doctors what they was German Jews—and they all can do some work—so they kept them in the camp. With seven thousand people, you need doctors—happened every day accidents, beating, killing, shooting . . . not to death, but to take out the bullets . . . so was like a regular hospital, a barrack. The equipment was not like a regular hospital—a lot of them died from the wounds, more than was saved.

For about two weeks I couldn't do anything. I had an infection in mine arm . . . start to be gangrene. In that time they used penicillin only for the officers, but they had something . . . they gave me a shot.

guards were more interested in obtaining money for carousing and prostitution than serving as killers or reliable underlings who carried out every Nazi command (Willenberg 1989, 97).

After a couple days, I went into the tailor shop with my arm hanging on a sling.

Mohwinkel shouldn't notice this that I was injured—was a secret from him because if he would know that I went out with the group, the commandant Fisher will be punished, or the other *Kapos* from the war prisoners . . . they will be punished, and I will be punished. The other prisoners in the tailor shop, they can tell what this was with mine arm, but they wouldn't say anything. They couldn't.

The night before I went out with the group to Majdanek to see my wife, my little boy Monyek, he was sleeping with me in the same bunk in the same bed . . . there on the Lipowa it was not so bad for us, was only four of us from the shops in a large room with two windows—we had blankets, we had a pillow brought from home. Monyek had a dream in a middle of the night with terrible yelling. "Dad! Dad! Dad!" He was so yelling, and he was jumping in his sleep, and I start to say, "Monyetchku, Monyetchku, I am here; nothing happened. I'm here; what happened Monyetchku?"

He woke up, and he said, "Daddy, I had a terrible dream."

"What was the dream, Monyetchku? What was the dream?"

"I dreamt that the Nazis shot you."

I start to laugh. "You see Monyetchku, I am alive, I am here helping you."

"I'm so glad, Dad; I'm so glad," and he went back to sleep.

When I came back from visiting Majdanek, I didn't tell him the story what I saw how his mother looks or what happened with Nunyek. I came home, he was waiting for me, and he saw me with the sling, helping mine arm . . . "What happened?"

I told him I was shot.

"You see Dad, this was my dream, what I had in the nighttime."

This dream was the night before I was shot. So what are you saying to that?[7]

---

7. In his depositions in the 1960s, Mr. Frank gave two other accounts of how he was shot in his upper arm. His 1965 account (*SSPF*, 7382–83) states that Mohwinkel shot at him at a roll call after Mr. Frank begged him to rescue his wife from Majandek; in 1969 he corrected that account, saying that Mohwinkel shot him after he protested that the Lipowa tailor shop couldn't meet Mohwinkel's production quotas (*SSPF*, 9767). Mr. Frank now states that Mohwinkel's actions in those two situations are correctly described in this book on p. 174 and pp. 100–102 respectively, and that the account of his being shot by a Ukranian in Majdanek is correct as told in this chapter.

26

Dora's Return

March 1943–October 1943

EVERYDAY I WAS TALKING with the Professor David, if he knows if Dora will be taken out from Majdanek, and he said he doesn't know anything. One time I talked to him, and he said that Mohwinkel told him that he is working on this to bring her over to his camp, to Lipowa. This took about six weeks, and he brought her over to me, and we was together, with my older boy—we was all three together.

When she arrived, I was standing near the gate. The watch-guys from the gates, they know me from so many years, almost four years. From the office from the David was in the same line from the gates, so I was near his office. When they brought her in, he took her over. She belonged to him—what I mean "belonged" is, he is responsible for her. She is another prisoner in the camp, he had to register her. And there was another woman, a German woman . . . I don't remember her name . . . also she was cleaning for an officer there. On the Lipowa, was a room, like a lavatory, a ladies room—she was sleeping there with the other German woman. In the daytime she was in the shop working.

ML: What was your wife's physical condition like when she returned?

JF: Her condition was not so bad because she found out there through the war prisoners that the Professor David told them that she should live with hope, that they'll take her out from there. The prisoners told her, "There's a possibility that you'll be together with your husband and your older boy." She start to hope; she was not sure . . . but after five-and-a-half or six weeks, David was waiting for her by the gates.

ML: What did she you tell about Majdanek? What it was like there?

180

JF: She didn't have to tell me anything; I knew from the war prisoners all the time what is there.

ML: But didn't what she told you confirm the transports, the selections, the gas chambers, the crematoriums firsthand? Wouldn't what your wife have told you been more vivid to you?

JF: When I ask her, she said, "Jack, let's not talk about this. Let's use our every moment what we are together, and let's not talk about what happened to me or what happened to our little boy. Let's keep what we can save. Let's make the best of it." Was a time before everything start, this was with a year before, when they took away my parents, with all my sisters and their families,[1] I had a conversation with my wife what will happen if they'll take away somebody from the four of us. What should we do? Should we go all together like my parents did, like my all family did together, to death? Or should we let go some from us? We was discussing a whole night this problem and we couldn't decide what to do. The end was, we both decide to leave this open. We'll act when something will happen like this. And my wife said, "What you'll do, what you'll decide will be OK with me," because she couldn't do anything, only me. She was believing in what I can do more than what I really can do. Her hope, you know?

ML: Even when she returned from Majdanek?

JF: Even when she returned from Majdanek.

ML: Do you think that in her eyes, her returning from Majdanek reinforced that belief that you had more power than you had?

JF: Yes, yes, yes. Not that I did, but she believed in that. Later, she said, "What you did Jack, I would never believe that I'll leave from there, because I can see that I'm only the one woman taken out." After this time what she was there, she told me that she was talking with other Jewish women what they was there cleaning in Majdanek; if they start to feel weaker, if they couldn't carry out the work . . . they had a German *Kapo* in the barrack, so if a woman got a little bit weak, they took her out to liquidate her. So everyday, "What you did was unbelievable." I didn't let her finish the conversation, because I know that she believes in something what this is not. Mohwinkel took her out because he didn't want me to be disturbed to carry out the work, the uniforms what they need to send to the soldiers on the front. That's what I knew this is; I was sure that this is the case.

When Mohwinkel took my wife into camp, he took her with the

1. The liquidation of the Lublin ghetto in March 1942.

idea what I told him, that she is a good dressmaker, she will work with me—she was always working with me in the tailor trade, so she'll be active, she'll work. When Mohwinkel came in, she was always active to do something, to show she is useful.

ML: What do you think it was like for her there, that she was one of the only women in the camp?[2]

JF: In her way, she was feeling that she is the lucky one, because she is with her husband with the one boy. One boy is gone, but she has one what she is alive to live for, to live for something. She was with me until November 1943, and for seven-and-a-half months or eight months, she was very happy. You know, life . . . you can never forget the people what they took away from you, but when you have something left, you try to live for them what they are alive, so this was her happiness, that somebody is alive. I don't know how to explain the feelings. It's a very, very strange feeling, but you feel a little bit better when you are with somebody what you can share your life with your nearest. In the moment, you are forgetting what happened a moment before, a month before, a year before. But it comes always back; you can never forget, but in the moment, you think about what is left.

ML: Time becomes very precious in the moment.

JF: That's right.

ML: In the moment you don't forget the tragedies that have happened before; there may be a powerful feeling of despair about what may happen in the future, but you're clinging to something . . . but you say that as if it's not very weak, as if it's very powerful.

JF: I think so, yes.

---

2. Dora Frank was the only woman in the tailor shop of approximately 450–75 tailors.

27

The Lublin Prison

November 2, 1943–Late November 1943

THE LAST WEEK from October '43 till November '43 was very quiet. We had a suspicion a couple days before that something would happen . . . they didn't beat up the prisoners like they used to do before if you didn't walk straight or you didn't do the things what they want.

On November 2, 1943, an SS man came into the tailor shop and went to Langfeld, and he told me I should take the tape measure, I should go with him to take a measurement for an officer. This was by me a little bit . . . I don't know . . . always when they told me to take some measurements for the big Nazis, they always came for me in the morning . . . ten o'clock, eleven o'clock, but this was about five o'clock in the afternoon, and I felt something. When something happened—I don't know why this was—always when something was about to happen, I had always the feeling that something *will happen*. Not always the same moment—the next day, or a couple hours later . . . when it was the liquidation of the small ghetto, I had the feeling that something'll happen in the ghetto, that's why I put my wife and my little boy in the hiding place.

I didn't mention anything to Klein and Gootmacher, because you had everything to keep in the way not to disturb the situation, that they shouldn't get excited, so I kept this like normal, like everyday when I take a measurement. I put on my jacket, took the tape measure with me, and went over to my wife—my little boy was a little bit further away from the desk where my wife was standing there. I went over to her and I said, "Dora, you see that the *Oberscharführer* came that I should go to take a measurement, but I have a feeling that something is cooking, something is not right."

She asked me, "Why do you feel this way?"

I told her, "All the time, for the last four years so long as I am here, five o'clock they never asked me to take a measurement. Five o'clock is almost the closing of the tailor shop. They have to prepare to go out for a counting, for the *appel*. I don't know if we will see each other again, or maybe this is just like the SS man says that I'll take the measurement, and I'll come back, but if not, I'd like to say good-bye to you. And I don't know how to get over to Monyetchku to say good-bye to him. You tell him good-bye for me."

I didn't want to say good-bye to my son . . . the emotions when he'll see how I feel . . . and I kissed my wife, and I was crying, and I didn't want him to see my tears.

I went with the SS man to the gates. Outside the gates was waiting a car; they opened the door, and I saw two SS men, two Nazis with machine guns in their hands. They let me in the car, and they put me in the middle, one guy with a machine gun from the right and one from the left side. They blindfolded me, and the car start to go. Knowing Lublin because I was born there, I know a little where the car is going with the turns what they made. And I had the feeling that they are taking me to the headquarters what was located on the *Kruel Leszcynskiego* Street. They took me into the offices there, and they tell me to wait in the lobby there. This was maybe about half-past five; I was standing in the lobby, an hour, two, three . . . this was already nine o'clock, already dark, and nobody is calling me to take the measurement. There passed by all kind of Nazi officers—they didn't say anything, and I didn't know them so I couldn't ask them anything.

About half-past nine, a Gestapo man came out, and he told me to go with him. I went with him out from the building, also with the machine gun on his shoulders, another guy in the back with me . . . they told me to go in a car, the car start, and they took me from there to the prison on the Zamkawa Street.[1] I came to the prison, they put me in a cell; was already about ten o'clock or a quarter to ten, was dark. Being in the cell, I heard the sound from chains shaking. I felt I am

---

1. The prison was one street away from Frank's birthplace at Shiroka 30. Since childhood he knew the long brick building, with its central tower and spire, that sat on a high hill above a wooded neighborhood. In the prewar era, it served as a general prison that housed civilian criminals, and after the invasion it continued to house these inmates. When the Gestapo requisitioned the prison, Gestapo and SS leaders housed their personal Jewish slaves there so they would not be deported and then killed in ghetto clearing actions.

with somebody there, but I couldn't see with whom I am. I was sitting on the cement floor a whole night. About six o'clock in the morning they opened the cell, and a Polish guard came in, and he took me out from there. And then I saw two guys was chained to the wall, by their hands and their legs.

They took me into a huge room with windows. I saw there is a tailor shop; I saw machines. I came in and I saw a lot of my friends what I knew them for years, people what I didn't see them for a year or for a year and a half . . . this was people what they was working for all kind of Nazis. Some worked for the Gestapo. Was also women what they was dressmakers; they was working for the wives from the Gestapo leaders.

Was there Pesach Rysfeld, an older man . . . in that time he was about sixty-five or sixty-six, but because he was an artist in his trade—he was a tailor—he was working from the chief from the Gestapo, Worthoff, on the Sklodowsky Street. Before they liquidated all the small, little shops outside the Lipowa . . . every big Nazi had a couple of Jews what they was working for him . . . I'm sure that Worthoff knew that they would liquidate, so he was hiding him there. Pesach Rysfeld had a wife, and he had two girls from his sister-in-law with him. One girl was about eighteen or nineteen, and the other was about twenty-one or twenty-two. Their mother was not in prison—she must have been killed before, with her father and her mother. When Pesach Rysfeld was by Worthoff as a tailor, the two girls helped to work by the tailoring business. Worthoff took them all, the four people, Pesach Rysfeld with the wife, and the two girls from her sister.

ML: That seems unusual to me that the two girls were taken out too.

JF: That's what the German wants to do. That's what he wants, that's what he did. Usual or not usual, they did all kinds of things what to you looks unusual; maybe he had something in his mind. I don't know why he saved them . . . because when they took me to prison, I was sure there was Jews what they could keep safe besides me . . . in that time, was still seven thousand on the Lipowa . . . I didn't know if they was killed, but in prison, I didn't know I would meet there Jews.

Then there was Joe Miller. He was also an artist in his trade. Pesach Rysfeld was a man's tailor—Joe Miller was a lady's tailor. The Joe Miller, he was only by himself. He was also working for the Gestapo there somewhere. I really don't know exactly from where because this was outside of the camp. I didn't know how many Jews are working for the Gestapo, or the SS, outside the camp; I don't know one or a thousand. What Joe Miller told me, he was working for the wife from the chief from the Gestapo. All the Jews what they was there, three hundred Jews, they told me later when I came in . . . they all was employed by the Germans, by the party people. There was four parties: the SS, the SR, the SD, and the SA, and the prison was run by the Gestapo [the SD], and all had different colors. The SS was wearing green or black uniforms, the SA gold uniforms, and the SD was green uniforms. Every Nazi had his Jew to use, one or two or three or five.

I turn around and I see the Professor David, the elder from the labor camp is there. Two months before this, David disappeared. Every time somebody else disappeared, we knew they finished them off . . . and we thought the same by him.

There was something about Professor David what will be very interesting for you . . . about in prison, what happened to me. In the beginning of Lipowa, about six months later when the barracks, when the shops, was ready, they open a canteen—in that time you still had your families, your houses, your apartments, you came in the morning to work, and in the evening, you went home. Lunchtime, you could buy a piece a cake there or a coffee in the canteen. Over there in the community, they arrest one girl because she was not wearing the armband with the King David star. She was a young girl, maybe nineteen years old or twenty years old . . . her name was Sver. Before the war, her family used to have a store from wholesale yard goods on the Lubartovsky Street. When I start to manage the tailor shop and I need something, I went into the canteen to buy something, and I met there this girl, she was the salesgirl from the canteen. David, he organized some food should be there, some pieces of candy, some doughnuts, little things. And this girl, Miss Sver, was there selling this. I came in to buy something, and I know this girl from before the war. Where I knew her—when I married my wife, I had an apartment on the same house on Lubartovsky Street 16, where the Svers lived across the hall—we was neighbors . . . and that's how I knew the three sisters from the family Sver.

When I came into the canteen to buy something—I don't remember her first name—I asked her, "What are you doing here?"

"I was arrested for not wearing an armband, the King David star."

They took her in on the camp, so the Professor David intervened by Mohwinkel, and he released her because of his intervention, and from his influence, he got her the job as the salesgirl from the canteen.

A couple days later, I saw the second sister; she was much older than the other was. The younger one was the head from the canteen, the older one was helping the younger one, and I found out that the younger girl from nineteen or twenty years old became the love-girl from Professor David.

Before I had my shop on the Krakow Street on Hotel Angelsky, I was living there on the Lubartovsky where the Svers lived . . . but in the meantime, when the war broke out and I became the head from the tailor shop, they gave me an apartment on the Grodzka Street.[2] Before this, maybe a year or nine months, they gave me an apartment on the Shientaduska, and over there on the Shientaduska Street was living a doctor, a gynecologist, what he was working I think, in a hospital what was only for German-descent women, and he was there in the beginning. He was a Jewish doctor . . . his name was Bromberg. We was living in this house on the Shientaduska, and the Germans put up signs on our doors—his and mine—that if Germans will inspect this house who lives there, they shouldn't come in our apartments, because I am the tailor of the *Obergruppenführer* Globocnik. Do you follow me?

ML: I think so. I'm assuming that all of the shop leaders who lived outside the camp and all the doctors had these signs outside their doors.

JF: Most of them, not all. It was to prevent that they should arrest you, because tomorrow you have to go to the shop to finish some work for this and this Nazi . . .

ML: So it was Jewish residence protection.

JF: I don't know what you want to call this, but this was the way. One night, I was lying with my wife in bed, and we heard footsteps from boots . . . you know, even the sound how the Nazis was walking, you could feel this is a Nazi . . . this is not just a civil person what is passing by in the hall, from the foyer in this building, walking on the steps, up to the second floor. We was already awake, was maybe about one, two o'clock in the middle of the night, and I said to my wife—we always had ready our clothes near our beds, if something should happen, *schnell* to put on your dress, the woman the dress or me the suit, to not be taken out nude, naked, with pajamas. We heard boots, steps, walking to come up on the stairs, and I figure, "That's it. This is our

2. All the shop leaders were given these apartments. See Chapter 4, "The Lublin Ghetto," pp. 41–42.

end. They'll come in; they'll kill us, or they'll arrest us"—always in fear.

But they knocked on the other door from the doctor. They went into the doctor's apartment, and we heard they opened the door; they closed the door, and later they opened the door and went out, but we was inside in our apartment, and you couldn't be anxious to open the door to look because that's what you need, to get killed. A couple of minutes later was like quiet, like nothing happened.

In the morning we went out to knock on the door by the neighbor, to ask the doctor's wife . . . we knew that he's supposed to go the hospital, and she said they took away her husband. They took away the doctor. That's it! They didn't say anything to this wife, nothing; they told him to get dressed, and he went with them . . . how many Nazis I don't know because I wasn't there outside my door.

I don't remember the name from this place in Poland, was already a place like a crematorium, but I don't know if this existed even from the time before the Nazis came in . . . it was a crematorium, not to burn mass people, but sometimes somebody leaves a will to be cremated, so they took him there. Was a special place where they cremated people, maybe criminals . . . this I don't know. But in fourteen days, fourteen days later, came a box with ashes to the woman, to the doctor's wife, with a letter that before the war in 1938, he made an abortion for a German-descent woman, and that was the reason she now is getting his ashes.

But going back to the Professor David and his girlfriend, why I mentioned this story, I was no more living with the Svers in this house, but in another house on the Shientaduska, so I didn't know what happened with her, with the Professor's girlfriend. He was maybe seventy years old, or in the late sixties, and she was twenty or twenty-one, this girlfriend. But because he was the commandant from the camp and he saved her life not to get arrested, so she became his girlfriend. Facts like this happened also with powerful men what they was *Kapos,* or they could choose a girl like the Schama Grajer, like I was telling you the story. Was a fine time.

ML: What was a fine time?

JF: I said in that time was a fine time to live, the things what happened, you know, with girls or with men—when somebody wanted a girl when he was powerful, he could get her.

ML: Are you joking?

JF: This was in a sarcastic way what I said "a fine time." Sometimes Jewish has expressions doesn't fit to understand if you are born in America. This was sarcastic for me to say this was a fine time. You follow me? Now you know.

So on the Lipowa I asked this girl, "What happened with your family, because we used to live in the same house; what happened with your father, with your mother, with your two sisters?" I don't remember what she said about her parents, but she has one sister Adja, she is working with her here, but she is not in yet, she didn't come today, or she didn't feel good or something . . . but the Adja is with her.

This is the end from this story, from this episode, until after a couple years when the ghetto was liquidated, and I didn't know what happened with the David, with the Adja, with his girlfriend; I lost contact with them . . . there was other things for me to think about, because later I had to think about them liquidating ghettos with the family and if I can still save someone. I still had my wife, two children; I had other things on my mind than to think about Professor David and his love-girl or her sister.

But when I came to the prison and I met David there, he came over: "*Herr Frank,* Mr. Frank, what happened with the Lipowa?"

And I said, "What happened with you? We was thinking you are dead." He told me he is here, and I called the name of his girlfriend and Adja, and he said, "Adja is here." The Gestapo man saved him with the sister Adja—but I don't remember what happened to David's girlfriend, how she disappeared.

———

When they took me into the prison, and in the morning they took me into the cell, and I met them all what I am talking about—a lot of them was very glad to see me, and a lot of them was not so glad to see me. The ones glad to see me, a lot of them was my friends; they knew that I was Himmler's tailor and did work for Globocnik, and they was thinking that maybe if something'll happen, they'll need my help, and maybe because of me they'll be saved. But some of them what they was there in prison, because I was Himmler's tailor, they was afraid I'll take away the power from them. I will be too big, and if the Nazis want to do something, they'll only save me, and they'll take the other tailors away . . . like Abraham Laderman, he was with his whole family . . . do you understand what I mean? I was on the second floor; there was another shop on the first floor from the prison. On the first floor was Laderman, what he was working for the chief from the Gestapo,

Worthoff. Before, he used to work on the Sklodowsky Street, the chief from the Gestapo gave him a room there, and when they liquidate the little shop from the Laderman, they took him to prison to hide him with his whole family. When they brought me, he was already there for six weeks.

They didn't show it; they didn't tell me anything, but I had the feeling, how they're acting between the other group, they didn't look so happy, so I figure they are afraid maybe because I am Himmler's tailor, maybe I'll be more powerful than the other tailors from the Gestapo. Instead to save ten tailors or five, or two, they'll save only me. Over there they was also afraid the next day they'll be dead, all of us.

ML: Did you and Laderman ever discuss incidents that happened to either of you while taking measurements?

JF: No, no, no. I never discussed. Because, was a little bit . . . if I would discuss with him, about Himmler, this will look . . . between Jews was a little bit jealousy too. I don't know if you follow me what I mean. If I would talk about Himmler, what I took the measurement, so I'll make myself in a higher position than he was. He was only the tailor from the chief from the Gestapo, but I was the tailor from Himmler. But for me was not a big reward because I knew this is only because they want me to take the measurement, not because I'll have a bigger reputation.

In civil life, when I had the customer from the publisher of the newspaper, I figure if somebody else would know that the publisher from the *Glos Lubelsky,* from the *Word from Lublin,* that I am dressing him, he'll recommend me to somebody else, or they'll see what nice clothes he is wearing, then I'll have more important people. But this was not a thing to discuss, was nothing to me, Himmler or not Himmler. They have one mind: to finish us off. In the beginning maybe I was not thinking about this . . . I knew they started killing— was not a mass killing at first, from time to time they killed people— but the point was not to discuss that I am the tailor from Himmler.

ML: Is that something you knew and decided, or did you once speak about it and then decide it wasn't judicious?

JF: I never discussed this that I made for Himmler things or a leather coat or something else. But the other people from outside, they came to me, "You took a measurement for Himmler?" They was approaching me to talk about Himmler all the time. I didn't talk about except when I came back to the camp after I took the measurement; I told the people, the friends from the shop, "You know to

whom they took me?" They said no, so I told them. That was only the
one time . . . but between us from the shop, between my friends what
they was near me, helping me to keep up with the hundred tailors, to
serve, to help them bring over the bundles and to take away, so with
them, we discussed. "Maybe this will save us longer . . . maybe the
war will come to an end." This was the discussion. "Thanks to you,
maybe because you are his tailor, maybe we will be saved."

But in the prison, I didn't have time to think if they are for me or
against me, I was thinking what happened with my wife and my
Monyek what I left there in camp; this was the thought of November.
The next day, I found out they brought with me to the prison a bundle with a leather coat I was making for Globocnik, what this was not
finished. In the morning, the Polish man what he guarded the door
brought in this package to the cell where we all was, and they gave me
a place to work. Was there standing a machine with a little table.

ML: Had the Gestapo supplied the equipment?

JF: This was not from the Gestapo, it was supplied by Poland. Before the war even, was there shops in the prison. They used to work
for the city; they made furniture, all kind of things to sell, by the Polish government, not by the Nazis.

On this bundle what they brought in was written there "Frank,"
for Prisoner Frank. I didn't open this, and this bundle was lying on
the table. I figure what this is, because I know I am in the middle
of the work for a leather coat for Globocnik. After a half hour or an
hour, the people was standing around me, asking me questions, and I
didn't have too many answers for them. I said, "Leave me alone. I
don't know what happened with my wife and my son," and they left
me alone by the table, and they went away to their places, because was
a very tremendous cell.

I was sitting by the table thinking, "What now? What should I do
now? To kill myself? Or to go back to work; or not to work?" All kind
of things came into my mind, and I couldn't come to any conclusion
what to do. But sitting there for a longer time, a half hour or something more, I decide that I lived enough; I lived too long to go
through this. This is enough; I want to finish my life. To finish my life
to commit suicide, I didn't have anything to commit suicide, or
maybe I was cowardly a little bit. I don't know; I didn't prepare myself with some poison to poison myself. So I decided I wouldn't finish
the coat what they brought in this bundle—I know from experience if
you don't carry out the orders what the Nazis give you, they give you

a bullet in the back of your head, and it doesn't take too long, and you are dead. And that was my decision—*that* was my decision.

I was sitting by the table, and that was my mind, and I wouldn't change anything what I decide to do. In the meantime after sitting a little bit longer, again people start to want to talk to me, and I said, "Leave me alone please . . . I cannot talk; I cannot think." They left me alone, and I was sitting.

This whole day passed by, till about two or three o'clock in the middle of the day when a Gestapo man came up, and he called out my name. I went over, and I said, "My name is Frank," because most of the prisoners, we didn't have names; we had numbers in that time, but I still had my name. The Gestapo man told me to go with him . . . the commandant from the prison wants to see me.

He took me in to his office on the first floor. The name from the commandant was Dominik—from the rank he was an *Oberstürm-führer;* this is like a First Lieutenant. He was sitting in the office, and on the other side of the desk was a chair, and he told me to sit down. It was for a long time what a Nazi in this rank was telling me sit down on a chair. I looked on his face, and he didn't say anything. He looked in some papers, and I am sitting waiting to hear his speech, what he will tell me or order me . . . I didn't know what.

After a couple of seconds, he told me, "I have an order from the *Obergruppenführer* Globocnik to help you here, and here you are safe. But I have also a package, I'm sure that you have this upstairs. This is the coat for the *Obergruppenführer,* and we have here a shop with tailors. I set up place for you, and if you need some help you tell me, and I'll give you all the help what you want from the other tailors what are there in the prison with you."

I was listening, and I said to the *Herr Obersturmführer,* "Can I say something?"

And very politely, he said, "Sure, *bitte,* you can speak; you can tell me what you'd like to say."

I said, "I left a wife with a son on the Lipowa." This was the 4th of November 1943 . . . this was the first day what I was there—"I will do everything; I'll carry out all the orders what you'll order me, because I always carried out the orders from the *Obergruppenführer* and from the commandant Mohwinkel . . . I'll do everything what you want, but one thing what I'd like, to bring over my wife with my son here. And then whatever you'll tell me, what to do, what to make, I'll do everything."

He said, "We'll bring her here, but we cannot do this right away . . . this has to go through channels. I'm sure you have an idea . . . this is a prison, and she is in a labor camp; this has to go through channels, through people, but we'll bring her here."

"OK *Herr Obersturmführer,* but so long as I wouldn't have my wife with my son, I won't start to do any tailoring business."

I know what I am going in for this, but I was looking for that; I was looking for the bullet; I was looking for them to finish me off, because I know what I am saying: I'll be dead.

But instead to kill me, he said, "That's OK, we'll try to bring your wife here, with your son, and if you don't want to start to work, we have plenty of food here; we'll feed you, and you can sit here so long as you want and not do anything, till you change your mind."

This was the end of the conversation. He told me I can go back, and the Gestapo man took me back to the cell.

ML: Was there a certain point where the routine in the camp, mainly in Lipowa, the Lublin prison, and Natzweiler-Vaihingen, was settled? You get used to what's going on; you only think about what will happen next; you live in constant fear—do you think there's a point where you reach a level of understanding with your captors? You know what their power is over you, and they know that they have you now: you're trapped; they've nailed you down, and they've reduced you to an animal or a frightened robot, and each acknowledges the other. Does this question make sense?

JF: What are you asking me—how I felt in that time?

ML: No, I'm asking: at the point where you realized, "I see what this is, and I see what their plan is, how they treat us, and they realize that we're living in fear, and they can do whatever they want with us"—when you realized that about them, and there was no more urge or possibility to resist—was that a level of understanding between the captors and the prisoners?

JF: Yes. In that time, I felt that I have no other way than to do what the captor wants me to do, because I couldn't think of another way—I knew that I have no power what I want to do. I had to do what the Nazi wants me to do. But at the same time, I still had in my mind to think that I'll carry out for a certain time, to a certain extent. What I mean is, I still had something to protect. I still had my family—if not all the family, I had a part of the family. I didn't think of something else to do but to carry out, because he has the power, and he can do with me what he wants. Because there was somebody except myself, I had to carry out what he wants me to do. But the moment when I didn't have nobody else, nobody to think that I'll save them, so I lost this fearfulness, and in my mind, I said to the Nazis, "That's it. You did everything what you could with your power, and you'll do the same thing with me: go ahead and do it right now." And I refused to carry out the order; this was something what I found out from people later after the war, that I am only the one without a machine gun in my hand to say that I would not finish the coat when they took me over from Lipowa to the prison. But this didn't help either, because when they saw that I lost my fear for them, they figured they'll find another way to persuade me, not with fear, but with kindness. They told me: there's plenty of space here, plenty of food to feed me, plenty of shelter to shelter me here, so if I don't want to work, it's OK with them. I felt that I have no power in me anymore to live and to carry out, with all the tortures . . . this was a torture for me every time, to cut off another limb from my body, first the parents, the other members of the family, and then later the wife with the children. But looks like they found all kinds of ways to use you and make you to do their way.

ML: So a reader of this will understand that at the point where you decided not to follow the order and they could do with you whatever they wanted, you were relinquishing everything. This was not defiance. Some people may think, "You were the only one who didn't have the machine gun and didn't have the hand grenades, but you stood up to them and you said, 'No, I won't do this.' " I think the spirit is different than defiance.

JF: I don't know if the spirit is different. In my feeling, today even, I felt this was a way to commit suicide. I was thinking many times to take my life . . . I don't know if I was a coward or I was weak . . . I don't know even if I would have poison, if I would have the courage to commit suicide. I was thinking this many times, but in another way I was thinking: maybe, maybe I'll survive. Maybe that's why I didn't commit suicide. Maybe I couldn't; maybe I didn't have the power, but in that moment I felt very strong, and this was the way to commit suicide. If I couldn't do it, I beg you, you do it, to the commandant from the prison.

ML: The way you say that: "You do it," the tone of your voice reminds me of a challenge, but it's ambiguous to me whether it was a challenge, because as you said, that was your way to commit suicide. There was a point where you weren't able to commit suicide through

Suicide at Dachau: touching the electric fence and hanging. Frank contemplated suicide numerous times, and is still uncertain why he was not able to commit it. *Courtesy of KZ–Gedenkstätte Dachau, Germany.*

the traditional routes, hanging yourself or taking poison, so you left the final act to someone else. Was there a little bit of a challenge also?

JF: I don't think so. I couldn't challenge him. I couldn't challenge against tanks and machine guns. And when I looked in his face, this was the machine gun; this was the tank. I couldn't challenge this power.

ML: Not that kind of defiant challenge I was talking about before. To me, it sounds like you weren't only trying to put him in the position of being the one responsible for finally killing you, getting rid of you, because you said you felt very strong, and you didn't want to continue anymore, and you also felt there might be a chance of surviving somehow. It sounds like you were ready to roll the die one last time.

JF: Not in that time. This was the end. I saw there was no way out.

ML: So when you said you felt very strong, where did that strength come from?

JF: I don't know. From desperation, from seeing there's no other way. You can't fight with the bare hands, tanks with machines guns, with hand grenades. And this was the power they really had against naked bodies.

ML: How do you think they viewed suicides? Do you think it didn't matter to them: it was just as well whether people killed themselves or they killed them?

JF: On the contrary, they was very pleased. They was looking for more suicide acts from Jews, because they will save bullets. Many times they said not to use too many bullets to kill. If you can kill two, three Jews with one bullet, you'll do a better job than to use three bullets.

ML: And probably if you can push a person to commit suicide, as you said, by "amputating their limbs" by taking away his family and by starving him, you won't have to support the person nearly as long until his natural death.

JF: That's right. But after the time when I am talking about, when I felt, "This is the end," seven or eight months later when they took us out from prison, there comes another mind to my brains that maybe I did a good thing when the other Jews persuaded me to go back to finish the leather coat. I was still alive—maybe I'll survive. So you see, your brains was thinking back and forth, and it was very bad when you were looking for the end, and it didn't happen. When the moment came where it gets a little bit easier, your brains start to think maybe there will be change. Maybe they wouldn't have time to finish

you off. Maybe you'll survive and tell somebody, if you meet somebody later, if there will be a world.

———

I came back to the cell and all the people there, the Jews, didn't
know why they took me down. The Gestapo man left, and I was free
in the cell . . . like nothing happened—I was not killed, nothing.
About six o'clock, usually they brought in a pot with food to feed all
the people from there, but for me they brought a dinner from the
hospital from the prison, better quality food. You follow me? I didn't
know, and the others didn't know what happened. They brought for
me a plate covered, with a piece of meat, with a soup, a special dinner
for me. I ate my supper, I was very hungry, I didn't eat from yesterday
evening! I didn't have no supper, I didn't have no breakfast, who
could eat? So this was the first meal what I had for twenty-four hours.

The two groups what I said before, one group was for me, and
one group was against me—the group what was against me, they said,
"Something is fishy here. Look, they brought a special supper for him.
What is going on here? What'll be?" So to me, after the supper, nobody wants to talk to me. I felt that they moved away, to stay away at
a distance.

We had our supper; we was sitting, then later a couple of guys
what I know them from before the war was talking all kind of things. I
still don't know what happened with my wife, with my son, with all
the people from everywhere. We was sitting for hours and hours, and
it became dark . . . I saw everybody has a little folding bed, most of
the people, the whole cell was with beds. They also gave me a folding
bed to lie down, with a very thin mattress with a little pillow. Was not
so bad, I lie down on my place; everybody lies down, some of them
whisper to one another to talk . . . what they talk I don't know . . .
and I lie by myself. One bed to another was maybe about ten inches
apart . . . you can understand . . . maybe about one hundred people in
one room. Also, everybody was together, women and men together,
no children.

The fifth of November, a Gestapo came up and he had a speech
for the whole cell. Everybody about eleven o'clock has to be downstairs on the hall; nobody can be missed, and also not only from the
second floor, also from the first floor, all the three hundred Jews, *except me*. I was only the one what was left by myself in the cell. They all
have to go down . . . the commandant has to say something to them,

but not to me. So you can imagine my feeling. I didn't know what to think about. This took maybe about three-quarters of an hour, then they all came back. The people from both cells chose a delegation from the other tailors to talk to me. The commandant said to them that they had to have the influence on me to go back to do the work in my line, and if not, he don't need no tailors here, so he'll take all the three hundred people out, with me, and he don't need nobody. I hope you understand: he put up hundreds of enemies against me, to force me to do the work what I make up my mind not to do, because I'll be responsible for three hundred lives if I wouldn't do the work.

ML: Do you think he knew you were trying to resist, and he was trying to break your spirit? Couldn't he have had another tailor finish that leather coat, and just killed you? Why were you the only one who could finish the coat for Globocnik?

JF: Well, he could do anything, but if he will do this, he will do something against the order from Globocnik that I have to finish the coat, that I have to finish what I start. Do you follow me?

ML: So he was afraid that if—

JF: I don't know if he was afraid. I don't know what was in his mind. He could kill me if he want; he could take another tailor too. But the Germans—I know from being with them for so long a time— if they have an order, they carry out the order exactly how the order is given to them. If Globocnik, the head from all the Gestapo and SS told him, "Here's this bundle from the leather coat what Frank, the *Jude* Frank, started. You have a shop there; let him finish the coat there"—this was enough. That's what I understand what the German is; this was enough for him to carry out the order from the *Obergruppenführer,* from the head from the party.

ML: Do you think also they wanted to make sure there wouldn't be a symbol of a man who refused their order?

JF: This I don't know.

ML: Because they took all of these people out, and they were hiding them there because they were all masters of their trades; it would have been disadvantageous if they killed them all. Who would make these articles of clothing and shoes for them?

JF: Maybe he wouldn't kill them all. Maybe was only a trap. Who knows? I don't think he would kill them, but he put up a whole army against me.

ML: And you can't think of it at the time as a threat or not—you can't call him on the bluff.

JF: No, no, no. I said it's a possibility—I don't know: I can't say yes, I can't say no, but I don't think Dominik will kill all three hundred, because this will not only involve one, what I was Globocnik's tailor, this will also involve the chief from the Gestapo, his workers, and he couldn't kill them till he gets the order from the chief. Do you follow me? And was not only one Nazi's order to follow—every couple of Jews worked for a couple of big Nazis, so I think this was a threat to make the Jews be afraid, or they should see to persuade me that all three hundred lives are in my hands. In the better way, between a Jew to a Jew, maybe Dominik felt this will work on me.

ML: What do mean, the better way from a Jew to a Jew?

JF: That I will be the savior, that if I go back to work I will save three hundred Jewish lives.

ML: And he was plotting that you would think that way.

JF: Yes. Like I said, they had all kind of schemes what they try to accomplish what they want, with violence, with good things, or with giving milk to children . . . they tried everything what's a better way— and maybe in that time, he felt that's a better way.

But this was not the end. If this wouldn't work, he also had a separate room for me . . . near the big cell was a small room what there was two Jews in the jewelry business. They used to sort out diamonds for the quality, or others things what they collect from the clothes from Jews what they killed. Was sitting there two Gestapo guys also, and they was watching the two jewelers when they sorted out the diamonds with other gold pieces. Do you follow me?

ML: I've heard about this at Treblinka, for example. Where were the jewels coming from? From Majdanek to the Lublin Prison?

JF: I don't know—from all over, from camps, from concentration camps, from private houses, I don't know. They emptied the room, was like twelve-by-fourteen with one window, a clean room with a table, with chairs.

In the evening, the same day, a group came over—I knew them from before the war, and they knew me—and they are talking to me like I am risking their lives, and I wouldn't gain anything by refusing to finish the coat or to do what the commandant tells me to do. The whole time what they are there, they tell me, they have no problems. Some of them was there for two, three months, and they didn't have no problems till I came there, so they was not very pleased with my refusing. For a couple of days went on the conversation only on this subject, to do what the commandant told them to, to persuade me.

They went to Adja Sver on the other side of the room, and they talked to her, that they had an order from Dominik that we both shouldn't be here in the big room—we all was sleeping in the same room before—we should be together, and they'll give us this little room where before the jewelry men was working there. In the same time, they start to work on her: "If you'll refuse, we all will get killed, because they don't need us anymore here. You don't have to be in a team with him there, but we have to carry out the order what Dominik gave us." Except for the order what he gave them, they start to persuade her in a nice way. They didn't talk with her about being lovers with me, but just to show that we are in the same room to carry out his order; what we do there is our business.

A couple of times a day, they start to talk to me, and this went on for a half hour or an hour, and then they stopped. They start to serve dinner—everybody had a small electric stove what they prepare food for their relatives—and after they ate and they brought for me something from the prison kitchen there, so they start again to talk to me about the same.

I tell them the story . . . "First they kill my little boy, and now I'm sure they killed my wife because I don't see her; Dominik says this has to take time to bring her back, and I know that if she and my older boy are not killed already, they'll finish them both off. I won't do anymore work, and if you think that you'll survive by working, you're mistaken too."

Especially Laderman from the first floor argued with me, because he had the family, and I didn't blame him. He wants to save their lives, so he said, "Jack, what will you accomplish not to work? You'll only accomplish that they'll kill all of us. Please, please, start to do something, because we have no other choice but to do the orders they are giving us. Maybe with the time this'll be a miracle what we'll survive. I know what you're talking about, but there's no other way. We are under their gun, and we have to carry out what they want us to do."

In four or five days, I start to be friends with a Polish watchman what he was staying by our cell; sometimes he let us out to the men's room or ladies' room and took us back, so you could talk with him a little bit, find out something from the outside. He did business with us, we paid him for everything: to buy something from outside and to bring in food, or some of us bought poison from him. He was in business, but he was like in the family, you know? After a couple of days, I ask him, "Maybe you can tell me what happened with the Lipowa?"

He told me, the 3rd of November, five o'clock in the morning, they took out all the people, in that time was seven thousand prisoners, and they took them all to Majdanek. He thinks they all was shot; they killed all of them.[3] If I will say this to somebody, maybe this is unbelievable, but this is the truth. From all the leaders from all shops, I was only the one what I was taken out from camp to the prison. Klein, Gootmacher, Fernandt, who used to take the bundles to the operators . . . they all went together to death, to Majdanek. That's how the end was from all the Lipowa Street, from all the people.

When I found out this, I tell the news from the watchman to all the friends what they was after me to start to work, and Laderman said again the same thing. "What will you accomplish? Every day they took away somebody from our families, and that's what they'll do with us. There's no other way; like we said before, we have to carry out, to live another hour, another day, another week, and that's how this is."

They start to talk to me again, and I start to feel that what we was friends before, I am now their enemy or they are my enemies. One was Pesach Rysfeld, he was one from the best tailors in Lublin . . . he was the eldest man there. He came over to me, and he said, "Before they kill us all and before they kill you, you'll have on your conscience all the three hundred Jews. Because of you, they'll kill us all. Please, please change your mind and start to do something, and we'll go down to the commandant and tell him you are working."

Also in the group what they chose to talk to me was Leah Dump, the dressmaker from the wife from Worthoff. She had two brothers, and she talked with me sometimes separate from the group to persuade me in a good way. She was working so hard the whole time to keep her brothers alive, and now comes up so a thing what the commandant said if I wouldn't go back to work to finish the leather coat . . . this is for the General Globocnik, and he will order that we'll be killed . . . what do they need all the Jews here for if they don't want to

3. This enormous extermination of forty-two thousand Jews in the Lublin district was code-named *Erntefest*, or "Harvest Festival." Himmler decided to liquidate all remaining Jews in the Majdanek concentration camp proper, the *Deutsche Ausrüstungswerke* and *Bekleidungswerke* labor camps (such as Lipowa and *Plaga Lashkewicz*), and the labor camps at Poniatowa and Trawnik because he feared prisoner revolts and increased organized resistance. Warsaw, Bialystock, Treblinka, and Sobibor had recently experienced resistance activity and uprisings (Marszalek 1986, 130; Browning 1993, 136–37; Hilberg 1985, 535).

carry out the orders? So in all kind of ways they was trying to persuade me to change my mind.

Looking on their faces, I figure, "What will I accomplish not to work? Maybe they are right." This took me about four or five days, and I start to feel also that I am doing something against them. Maybe they'll kill them because of me, because I won't finish the leather coat for the bandit, for the *Obergruppenführer* Globocnik, and I said, "All right, you won." And they start to hug me and to kiss me, like the war was to an end, like we survived already . . . but we knew we survived only for the moment.

I took out the pieces, the fronts with the backs with the sleeves, and I start to do something. But my heart was . . . I felt I am falling apart. I was not anymore the man what I was six or seven days before.

About eight or ten days later, they brought from Majdanek five or six guys from the Jewish war prisoners, what they was with me on the Lipowa. Before they liquidated the camp, they took them away a week or two weeks before, and they stayed on the Majdanek the whole time, and they sorted clothes. Before they killed the people, they had to undress themselves, and the war prisoners took the clothes, the suits, the dresses, to check if there are not some gold or diamonds hidden.[4] When they brought the war prisoners to the prison, Laderman came up to me and said that maybe we should go down to the commandant. Laderman talked like he is thinking Dominik is a human being, so nice when he talked to you . . . that was the scheme from some of them: you was thinking you talked to a friend. But Dominik knew sooner or later that if he received the order, he'll finish us off.

Laderman said because I am the tailor from the *Obergruppenführer* Globocnik we should go down and use the influence what we had, if you can call this an influence, to say that we know how the work is going, how long it will take, and we need more help. We should say that the Jewish war prisoners are tailors; maybe we can take them with us so they shouldn't be put in the other cells with the other prisoners. We told a Gestapo man that they should announce us to the commandant, that we have something to ask him about. We went over to the office from the commandant, and we tell him there are five or six tailors from the group from the war prisoners. In the meantime,

---

4. Prisoners who did this kind of work were usually killed afterward so there wouldn't be any witnesses to the killing operation. However, sometimes this wasn't the case, as described here and in Willenberg's account in *Surviving Treblinka*.

they brought more work for me, to make a uniform for the commandant from the prison, for Dominik, so he said OK, and he took three
guys from the Jewish war prisoners, and said they should go to my cell
to work with me—I should be their leader. Laderman took two guys,
and there was another one or two other guys what they went in the
shoemaker shop.

When the couple of prisoners went to work, I asked them what
happened with all the people on the Lipowa. They tell me the story
that on the third of November, in the morning, all seven thousand was
undressed, they had prepared a ditch, and one saw my wife with my
older boy. They both was shot together with the others—my wife was
holding the boy by his shoulders and that's how they fall down in the
ditch.[5] The war prisoner was reluctant telling me this, but was not too
painful for them to tell me the story, because they was there for weeks
carrying out the work, to segregate the clothing after they undressed,
before they went to the gas chamber, or was shot and fall to the ditch
. . . was to them a routine what they did for weeks and weeks.

Always I have the same picture when my wife went to the ditch
with my older son and she was holding her hands on his shoulders,
and that's how they was shot and fall down to the ditch—that's what
comes to my mind. Always the same thing.

After a couple of days, I tried to pull myself together . . . I couldn't
do anything anymore. Myself with Adja, we went into this little room,
and for five, six weeks, every night when we went in we was crying. She
had a family too before, a husband with a little girl, what she doesn't
know where they are. You can cry all your life, but you get used to
everything with the time. You get so used, you feel there is no other
way. You wait only for the moment when they'll kill you. This was always in your mind. But after a certain time, you felt that you are dead.

5. For these liquidations at Majdanek, between 16,500 and 18,000 Jews were
slowly herded into the camp, forced to strip naked, made to lie down in previously dug
slit trenches in groups of ten, and executed by SD commandos using submachine
guns. The Nazis attempted to blare recorded music over loudspeakers to drown out
the gunfire, but camp inmates were aware of what was taking place. Victims about to
be shot lay prostrate on top of the still warm bodies who had just been killed, thus
gradually filling in the trenches during the eleven- to twelve-hour murder process.
Mercy shots were not given to those who had been wounded (account summarized
from Marszalek 1986, 131–34; Browning 1993, 138–42).

28

The Safe Haven of Despair

Late November 1943–July 23 or 24, 1944

ONCE IN PRISON they took us down for a walk. Everyday we had an hour or an hour and a half to be outside. But one day, after I was about two or three weeks in the prison, they put us away in a line, instead of walking . . . always we walked around, and they gave us an order not to talk to each other . . . but in that time, instead of walking, they made a line, and we was standing in form. There came down a whole bunch of Gestapo henchmen, and they was standing across from us. A couple of minutes later, they brought down a German Gestapo man from the prison cell. He was wearing the uniform, and he was a high-ranking officer, like a captain or a lieutenant. They brought down later a Jewish woman, walking like a free person; she was standing, and I didn't know what she is waiting for. We all saw her . . . really a beautiful face, a beautiful figure . . . and a couple of minutes later, they gave a whip to the officer, to his hand. We was standing about a hundred feet or seventy-five feet from the bunch where the Gestapo was standing.

They gave us a command that we should look where the Nazis was standing. They told the officer to whip the woman, to give her some lashes, and looks like he didn't hit her, he refused. Then another took over the whip, another from the Gestapo, and he told her that she should undress herself, and he told the man to watch how beautiful she would look later. She undressed herself, and she was naked. We heard screaming, screaming from the woman, and the sound from the whip. He whipped her, and in a couple of seconds, you didn't recognize her body, her face, everything, the whole body, with her face, was blood.

When she fall down on the ground, they took her away, and the

204

Gestapo man, what he first had the whip in his hand, two Gestapo men took him away separate.

This was the end from the spectacle, from the show-time—they made a show, like a theater play from this. The all bunch from the Gestapo went back, and some of them what they was watching us told us to march, like nothing happened. And later we found out, the Gestapo man what he didn't want to whip her, we found out that this woman was the mistress of the Gestapo man. She was cleaning his apartment, they was together—and the Gestapo accuse him that he is living with a Jewish woman. How much punishment he received, I don't know; I can only say about the woman. I don't know if they whipped her until she was dead or not—the whole ground was with blood from her body. Before she was undressed, looking at her, she was beautiful, and in a couple of seconds, we was standing like we couldn't talk with one another a word.

ML: I think the technique of punishing someone publicly brings more people into servility because it terrorizes the observers all at once, immediately, where the effect of the terror on others isn't as great with torture in private. In that case, the effect of the terror is more gradual as the rumors about it spread, as people disappear, as the climate of fear builds.

JF: Possibly, possibly. It was their system. When they did the hanging with Jewish prisoners on the Lipowa, they always gave a command that we should look where they was hanging. And they was watching the groups from us, and if they caught somebody what he couldn't watch, they went over, and they killed him; they gave him a bullet . . . they always shoot in the neck in the back . . . because he didn't hold his head exactly in the way like the others in the group. That was the system all the time.

———

Some of the people had little electric stoves, very little, and the Polish watchpeople brought some potatoes, other food, and most of the people what we was in the prison had some money—was like a market, buying and selling. If not money, they still had some fur pieces, a woman had a fur coat or a fur jacket; they gave away for the food what the Polish watchman used to bring.[1] The prison food was

1. Prisoners who had been "privately employed" by SS and Gestapo officers were allowed to take some possessions with them to the prison. Those who had been in

not sufficient to live, but there, we was not treated like prisoners. Was like a house arrest—you couldn't go out. The toilets, the men's rooms or the ladies' room was outside the cell. If you want to go out, you knocked on the door, and the watchman had a little opening on the door. He asked you what you want, and you said you want to go out to the men's room or the ladies' room, so he let you out, and when you came back, he let you in. In the bathrooms was running water, so every morning when you went to do the things what a human being is doing, you wash yourself. Once a week or once in two weeks, they took you to a special place in prison to take a hot shower, warm water, so to keep clean was not a big problem in prison for us.

Comparing the conditions to what we had outside, even on the Lipowa—I don't know the conditions too much from the other craftspeople what they was my associates from before the war . . . I knew them, and they knew me . . . but we didn't talk about the conditions what they had before they took them to prison. They didn't have it bad there, because they was almost free. They couldn't go around in the streets to go out, but in the places where they was working for the Gestapo or some was working for the regular army, the watchman took them somewhere to work, and the watchman came back in the evening or in the late afternoon to take them back to their places if they was working outside.

In comparing to outside, what I had, like I said, a little bit better on the Lipowa than the other ones . . . the better thing was: when a German brought a bundle with material, between the material was hidden a piece of ham or a piece of bread or sometimes a whole carton of German cigarettes, and this was like if you have a diamond, a nice piece of jewelry—was some selling and buying, to exchange cigarettes for bread, from bread to cigarettes—but to get cigarettes or a piece a bread more than the rationing was something special. Sometimes I had a little more so I gave away to the nearest, to Klein, to Goot-macher, so we shared the piece of bread together or an apple, two apples sometimes.

The conditions from us in the prison . . . we was like the elite, the chosen. We had a little bit better than the regular prisoners . . . a little bit more food—this was the better thing what we had. And in prison, was more freedom. The Gestapo or the SS didn't watch us always to

labor and concentration camps, including war prisoners, had only the clothing they wore and whatever they might have concealed.

find some excuse to beat us up like they did with other prisoners in the camp. You saw them only when they took us down for an hour a day or a half hour, downstairs on the lot what we was marching around on a circle. When we marched, they gave us an order not to talk from one to another. Was not far away from one to another, so you could whisper something, if the German shouldn't hear or shouldn't see. But when we was inside in the cell, was like house arrest. You felt much better than in the labor camp.

Even with the conditions, we all was thinking that they'll kill us, sooner or later . . . especially in the prison we was not too busy in our trades like we used to be . . . like I used to be in the camp, very busy in the shop with all hundreds of tailors making thousands of uniform jackets. In prison I almost didn't have anything to do, just sitting, sitting—this was very, very bad for me to sit and not to work, and later when I decide with the encouragement from them all to start to work, not to refuse, because they all will be in danger to be killed, I really didn't have too much to do. From time to time they brought some uniforms to fix, trousers, but not really too much, and for me this left me to think only about my family. I couldn't work, so I didn't have the strength, the mind to work. So I sit. Before when I had at least the last couple of people from my nearest, my wife with the little boy, I still was working for something, feeling that maybe, maybe I can save them. And when they was gone, I just sat at the table without feeling, like a robot.

After when I lost everybody, I wanted to survive, but I didn't believe that I would survive. You just received an order, and the thinking was if you'll make the coat and you'll stretch for time, maybe the war will come to an end. Maybe the end will be the next hour, the next day. On the Lipowa we didn't know if this'll be for five or six years, so this was the thinking: so long as they let us live, we'll do what they want us to do to work, and if we work, they won't kill us; they won't finish us off.

But this was not the case. We didn't know that they had a plan— was not the work what they need us for, just to eliminate the Jewish nation. Everybody what was a Jew, even all the Jews what they convert themselves to other nationalities, to German Protestants or Catholics, if their father or grandfather or great-grandfather was a Jew, they took the same people to the same concentration camps to be with the regular Jews what they was not converted, and the end from them was the same thing.

ML: Throughout the whole camp experience, did you fear the SS, the Gestapo, the guards all equally? Were there places, times, and people whom you feared more than others?

JF: In the beginning, I was very fearful. When I went to a higher-rank Nazi guy, I was more fearful than with the others what was not so high in the rank. But fear was always there. But later on, after a year of working for them, and seeing them from almost every day, from the lower ranks to the highest ranks what I knew them, I didn't have no more fear like in the beginning; I figure what will be, will be. If you get used to the devil, you try to stay alive with them, to do what you have to do, to get used to the fear.

ML: How did getting used to the fear influence your attitude about death?

JF: In that time, you didn't fear death. You was afraid before that when you are dying you will suffer. You became almost used to death. When you saw between life and death takes only a couple of seconds, and when you saw somebody, he was standing alive, the Nazi was talking to the Jew, and in a moment he gave him the bullet. He shot him in his neck in the back; took a minute, and he didn't move anymore. I saw this many times, many, many, many like this, standing one second he was alive, and one second he didn't feel anymore—so the death was only *before* the person died. But later, when they took away everybody from me, I didn't fear anymore. I was praying to God not to suffer, the end should be like the other ones—takes a second or two seconds to be shot—but the suffering was the fear. I didn't fear that they'll kill me, because I knew they'll do it anyway.

———

The nearest people what I was talking with them was the Professor David, and later Adja when she became my—when they forced me (I say forced me)—when they made up their mind that we should be together, so we was sitting together like a group talking. We had a lot of time there to think about why they put us together, and the discussion was, on both sides, this was only to use us for their purpose. They used her to combine her with me, because maybe they'll need from me more leather coats or more uniforms or more something else, so she knew that they're using her. She didn't do anything—she was not a dressmaker—she was only saved because her younger sister was the lover from Professor David.

For two-and-a-half months the relationship with Adja was a friendship relationship. Most of the time we both was talking and crying; she was crying about her parents, and I was crying about my whole family, but with the time, she start to cook inside the little room and to serve me some food, to go over closer to me by the table and to talk.

"You can see, Jack, we don't have too long, we'll be the next. We have nothing more to lose, because we lost everything. But we still have a minute or an hour or a day; let's be together—let's love each other. While we're still living, let's do everything what is possible to forget the moment."

She didn't think she would be taken out from prison if I should be taken out. Sometimes we was talking, and she encouraged me that I shouldn't worry so much like I should be killed like the other prisoners.

"Still, the Nazis know that you are Himmler's tailor, and they have an order not to kill you. Why would they save me? They did what they did with us, they forced us against our will to be together here because they had a purpose about a leather coat what you had to finish."

And I tell her, "Don't try to make me feel better . . . why will I be the one? You see, before I was more important, I did some work. Now I don't do even in my trade, so what will save me? What are you talking I'll be saved?"

About five months or five-and-a-half months we was romantically involved . . . not like to be romantically involved all the time. She was pretty—a young woman in the twenties, and I was in the twenties also in that time—but after the romantic scene, we went back to mourn. Most of the time we talked about our families, how they went away . . . almost was an old story. It was about two years when they disappeared, my family[2] or her parents with her sister. You talk all the time, you don't forget . . . after a couple hours you stop talking about this; you start to be very moody, miserable, crying, so we start to pick ourselves up again, to change the atmosphere. We start to have the meal, to eat, some soup she cooked; it was like a small family. We try to change the conversation, but we couldn't get something to talk about, not a book to read, or a paper to have. Sometimes we found in the toilet room a piece of newspaper, from weeks ago or months ago, and we was reading ten times the same article. We receive some news from the outside, but only through the Polish watchpeople from the prison.

2. Frank is referring to his parents, sisters, and their families.

When you ask them something, if they think there are some Jews living outside, they said no; there's no Jews. Was not too much information what you could get, but some of the other Jews what they was there a couple of months longer, they was more acquainted with them, and sometimes they ask them questions, and they tell them news, and they came back and spread the news what they found out. Was nothing really too much to talk about, because we found out with the liquidation from Lipowa that there's no more Jews, except some—you could count them on the fingers. They was hidden by some Polish people; some Poles risked their lives, that I have to say, and they saved some . . . but a very, very, very small amount.

On the 20th or 21st of July, we heard from the Polish watchman that shortly they will liquidate all the Jews from the prison. We was there for nine months, since November, and in July of '44, the Russians start to bomb Lublin, and they bombed the prison.[3] One side of the building they destroyed. The commandant decide that they have to evacuate from there. Some Jews from the three hundred inside the prison, they had still some money hidden . . . some had a gold piece or a diamond hidden in their coats, and they gave it away to the guard to buy them some poison. When the rumors start to go around that they'll liquidate the Jews, there was a young man, the son of Greenwald, a lady's tailor for the Gestapo—he prepared himself poison, and he poisoned himself. From the suicide I see the picture now. We didn't know that he poisoned himself; all of a sudden he was sitting, his hand was on a table, and his head was falling down. The color from his face was blue—not white or red coloring what a face has. Everybody start to yell, "Get me some water, get me some water!" They start to resuscitate him or to help him . . . a couple minutes later, they laid him down on the floor; he was dead. And then the Polish guards took him out a couple hours later.

On July 23 or 24, a Gestapo man came into the cell, he took out thirteen from the twenty-eight or thirty people in the cell, and I was

---

3. From documentary evidence, Hilberg establishes that "on July 20, 1944, BdS Oberführer Bierkamp issued a circular order that inmates of prisons and Jews in armament enterprises were to be evacuated before the arrival of the Red Army. In the event that sudden developments made transport impossible, the victims were to be killed on the spot" (Hilberg 1985, 539–40). It is probable that the Jews in the prison in Lublin would have been subject to this order for evacuation and liquidation.

between the thirteen,[4] and they tell us to march downstairs. When the moment came when we took our jackets, I turn around, and I saw the two daughters from Pesach Rysfeld . . . I saw about two or three with heads down on a table; they poisoned themselves. They took us downstairs, and they kept us for maybe a half or three-quarters of an hour. Downstairs on the lot from the prison was fifty or sixty Jews, and they also took down the rest from our cell. They put them all together; they made like a pyramid—they wired them around with wire so that somebody shouldn't move out from the line.

They put the thirteen in a truck, opened the gates, and they took us out from the prison. From the moment when we left the prison, maybe for a mile or a quarter of a mile, we heard shots. We figured they killed the 287 people.[5] We was riding for hours and hours, and we didn't know where they are taking us.

ML: Even though Professor David had influence on his side originally, why wasn't he taken out from the Lublin prison?

JF: When the Professor David was the commandant from the Lipowa, over the Jews, I don't know if he believed that other Jews will survive, but because he is a German from Germany, and he had the Iron Cross from the First World War, and the Chief from the Gestapo chose him to be the commandant, he had a feeling that he'll survive. But when I met him in prison, later, when we talked, he had the same thoughts as the Polish Jews, that sooner or later they'll finish us off. He couldn't produce anymore for the Nazis. Why should they take him to Radom, and from Radom to Auschwitz and to Natzweiler, and to carry him around on the trains? You need space for somebody what he can produce something. David couldn't produce anymore, or others like David. And another thing—I'm sure they knew already that's it's getting late for them, because the Russians was five or six kilome-

4. The thirteen included Mr. Frank, Abraham Laderman with his wife and two sons, and Leah Dump and her two brothers. Frank cannot remember the names of the others.

5. If there were sixty to eighty people from the first floor who were already taken downstairs, approximately twenty-eight to thirty-two from the second floor, and an unknown number of additional prisoners from the second floor ("the rest from our cell") this would not account for all 287 people. Mr. Frank remembers only glancing at the group when he was taken to the prison yard, so it is possible that he could not make an accurate observation or that the prisoners not accounted for had been taken elsewhere to be transferred or killed.

ters from Lublin. When they took us out from prison, I saw the Russian jeeps with the Russian tanks, almost near the German jeeps with the cars and trucks. The Russians went in this side, and the Germans went on that side, and they just looked at each other. I saw them with mine own eyes, not just me, all the thirteen of us. They kept us longer because they want to use us, to get the last drop of blood out of us, and later they knew we cannot escape; they'll get us when the time comes when they want to finish us off. But so happened they didn't figure out exactly, so it was too late—who knows? I don't know. I was asking many times, why me—why did I survive, but nobody can answer me.

ML: Considering your experiences as a whole—when you're in a camp, whether it's a labor camp or in the Lublin prison, how much do you think a person should be willing to give up and compromise to continue living? How much dignity to feel and be an individual should you be willing to give up; how many around you, if such a price can be expressed, might you be willing to give up so you can continue living?

JF: I don't know how to answer you this kind of question, because it's according to how the others from the other side, what he wants you to give up, what kind of power the other side has. If the other side has a power from a tank or from a hand grenade or from a machine gun, and he wants you to give up your dignity and your manhood, from your personality and from your family and from your children and from your parents—you're thinking that against so a power, you'll do everything what he tells you to do; maybe you'll save yourself and the other people around you. How much to give up is according to what the power is demanding from you.

ML: If the power is to torture and to kill, that power dictates your choice for you. With a power like that, you're willing to give up everything and to compromise everything to continue living.

JF: That's right. You have no other choice. Even when you try—and I tried—to take myself and to put myself in a position to refuse to do, to refuse to carry out an order from a Gestapo commandant from a prison, this was the power I took against me, because I didn't have nothing else to lose. But when you have something to lose, it doesn't matter if the other side is much more powerful than you: you carry out everything; you give away everything what they want you to give. You have no other choice. If you can't find some way to revenge, you do something what you think you can to win something, so you try.

There was many places . . . the Warsaw ghetto, the partisans . . . they was trying. Jews was trying to not to go to the slaughter like most of us did, because we didn't have no other choice. And if you had a choice, you tried to use the choices what you had.

But when you lose everything, the other side, I mean the Gestapo or the SS, they still had a system to bring you to their way. I could refuse an order like that from a commandant from the prison, but looks like I didn't hurt him too much with my refusal. They was prepared again to use their psychology that even when I don't want to do this what they want me to do, they'll find a way. It's just a matter of time—a day, an hour, a week, two days—they found a psychological way to bring you back to the way what they want you to be. If they felt that you want to die, that you are asking that they should kill you, they didn't kill you. They was waiting for a little time longer. They was waiting for when they want to kill you, not when you want to be killed. That's what I found out in that time.

29

The Chicken Coop

July 23 or 24–August 10, 1944

ML: WHEN YOU WERE TAKEN out of the Lublin Prison and then taken to Radom, that was the first time you'd been outside a confined place for several years, or at least in the eight months you had been in the prison, so I wanted to know what the countryside was like when you were going there. I know it's not a long trip.

JF: Was a long trip, even by car. We went with some from the Gestapo, the driver, and one guy with a gun, he watched us. The feeling was we saw the world. In all the months in prison we was sitting inside, except what we went out for an hour, three-quarters of an hour to walk downstairs on the open air. Otherwise we was inside the whole time, twenty-three hours.

ML: Did you know that area between Lublin and Radom very well?

JF: Not very well. About forty, fifty, sixty kilometers I know very well, because was outskirts from Lublin state. Was about 225 kilometers from Lublin to Radom. Took four or five hours to drive by car.

ML: Was it mostly farmland on the way?

JF: Was a lot farmland, yes, but we passed by little towns, between Lublin and Radom. Poland is an agricultural country, more farmers.

ML: Did anything appear different than it had before the war?

JF: No, it was the same. Only the difference was, on the road from time to time you saw some German soldiers. Most of the time you saw German soldiers, not the Gestapo or the SS—they was only with us— otherwise Polish life went on. In my estimation, in what I saw, was like a normal life for them, not for us.

ML: What was Radom before the war?

JF: Radom was more factories than Lublin. They produced there leather goods from animals. They took off the skins. Like here, De-

214

troit with cars, the name from Radom was there they made leather. Lublin was more stores, business, retail.

ML: When you got to Radom, do you remember anybody you met there, who was already there, in those eight days?

JF: When I came to Radom, we was not free. They took us with the car from the prison, under the gun, to the camp. Was there also a labor camp, and I met there about three-thousand Jews. Women with children, with men . . . all families . . . they didn't separate them there. Like I said in the beginning, there was some commandants, leaders from the Gestapo, from the SS, they was managing their camps different. The difference was they didn't separate the families, the women with the children from the men. I met about three-thousand people, but I didn't meet nobody what I know from before the war.

ML: What about people whom you just began speaking to there, to try to find out what things were like or how the camp was run?

JF: When we came, we couldn't . . . they speak to us; they want to find out from where we came, if there are more Jews from where we came, why we are only thirteen. So they want to find out from us. When we asked them about conditions there, they said they don't have so bad there; they don't beat them, just everybody was busy, to do their work. Was all kind of shops, like in Lublin, but they had a better life when they were in camp. There when they liquidate the ghetto—they had a ghetto also in Radom—when they liquidate the private apartments, houses, from the Jews, they took them to this camp, all the families. In Lublin when they liquidate the ghetto, they took away most of the people from Lublin away from Lublin. In the beginning, we didn't know where they took them, but later we found out that they took them to kill them. This was not the way in Radom.

Radom, the camp was a little bit better. Was more administrated by the Jews by themselves. This camp also belonged to the SS, but they didn't bother to go around in the camp from the daytime. I remember in the morning, when the commandant came out after the counting, the Jewish commandant, his name was Friedman, gave over the list that everything is in order, and nobody is absent or missing, then the whole day we didn't see the SS there. Always in the Lipowa you saw walking around the bandits, always they find something . . . one didn't walk straight; one didn't greet them right. Over there was a big difference, but I was not there too long—the Russians start to attack, come nearer to Radom. We had to move.

ML: Can you describe how the camp was laid out?

JF: In the Radom, I don't have a very big idea how the camp was laid out, because I was not too long there, like I said, about seven, eight days. In the seven, eight days, right away, when we came into Radom, we still had our civil clothes what we was wearing. When we came in, they took us in and shaved our heads and gave us stripes uniforms. The couple days what we was there, the thirteen was keeping ourselves together and to talk. This life for them was better, but for us was much worse, because we was already used to the life from Lubliner Prison—they didn't bother us in the cell where we was working in prison, too much, but there in Radom, even the Jewish commandant gave us work to do for outsiders, to carry things, to move furniture from barrack to barrack. They gave us an empty barrack and we had to put in our bunk beds[1] . . . one section was on top, two or three on top of them.

ML: And were the other twelve from the Lublin Prison working on that too?

JF: We was together; we almost had the same type of work. Matter of fact . . . this also came to my mind—if I remind myself I can never forget—I was a little bit on the heavier side. The other ones was very thin, but because all the time what I said I had a little bit better with the food; I had a little bit more food to eat, so comparing to the other ones, I was *fat*. I was not a tall guy, but in the height, I was looking more heavier than the others. Because I looked healthier than the other ones, so the Jewish commandant gave me heavier work to do. For instance, they brought a very big truck with the bunk beds, and this was very, very high, maybe about two stories, or a story high—in my eyes looked like two or three stories high. They told me to climb up on top, with another guy, we both should take a bed and let it down so that the others from the thirteen should catch. The other guy had a ladder to climb up; he took one end of the bed, and that's how we took them down from the truck to the ground. I was on top, and I was scared. I climb up—it took maybe about a half-hour almost. I couldn't get up. I was not on the ladder; I have to climb up in the middle of the truck, to keep myself by the beds, to keep myself safe not to fall down. I never in my life did this kind of work—the work what we did for the days what we was in Radom. And the other

1. These were wooden planks called *Pritschen*.

Radomers was all occupied, in the tailor shops, in the shoemaker shops, all kind of shops, like it was in Lublin.

ML: Did you have any contact with those people at all?

JF: Only the contact was very short. The people what they was there, they start to worry much more than we, because the thirteen, we was already used to be transferred from one place to another, over almost five years, in that time. When they heard the rumors that the Russians are coming nearer to Radom, and the camp will be liquidated, so they didn't know what will happen to them. They was more occupied, so you couldn't talk to them too much . . . I could understand—they still had their families, so they was worrying what'll happen to them.

ML: Did they know that most of you of the thirteen had lost your entire families already?

JF: When we came, they ask us, and we told them.

ML: And did they know that that kind of liquidation and killing was going on?

JF: They already knew; this was in 1944 already. Everybody knew. But like I said, the commandant kept them a little bit better, to give them a better life for the time what they was working, so they was thinking maybe the war will come to an end, and they'll survive. They hope—this was only the one thing what's left for some of us, to hope. For me there was no hope anymore, because I knew, sooner or later, they'll finish us off, all of them, all of us.

ML: Do you think that idea had developed in you already from being moved around so much, as well as your seeing all of these liquidations and narrowing down of ghettos?

JF: Oh sure, they took away everybody systematically. First they took away my parents with the sisters and the brother-in-laws and the children and then a year later, first one boy, then the other boy with my wife, so I saw their system, how they are working. I know exactly, because all the time, I was always with them or near them, to serve them. All the time they called me, every day, four or five times a day, to take their measurements or to take their clothes to fix, so I knew their system. You couldn't even share the thoughts with your friends in the Lipowa at that time. Because what was the talking for? We couldn't escape; we couldn't do anything to improve our situation . . . when you're hungry and you're barefoot, and they take away your nearest, you lose the mood to do something. Even if you would do something, you feel that you are lost. And they prepared your mind until the end. The mind didn't work at all. You didn't have a name. All right, if they need you, they call you by the number. So they prepared you for this, for a long time, years and years.

ML: During this process of losing your identity and losing your will, did you recognize that it was taking place? I know you knew when you were losing members of your family, when you were extremely hungry, when you didn't have anything and you couldn't escape, but as this went on, did you feel that you were becoming more and more lost and depersonalized?

JF: I didn't want to have this feeling, because I knew this wouldn't help me if I'll feel this way. I was trying to go on with life. Even later when I lost everybody, the mind might start to work: "Maybe I'll survive. If there will be somebody, if I will be alive and I will meet some people maybe they will listen to this story about how this was." Even later, after the surviving, most of the people didn't want to listen. "Forget about, forget about"—that was the answer from the people when you want to share your feeling. Later I was feeling I didn't deserve to survive. Why should I be alive and they all should be dead? But when I met people even after the war, they was not so anxious to listen: "We know that you was suffering; try to forget." I think they meant good, but for me, I didn't take this for the right way. I felt that the world should never forget, should never forget in centuries what happened in this time.

ML: At the time you were at Radom, did you think about telling people what happened very often or was that only a small, occasional thought?

JF: No, in that time, I didn't think this way. At that time I was only thinking—I have to say that that's how this was—in that time I was thinking, "Maybe tomorrow. Maybe the next hour, maybe the next week, maybe the war will come to an end," because I saw the Russians was taking over the places around Lublin. We heard rumors, if this was true or not, the Allies, the United States and England, they are bombing Germany; they was near to the end to win the war. My mind in that time was only that maybe the end will come, and I'll survive. And that's what happened. I survived, but through a miracle—they didn't have time to finish me off, to kill me.

ML: At this time, because it was only you and twelve others, did you ever think about the time in the Lublin Prison where you refused to work, and all of them gathered around you and told you that if you refused to work they would all be killed, and it would be on your conscience? Did it ever come to mind that they were killed anyway?

JF: I was sure that this will be the way, what you just asked me. I didn't think this—I was sure that this will be this way, because I went through schemes like that to ask a group if they need shoes or boots and then to give them the boots and kill them. I knew that this is only an excuse to keep the three hundred Jews in prison, to hide them, to take out just thirteen and to kill the rest. What are we so special to them that they'll let us live? It's only that they have their purpose. By me, and also by the others when we was talking, it was only a matter of time. They had maybe some work that we have to finish for them, and then they'll do the same thing what they did with the other ones. We knew this.

ML: Did you ever discuss this in Radom with Laderman, because he was someone who strongly argued for you to go back to work?

JF: We discussed this many times, but he believed more that he'll survive than I did. He said, most of time, "You used to be an optimist, but you became a pessimist, and you don't believe in nothing. But so long as we still have our lives, then there is hope." And I said, "You have it your way, and I am thinking my way." This was the end of the discussion. We didn't agree with this thought.

ML: And many times you had the discussion and it was always the same?

JF: Was almost the same. Was no new ideas to discuss. Every minute, every day was the same miserable life, so you discussed all the time the same thing. Was not like you are free, you take a paper, you read, and every day there is news to talk about. With us, it was every day the same thing.

ML: Can you tell me what Friedman was like, the Jewish commandant?

JF: Friedman . . . if he had to or not, I cannot discuss about this, because I don't know how I would be if I would be in his position. Maybe I will be different. But I cannot accuse him. He was not a murderer, but from time to time he went around with a stick and gave a couple a lashes to run, to run faster to the line to be counted, to prepare for the commandant, because the counting had to be just an hour—to carry out everything on time. He was not an angel, but he was not a murderer either, so take this in between.

ML: How did the other prisoners view him?

JF: They had the same feeling what I am telling you. This was his friends, his people from Radom, but maybe some of them he treated a little bit different . . . by different, I mean instead of hitting them with the stick, he hit them with his mouth, verbally—he was yelling, "Run! Run! Faster! We are late!" Nobody what they was friends with him before the war was friendly with him in the camp anymore.

ML: Since Radom was the first time you had to wear prisoner's stripes, were you afraid that your status as tailor would no longer mean anything?

JF: Yes, at that time I had this feeling. The feeling was "That's the end from my life." It's not just that they gave me the stripes, because over there, in Radom, there was some prisoners from the Jews wearing the stripes uniforms, and some of them the civilian clothes—you was not forced to wear the stripes, but if they gave you, you was wearing them. But you came into an atmosphere, into a place, where you don't know nobody, even when they was Jews—like when you take out from a chicken coop a chicken and you put him in another coop. Did you ever see chickens how they're fighting with the new chicken?

ML: No. What happens?

JF: I saw in life. They take out from a chicken coop one chicken, and they put the chicken with another coop, with another group, and they start to fight. The jealousy between chickens—this was the feeling what I saw sometimes in my life. I remember I was between people what they don't know me, and I don't know them, and that's what they did: they gave me work what they knew is too hard for me. But that was the feeling. In me was not a friendly feeling, but I couldn't help it; I couldn't feel different, because you had to carry out what the Jewish *Kapo* tells you or what the German watchman tells you. The difference was only the Jewish *Kapo* didn't carry a machine gun, but he carried a stick or a whip. I wouldn't say all Jewish *Kapos* was carrying out dirty work; some of them, they talked to the prisoners. Somebody couldn't walk, couldn't march so fast, so the *Kapos* told others what they was nearby that they should help him, to take him under the arms. If the German saw that you couldn't walk, he would come over with the pistol and give you the bullet in your head in the back. So you have some *Kapos* what they tried to help somebody what he was feeling weak.

ML: Where were you, and what were the people around you doing when it was time to evacuate Radom? How were people preparing?

JF: We didn't do nothing; you couldn't prepare nothing. We was just sitting to wait for the order to go out from the barrack. We didn't have nothing to take with us. We didn't have a valise to pack our suits or our shirts.

ML: Were there other Radomers living in your barrack, though?

JF: Yes, they were just sitting with their families.

ML: Did they have possessions to pack up?

JF: Maybe they have, but they didn't take with them anything. They didn't have too much, but maybe somebody had a pair of pants, a pair of extra boots maybe, but they didn't take nothing with them because was a very hot day in August. We didn't know where we will march, but most of us, especially the thirteen from us, we was thinking that we will march to the end, to be shot on the road.

30

"This Is the Last Stop of Your Life"

August 10–15, 1944

WE FOUND OUT THEY ARE TAKING us to Tomaschow-Lubelsky. I remember if somebody couldn't walk, they had a horse and buggy, a little carriage with a horse, and when they pass by a woods, they went in with the men, two or three. We marched further, after a half a mile or a quarter a mile, and we saw the same carriage from the back would be empty, from the people what they took.

Was also a very hot day, and we didn't have no water, and we passed by a pipe with water running through it, so some of them would run out from the line to this little place where the water was, dirty water—who knows! They never stood up; they killed them right away with a machine gun—five or six. And we marched further. Later, I found out, after the liberation, I see the war pictures on the front line, when the soldiers are fighting and some of them are getting killed, they let them lie, and they run with the guns further. The same was with us. They didn't let you look even—*Schnell! Schnell! Schnell!* Some of them was beaten with the gun or with whips, and that's how this was with the march about 150 kilometers.

ML: Did you stop at night for sleep?

JF: Yes, we was sleeping two nights on a field. Around us they concentrate us all together, and around us, with machine guns, was the SS. That time, one from the thirteen, Leah Dump, she escaped.

ML: How did she do that?

JF: She was with her two brothers. She was in the middle, one brother was on this side, one brother on that side, and I was lying near her brother—the all thirteen was together, but so happened I was lying the second from her, and she raised her head. The brothers was sleeping, but I was not sleeping, and she saw that when she raised her

222

head, I moved my head. She decided to escape, and she asked me if I can look around if the SS are not watching. I raised my head, and I didn't see anybody from the SS: looks like they are sleeping too. She crawled out from our line, and I was having my head down to see how she was crawling on her fours, with her hands on her legs. And after a couple of minutes, she disappeared from my eyes' view what I could see anymore, and I didn't know what happened with her. The brothers didn't know. When they woke up, she was not there. They asked me, "Where's my sister? Where's Leah?" I said, "I think she escaped, but I don't know if she's alive or if they caught her, or they killed her." She found out that I am in the United States; a year after the liberation, I received a letter of her that she is in Israel.

ML: When you were on this march, did you encounter or see any Polish peasants who came out from their houses or were near the road?

JF: In that time I didn't. The march was most of the time over rough land, not towns. But I remember one town we passed by, and there was some Polish people what they was standing outside, and on their faces, we saw smiles. They was happy to get rid of us. That's the picture I saw on their faces.

ML: Who do you think was affected the most by the march?

JF: Most of the elderly was affected because they couldn't walk. We went out from Radom—I'm not sure, but that's what I heard—about 2,800 or 2,900 people, with the women and children. We came to Tomaschow, after the 150 kilometers, about 1,700 or 1,800. That means about a 1,000 or 1,100 people was killed on the march.

ML: Do you think a lot of children also couldn't weather the march and died also?

JF: I really don't know, because you didn't look too much behind. You had in your mind yourself, not who was behind or even the next to you. There was four in the line, or five; I can't remember exactly. Nobody cared about the next one, except the women was keeping little kids on their hands, marching with the kids. How many from the women with the children was killed I don't know, because I didn't look behind. Nobody looked behind them.

———

At Tomaschow, they took us to a place on the outskirts where there was a big building—a mill there what they was making yard goods. In the building was pipes on the top from the ceiling and around the walls, very large pipes like machinery, and we saw wide doors to come in. We didn't want to go in because we saw smoke from steam pipes, very, very, very wide ones, like thirty, forty inches the width, with all valves, so we was sure they'll take us in there, and they'll put in gas, and they'll finish us off there, with the women and children. When we came over there, we was in line all the time, but walking; the line didn't keep so straight, so they lined us up. They opened the wide doors, and they said, "You'll stay here."

There was no toilets, was no water, was nothing. The first row from us, when they came and they gave a look, they said, "We don't go in. If you want to kill us, kill us here." The commandant came over—he was an *Oberscharführer;* his name was Heckart—he said, "What are you afraid of? This is not what you think. If we had in our minds to kill you, we would kill you there on the road when you are marching. This is just a building where they made yard goods." After a half-hour or an hour, they had a speech for us, and we decide what's the difference—we'll die this way, or we'll die the other way—so we went in.

Showed out that he was telling the truth. Was a factory from yard goods, from wool what they was making before. They had moved; they cleaned this out empty. All seventeen hundred or eighteen hundred from us went in. But excuse me for the expression, we pissed, and we did all kind of things, unclean things, everybody, on this place. Outside was standing the SS; they closed the doors, and you couldn't go out. There was skylights; there was no windows, and was open so the air should come in. But there was no air at all, you was choking to death almost. The people, every family was together; they made a little place in the side . . . but the stink . . . the air was terrible, terrible.

We was there about two days, and we had no food to eat. When we left from Radom, they gave us some bread what we had with us, but on the march from Radom to Tomaschow, there was no food or water either . . . maybe some from us kept what they had. There some who died here, but nobody looked; nobody knew if they were dead or not. This place was so big; I didn't look what this is from the other end from this place, you know what I mean? You are thirsty, they put you in a filthy place where you don't have a place to urinate and to have your bowel movement; you had to do this behind you— this is even worse than to be hungry, even worse than to be dead. When you're dead you don't feel anymore. Here you feel every moment the filth: you have no air, you can't breathe, and if you're breathing you're breathing in yourself filth. This is the worst thing . . .

I don't know how to express myself . . . there's no expression for this what this was really there. And we was there, this life, this way, for two days, I think, two nights and three days, till they took us to a place where there was a cattle train, and they took us from there to Auschwitz.

I heard about Auschwitz, that they have gas chambers, and they are burning people alive, but that's what I heard from rumors . . . I believed that this is so, but I had not been there. When we came there I found out that this is true what I heard before I came there. When we arrived, there was standing there waiting some *Kapos* with the stripes uniforms, Jews. We asked them, "Where are we?" And they told us, "You are in Auschwitz, and this is the last stop of your life." They greet us with this news: "This is the last stop. You have something with you? Give it to me. Gold, money, diamonds? Give it to me, because this is the last stop."

This didn't affect me at all, because I didn't have nothing more to lose. I lost everything. What I had to lose was only the misery what I went through for the last couple of days, what I described with this life in the mill there, so for me was nothing to think about how what I heard from them will affect me. And from the experience, I knew this life from the camps. The *Kapos* asked this question about gold, valuable things to the general people, when they opened the doors, before we went down from the cattle trains. This was the same in other camps; was also when they transferred you to a new camp, from the other camps in Poland even before Auschwitz. When we came to Radom, they ask you if you have some diamonds, some jewelry; they'll take away anything from you here, so this was nothing. I knew this kind of language, this kind of conversation.

A lot of people lost their consciousness. They was walking like mummies, not like real living people. But I was conscious, I was fully aware of the situation, but when they gave out orders to move, I just moved; I didn't have no control over anything. I just did what I heard—the general order to all of them to step out from the train and to make a line. That's what we all did. In this moment, you don't think; I didn't think, and I don't think that anybody was thinking about something else, only to carry out what they tell you.

After a minute or two from the time when we went out from the train . . . the Gestapo, the SS, I don't know what part of the party it was—they came with dogs, and they surrounded the whole group from the 1,700 or 1,800. We march for maybe about a kilometer or

maybe about a quarter a mile under the guns, and they start to take
away the women with the children from us, to segregate us. The men,
they took us on one side, and the women with the children, they took
on the other side. This was the same thing what I was in Majdanek
when I was there.[1] The same yelling, the same crying, the same begging, the same falling on their knees to keep their children, to cover
themselves on top of the children that they shouldn't take them. They
all went over with the dogs, and they kept back the dogs, and they put
the dogs on them, not to bite them, but near, almost near their bodies—was the same picture what I saw in Majdanek, the same system in
Auschwitz. The same feeling from the people, from the women and
children, the same tragedy what I saw there, I saw in Auschwitz. Was a
repeat, was a continuation, like nothing changed, went on the same
thing.

When they had the women with the children, they took them
away somewhere, and they was keeping us surrounded with machine
guns. They kept us about four or five hours, then they took us away,
and they put us back on the cattle trains. To go inside takes ten minutes, with the whip and with the sticks . . . doesn't take too long to go
in a jump, and whoever was not able to go up—because was no steps
there—we give them the hand to carry them up, to help get them in
the train before they give them a couple of lashes. After an hour or
two, the trains start to move, no more women, no more children. We
was only the men. I don't know if we was about 1,000 or 1,100 men
in that time.

In that moment when I went back to the train, I start to think a
little bit differently than when I left Tomaschow, with the conditions,
with the train what we came to Auschwitz, because already knowing
their way, how they are operating, if they are taking me out from
Auschwitz, I have a chance to live a little bit longer. If I am supposed
to be killed, why are they taking me out from Auschwitz? When they
took me out from Lubliner prison, when they took me out with the
thirteen, we went to a place to live. How long? It doesn't matter, but
to live not to die. In that time in the truck, I heard shots that they
killed the other prisoners from the prison, and I came back to think a
little bit at that moment, that they'll take us to another camp. Now,
on the train from Auschwitz, I was talking to Jack Silberstein, and he
was sitting near me on the floor, so I told him, "I think we'll suffer a

1. To compare impressions, see "The Liquidation of Majdan-Tatarsky," p. 162.

little bit longer before we die." He was listening to me, and he didn't say anything; he was sitting and mourning about his little girl and his wife. They stayed in Auschwitz.

ML: This realization you had that your life was going to be prolonged and that would mean more suffering, how did that realization affect you?

JF: I don't know if this affected me or not. How could this affect me? I didn't have no control over me; somebody was controlling me.

ML: What I meant by "affecting you" was that at many of the previous stops and changes of events before this, I had the feeling that you were ready for it to end, that you had had enough, but then you realized that being taken out from Auschwitz meant it wasn't going to end.

JF: The answer is: from the time when they took away my wife with the older boy, I was looking for an end, but I was looking the whole time after this for an end, and I couldn't get to the end. Like I said, I don't know if my will was to live or I was a coward to kill myself; I didn't even have anything to kill myself with.

ML: At this point when they put you back on the train, was it a twisted, strange frustration that you didn't want to live anymore, but even that couldn't come to be?

JF: No, I didn't think at all anymore. If I have to suffer, I'll suffer till the end will come. The whole time I was thinking "I want to die," but I didn't do nothing to kill myself, so I never thought to kill myself. I was praying that death should come, that when I should go to sleep, I shouldn't get up in the morning, but I never was thinking about committing suicide.

ML: On the train, you didn't feel frustrated that they weren't going to finish everyone off then. Whatever would be, would be.

JF: That's correct, that's correct. The feeling was that this couldn't be worse than this was a couple of hours before or two days before or a day before—couldn't be worse where they are taking me or what they'll do with me. So I didn't think anymore what they'll do. What they'll do, they'll do. There is nothing what I can do to change the situation.

ML: So you experienced no attachment to either life or to death.

JF: That's right, that's correct.

31

—

A Contact from Inside

August 15, 1944–March 25, 1945

WE ARRIVED THE NEXT DAY to a concentration camp in Natzweiler. The regular SS guys went out from their passenger car; they opened the locks from every car, and they let us out. We came to a wide place like in the woods, no houses, just free land. They separate us to three camps: Natzweiler, Vaihingen, and Unterriexingen . . . all belonged to Natzweiler, not far from Stuttgart in Germany.[1] They took my group to the Vaihingen camp, and I saw the camp was not a so a big camp. Was no crematoriums, and we was a little bit relieved from the fear that they won't finish us off there. We was out for almost two days and a night without food and without water. In Natzweiler there was some war prisoners, prisoners from German descent . . . socialists, communists, I don't know what nationalities, a couple hundred. They had already there a kitchen with food, some water—they gave everybody a portion of bread. The day was already over almost. They count us, and they let us into the barracks. Just a bunk bed, no mattresses, no straw sacks, nothing. Everybody received a blanket. The striped jacket what you was wearing, you put under your head, if it was not cold outdoors, for a pillow. This was in all the barracks from all the camps the same conditions.

The next day, six o'clock in the morning, they let us out from the barracks on the outside, and we lined up all of us, and Friedman, the commandant what he was in Radom, he became the same position in Natzweiler. This was also the case from the *Kapos*, they was all the

1. There were more branches of Natzweiler than Mr. Frank mentions. The other branches were Bruttig, Sandhofen, Markirch, Neckarelz, Kochendorf, Hessenthal, Ellwangen, Wasseralfingen, Leonberg, Echterdingen, Gesilingen, Tailfingen, Dormettingen, Bisingen, Dautmergen, Schomberg, and Schorzingen.

same from Radom also—the same system from one camp to another. Matter of fact, what I was talking before about Jack Silberstein, Friedman was his brother-in-law. They was married to two sisters. When we came from Radom to Tomaschow, and in Tomaschow they took us in a cattle train to Auschwitz, they took away both the Friedman's wife, with his children—I don't remember if he had one or two children—and also the wife from Jack Silberstein, with his little girl, four or five years old.

Silberstein had a little bit better in Natzweiler, because Friedman gave him a job, an inside job to give out soap. Everybody receive a piece of soap to keep yourself clean. The piece of soap was maybe about a half-ounce—was like not soap but like a piece of stone—I don't what this soap was made. And the people was mad on the Silberstein because if somebody came in and his soap is gone, he need another piece of soap, Silberstein said he is not allowed to give them. So this was the work.

The main thing, like I said, there was *Kapos* there, and of all the *Kapos,* there was only one what he was like a gangster, like a bandit, like a killer. This was in Natzweiler, but he was from Radom. This was Morgan Kirschanzwig; he was only the one. Actually there was two of them: the other I don't remember his name—I don't remember if he commit suicide. I think the other one commit suicide, and the Morgan Kirschanzwig was beaten to death after the liberation by his people from Radom.

They was cleaning the yard in the camp, after snow,[2] and I saw—at that time they told me also to clean up the snow . . . not only what I saw, but many around me what they was digging, to clean up the snow, they saw. One man, he didn't feel good or something, he didn't dig the shovel too deep, or he didn't do anything, so Kirschanzwig went over, he took out the shovel from his hand, and he hit him with his shovel over his head, and he fell down, and he was dead. But the other ones, they was also the same way . . . the marching from one place to another, always they beat—with a stick or with a leather whip, like the Nazis used the same whips. They find some whip, and they was carrying. They act like this to show the SS or the Gestapo that they carry out very nice the work what they want them to carry out.

———————

2. This event took place in the winter, several months after Mr. Frank arrived in the camp in August.

On the first day at the Natzweiler, eight o'clock, the SS commandant came out, and Friedman went over, and he gave him the report
that he count us, how many we are, everything is in order, and the
Oberscharführer Heckart, the same from Radom, he left. Friedman
had a speech that today we'll take a rest, and the next day, we'll go
outside to work. They are building there an ammunition factory or
an aeroplane factory under the ground. They call this in German a
Bombenstelle, the building underground. They'll take us every morning; there'll be two shifts—in the daytime and in the nighttime. They
start to segregate how many will go out in the daytime, and the other
group on the other side, they will work in the nighttime. And I was
between the group what I had to go to work in the nighttime.

They took us there outside a kilometer or two kilometers from the
camp, what they built there the ammunition factory or the plane factory . . . we didn't know exactly what they are doing there. Looks like
the work went on from before already, for months or for years. They
let us down in an elevator, deep down . . . when I came down, I
looked up to the sky, the sky was only so big like a box of matches, so
deep we was there. They gave me an electric jackhammer, what you
dig granite or asphalt, cement. Was walls from granite—we had to dig
from the walls to take out some parts. The electric hammer was so
heavy I couldn't even lift the hammer. In the place what they let us
down was no watchpeople from the SS, so I was standing a whole
night and not doing nothing. I was shivering; it was cold. Underground it was very, very, very chilly, even in that time in August. In
the morning, they took us up, and they already had there on the
Bombenstelle some food, some coffee with a piece of bread after the
night-work, before they take you back to the camp. They count us
again, and they let us into barracks, and we went to sleep to get ready
for the evening to go back to work. Working for two nights already, I
was thinking, "Now I wouldn't live too long with this," because I was
not used to do this heavy labor. I figure I wouldn't survive. I was
thinking maybe I can do for myself something to save my life, but
what can I do?

When they took me up, because I was a little bit healthier than the
other prisoners, looks like my mind was working better a little bit, the
brains was working better . . . so I figure . . . I was looking for something to improve my situation—maybe there is a way to do another
type of work. There is other work on the night shift there, and I
didn't know how to get to this, because the Jewish commandant

wouldn't do for me anything because I am from Lublin. In the morning, when they took us up with the carriage and the cable from where
we was working, the same time about six o'clock in the morning, a
German in civil clothes, not in a uniform, came over to the group
what they took us up, and he asked, "Who can operate a crane?" I
raised my hand . . . a couple of them raised their hands . . . only the
mind was working how to save your life, if only for a moment! Let
him catch me that I am lying, and *then* he'll punish me, but this moment maybe I'll have a couple of moments better in life.

The German came over and took three of us—and I was between
the three—away from the group, about two hundred or three hundred yards to a big crane. The iron rope was ripped! To go on top, up
to the crane, and take off the old cable, and they'll hand you another
cable, and I should put in a new cable there in the crane! I am a short
guy, and fat too, you know, and you go up the crane, and you go up a
ladder, and from one space to another on the ladder, my short legs
couldn't reach the next one! I was crawling . . . how I did it I don't
know, maybe two or three steps! And the guy who chose us, he was
standing downstairs, and he was looking like I am suffering to go up
. . . there is maybe thirty or forty steps before I get to the top to put
up the cable! And he called me, in German, "Come down!" I said to
myself, "Here's the end!" I came down, took maybe about fifteen
minutes, and he helped me on the last steps.

The other two men what he took, he put them where the crane
took some dirt with little wagons, and one put the dirt in the wagons,
and the other took the wagon to a certain place to empty out, and
then they came back, you follow me? This was their work, and I said I
am a mechanic, a crane mechanic, so he took me to put up the cable.
He said to me, "I see that you didn't tell the truth. You're not a mechanic from cranes. But now tell me the truth, and don't be scared; I
wouldn't do nothing bad to you." I told him the whole true story
about being Himmler's tailor and coming from Lublin, and they put
me to the night shift, and I saw that this is the end of my life, like I
was telling you from before.

He said, "I understand that's the truth what you're telling me.
And I'll help you not to go back to the work what you did before." I
start to thank him, and he said, "Don't thank me so much." I want to
kiss his hands—I don't know what to do—for me this is life and death,
everything, just to do a job that they will not kill you off because you
are too slow or too weak.

"Your work will be: you'll go inside to the crane, inside a little room where the operator sits, and you'll have a big oilcan. You'll always keep the oilcan in your hands, and when a uniform man passes by, you'll go around to openings from the crane, where there is the motor, and you'll try to oil it. This will be your job. And you'll sit only here and watch through the window if a uniformed guy passes by." In an hour or two hours, he brought me a sandwich.

Two days later, he said that he is going on vacation, so I figure again this is the end from this—and I never went back as a mechanic to this type of work.

After the liberation, when I was in Germany, I went back to this place Vaihingen, and I was trying to find this man. I knew his name; he told me his name, but I never wrote it down, or I forgot, and after the war, all the years, I am trying to remember the name to look him up in Germany. Why I was looking for this German is—I found out later that this German was an electrical engineer, and the all *Bombenstelle,* the all place was so tremendously big, with all kind of equipment—he was a head engineer. If something went wrong when he went on vacation, everything was dead. If there was a short somewhere from the electric, they was waiting; there was nobody what they could fix. All the machinery was stopped. I found out later that the Nazis took him as a communist or a socialist. They told him, "If you'll register to be in the party, we won't arrest you." He refused, and he was supposed to be arrested. Why they didn't arrest him was, he had a brother . . . when Hitler was supposed to come to power, was seven people in the Beer Hall Putsch in 1926, preparing to take power, and his brother was one from the seven. The brother, because he is a big wheel, arranged it so they can take him to the regular army, to the *Wehrmacht,* or they will arrest him and send him to a concentration camp. They didn't want to take him to the army, but in a camp, the party will have an eye on him. So this guy what he helped me, managed so that he was an electrical engineer, and he was working on the *Bombenstelle.* Because he helped me, I tried to find him; I went to Vaihingen, and I was asking all kinds of people, and they asked for a name—and I couldn't tell them. I only know what I heard about the brother, but no German knew. At that time, the Germans was interested to do something for a Jew . . . they start to be friendly to Jews in the beginning after the liberation. They want Jews in their homes. A doctor took me in and gave me two rooms on the *Schubertstrasse* in Dachau, after when I moved away from the camp.

After the two days with the engineer from the crane, they take me back to the camp, and again I figure this is the end—what can I do to get out from the night work? I don't know nobody for any special favors for me. Thinking so I fall asleep, and a couple hours passed by, and they took us out to be counted, and the SS commandant came over, waiting that the Jewish commandant should give him the report that everything is correct. The Friedman went over to him and gave him the list that everybody is there, and in a half hour we'll leave to the building where we are working outside. When the *Oberscharführer*, the SS commandant, passed by my line, I walked out from the line, and I start to talk to him, I stretched out and I told him, *"Herr Oberscharführer*, I was the *Schneidermeister* for the *Reichsführer* Himmler, and if this is a possibility, I would appreciate if there is here a tailor shop to do my work for the officers, from the *Deutsches Beherrscherin*,[3] from the people from Germany."

I was stretched out like a soldier, and that moment, I felt that he'll kill me, but what is the difference? I knew that I'll die this way, or I'll die another way—let there be an end from the suffering—and I took a chance. It looks like the idea was not bad, and he called out "Friedman! Take out this prisoner and keep him till we open a *Schneiderie*, a tailor shop, and he'll work for the officers for us." This was the end from the *appel;* they all went out to work, and Friedman sent me into the barracks.

The next day, a *Kapo* came into the barrack, and told me I should go into a barrack where Friedman has the office . . . he has to tell me something: "This afternoon, I'll take you to the commandant, to his office, and he has to talk with you, to make for him something . . . I don't know what." At the time that he should take me, I came into the office from the Nazi commandant, and the Jewish commandant was waiting out in the lobby for me . . . the Heckart told me that he has a friend, outside, a woman friend, and she has some work to have done, so he wants me to go there—and what she'll tell me to do, I'll do.

The next day in the morning after the counting, the SS man called out my name, and he told me he'll take me to the commandant's friend's house. We was walking for maybe a mile or less than a mile, and I came into a private house. Was there a young woman . . . I find out that she was the mistress from the commandant. The guard what he took me over, he left me there on her responsibility. He talked with

3. Literally, "the German rulers."

the woman, and she told him that I'll be ready in a certain time to go back, and he should bring me in the morning again too. He left this house.

The mistress was living in her father's home, and her father was a shoemaker . . . he has his shop there, he still was making shoes there. The woman has a little boy, and they was living with the father because the husband was killed in the war. She gave me some material that I should make a dress for her . . . so she asked me if this table was good, she had a pair of scissors—there was a little machine. I start to work; after working a couple hours, I ask her for some paper to make a pattern, and then I take her measurement. This was about eight o'clock or nine o'clock already. About twelve o'clock she came in and told me that I should stop the work, and I should go in the other room to eat lunch. This was the first time, in years . . . she was sitting by the table with her father and the little boy, and I was sitting by the same table, and they gave me lunch. I didn't have two eggs with a big piece of bread, with a cup of coffee, in years. Looks like this was a different kind of German—the attitude, how they acted toward me was entirely different what I was used to for five years or more. Even with the food, I didn't feel comfortable to sit by the table. Was to me like . . . I don't know how to tell you how the feeling was, but by me, was like I am sitting with the SS. But I made her the dress, and then she prepared more food for me . . . every day, they feed me.

Every day they used to take me out from the camp in the morning, about eight o'clock the watchman left me there, and he came back about half-past four to take me back to the camp. This went on for about three or four weeks . . . I had gained five, six pounds, maybe more from the food what they feed me there. That's why I had the opportunity to survive better, even when later they took me to the hospital in Dachau;[4] maybe that's why. Most of the time, my condition was I was better food-wise, I was better off than the other ones. So I stretched the work—what I could do this in two days, I was working for two weeks.

But in the meantime, I didn't mention this to nobody—I was afraid to mention something like this—her father, the shoemaker, he start to be with me the best friend. The whole time while I was sitting by the table and eating, he talked to me politics, but the whole time, I was sitting and only listening; I didn't open my mouth to say any-

---

4. This incident is recollected in Chapter 32, "The Dachau Shower."

thing. And he said, "I understand you; I understand you very well. I understand you are afraid to talk. But one thing I'll tell you, keep up this way that you should want to live. Any day, or in a short time, the war will be to an end."

Looks like her father was more to not supporting the Germans . . . he believed the Germans lost the war. I didn't trust them; I didn't trust nobody . . . in the time what I know the Germans when I worked for them, I had a couple what they was talking like this, but I never, never opened my mouth, because I knew if I say something, I can be dead. In that time I had my family—so in that time I kept quiet; I was only listening. Even sometimes a German said to me, "What are you—a mute? You can't hear, or you can't talk?"

I said, "I can hear, and that's what I can do." Only to hear, only to listen. But the shoemaker, the father, when he told me I should do everything to try to keep alive—because in a short time I'll be liberated, the Americans and English are very near—this is the first time what I took the risk to ask him one word.

"How do you know to tell me this? Maybe you think that you're telling me this because I am a Jew, and this is the last minute what I can live?"

He said, "No. I heard this on the English radio that we are losing, and we already lost everything." This was in March in 1945. And a couple of days later, they took me with all the prisoners from Vaihingen, Unterriexingen; they took us all to Dachau.

ML: At first you didn't trust the family, and as he told you more of his opinions, you didn't say anything. It sounds like you had to lead a double life, because they were treating you like a person there, but you were still a complete prisoner in a concentration camp. What was this like to go from this house during the day back to the concentration camp at night?

JF: In this moment I took a risk; like I said, I didn't have too much to lose, because I didn't know that the end will be they'll take me to Dachau, and I'll make myself sick, and I'll get taken to a hospital. Even in that time when I asked him this, I was not sure that I'll be alive or I'll survive, but so long before I die, I would like to hear that the end came to the Germans. I believed him when he told me this, because of how he told me this, very quietly; even the daughter was not present, the little boy from five or six years was not in the room. So the way he told me . . . and I knew him already for ten days or two weeks, that they was feeding me, and I was doing something for them

. . . and he talked to me that he hated the lover from his daughter. Like he was talking, he said not pleasant things from the lover from his daughter, but looks like she was a grown-up woman and he couldn't tell her whom she should have for a lover or not. That's what I understood in that time and how I understand this now too.

ML: How do you think she became the lover of the commandant?

JF: I don't know. The father told me that her husband was killed on the Russian front. Because the commandant used to live there, even before the war, looks like a very small town, and they knew each other from before the war maybe . . . I really don't know. But the father-in-law told me the husband had been killed on the Russian front, and from that he was very mad from the death from his son-in-law, with the whole situation . . . they was living somewhere in Germany, and the daughter had to move to his house.

A family affair—this didn't interest me too much. My interest was to listen to what he is telling about the war. But in the meantime when they let me out, I had a couple weeks what I was living like a *mensch,* like a human being, and this gave me health to survive, to live longer. Even when I became sick in Dachau, I was not so like the others sick . . . was one from Radom; I don't know if he is alive or he died in that time in the hospital when they took me in. He was sick from typhus—before they took me, they took him. He was very thin; he couldn't survive. He was like a skeleton.

ML: Were there any close calls at their house where the commandant suddenly showed up, or an SS man?

JF: Nobody called in . . . I don't remember. In the morning, they took me in, and the commandant, he asked me, I think twice or three times, when I'll be finished there. I said she gave me some new work. He said, "That's OK. You do what she is telling you to do." And the SS guy, he's not supposed to leave me there, he's supposed to watch me the whole time.

ML: So what do you think he was doing?

JF: I don't know. He didn't carry out the order—that's what I think. When you send out a watchman with a prisoner, you have to watch him, no? That's what I think. But when we came he was sitting there for fifteen, twenty minutes, and he said he'll be back. And he came back to take me home.

ML: When he came to take you home was he drunk?

JF: No, no. I don't know, but I saw he was walking very straight with his machine gun.

ML: Did you ever have any conversations with him as you walked back and forth?

JF: No, never. We had conversations: "You have a good life there. You are out of the camp." That was the conversation.

ML: Did you share any information you received with the other prisoners back at Natzweiler?

JF: No, no. They knew that I'm going out to work. But also other prisoners went out to work, but not to a lover from commandant.

ML: So you didn't even pass on to them what you learned about the approaching end of the war?

JF: God forbid.

ML: Why do you say "God forbid?"

JF: God forbid if I will tell somebody and he will tell somebody and somebody else will tell again somebody and the whole camp will know, and the *Kapos* will find out, and you'll be dead right away—what are you talking? This I couldn't change. First of all, what will they do? Just to give them a little satisfaction in life? What will they do with what I'll tell them? And I didn't know by myself if this is true what he is telling me. I had to take this for truth.

ML: Why would you have been killed for spreading that rumor?

JF: I don't think this is a smart question what you are asking me why. What do you mean "Why?" You put out rumors against Germany, you will not be killed and you are in a German camp? This is a rumor against Germany—they are losing the war.

ML: It wouldn't have to be passed to the guards; it could be kept among the prisoners.

JF: There are *Kapos* there among the prisoners that are working for the Germans!

ML: And they would report any rumors?

JF: I don't know if they would or not. But you had a right to think this way. I'm sure that others had some secrets too, other secrets maybe from us from the camp. They didn't tell me. Nobody tells somebody else what he knows. And was not too many secrets what you could know. So happened that I was two weeks with a German family.

ML: You described that you gained about five or six pounds at that time, so did the other prisoners notice that you weren't as thin?

JF: They didn't know that I gained five or six pounds. I knew. Like I said, I was always on the heavier side comparing to the other ones, because if I had more, if I was better fed from six months ago or three months ago, I still didn't lose so much weight like the other ones what they was hungry for two years. And from time to time, like I said, I had a little better than the other ones, so I kept up my strength more.

ML: I'm very interested in what you're saying about secrets, because in a book I read about Auschwitz,[5] prisoners would boast to each other about their secret benefactors outside the camp who'd bring them food, or with whom they had connections, and they'd never want to reveal who they were, but they spoke about them with reverence, almost as if they had special help from the outside, and that they were smart enough to organize this. But you're describing complete secrecy, where you never shared anything.

JF: Because this is different what you are telling me. They had a contact with outside. I never had contact with outside. I had no contact with anybody on the Lipowa. I just receive this appreciation from the Nazi, or the doctor from the *Wehrmacht* was satisfied from the garment what I made, so I received as an appreciation a piece of food or other things, but I had no contact with nobody.

ML: This time with the shoemaker was the first contact with the outside . . .

JF: Well, was also not a contact from outside. Was a contact from inside. I didn't make with him no business.[6] He was only talking . . . two weeks . . . he is a living life, so he talked to me. You know what I mean? He talked, but I didn't talk with him. This was only the first time when he told me to keep up . . . he even told me when I finished my work that his daughter will talk with the commandant, her lover, that maybe he can send me into the camp some food, some bread or something. I don't know if they talked or not, but I never, never received any privileges after I finished the work, you know what I mean? This was the end.

When the mistress didn't have no more work for me, they took me back to the camp, and the next day, the commandant made me a

5. Levi's *Survival in Auschwitz* (1986). I refrained from mentioning it by name not because I thought that Mr. Frank wouldn't have heard of it, but because in an earlier conversation, he strongly stated that he didn't have to know what other historical works said, since he had lived in the camps and had daily contact with the decision makers.

6. Frank distinguishes between a fortuitous association with someone that he was assigned to work for and a contact that one might actively pursue for the purpose of trading for food or other goods. The latter was "business" or organizing, and required more active negotiation on the part of the prisoner.

little shop outside where they made the ammunition. On top they had a shop where they made tools for machine guns and other *Waffen*. They took away a little space, was like a walk-in closet. Somebody brought a very small machine, and the Nazi brought me some things to repair and to clean, some uniforms, and he also brought me some women's things to fix. Every day they brought me to the shop, and I was doing the tailoring work for them.

I was there for eight months, from August till March 1945. In March '45, there came an order that they have to liquidate the camp, the branch Vaihingen.[7] The Americans start to bomb around Stuttgart day and night, and the Jewish commandant had a speech for us when they count us, and he said to get ready—we are leaving from there to other camps. From the all, they made three or four groups. Every group went to a different camp—and I went with a group that went to Dachau.

7. This date is in conflict with the history of the camp in Feig's *Hitler's Death Camps: The Sanity of Madness* (1981, 226). Feig reports that the first evacuation convoys began on August 31, 1944, and were concluded by early September 1944, followed by the liberation of the camp by the French First Army on November 23, 1944. According to Frank's certificate of Incarceration and Residence (No. 315355), completed on March 10, 1955, by the Allied High Commission for Germany, International Tracing Service, Frank departed Vaihingen on March 3, 1945. On the certificate, it states that one of the documents relied upon was the KL Natzweiler List of Prisoners. If this information is accurate, the Vaihingen branch would have continued to operate into March 1945, and would not have been liberated in November 1944.

32

The Dachau Shower

March 25–April 4, 1945

I CAN ONLY SAY what I was thinking; I don't know what the other ones had in their minds, but always, when I had to be transferred from one camp to another, always the mind was working that this is the last camp—they'll kill me there, together with all of the other ones. Leaving Natzweiler, we came out in the lot. They count us, and they put us on the line, and we walk maybe about a mile or two miles to a train station, and they took us from there to Dachau. When we came on the front from Dachau, I saw an iron gate with a sign on top: *Arbeit Macht Frei.*[1] The same I saw when I came to Auschwitz for a short time, so was nothing new to me. Arriving here was a little bit more orderly than what was in Auschwitz with the dogs and the separating the women with the children. They only yelled in German . . . the German voices was all the time loud—*"Schnell! Schnell! Schnell!"*—to go out from the cattle cars—but was not like in Poland, when they took us from Tomaschow to Auschwitz.

They took us in to a special field, and they let us into a barrack, and we was there standing waiting what the new orders will be. A Nazi came in, and he said, "This is your new camp, and you'll be here." At that time was no more Jewish commandants . . . nobody was in charge, but was not chaotic at all. We came in, we was sitting, everybody took his place . . . was a little bit chaotic when you came in.

---

1. Usually translated as "Work will set you free," the ironic slogan typifies the conscious practice in the Nazi-camp world of concealing the true nature of things. Although Nazi press releases and instructions for the discharge of prisoners claimed that their hard work and irreproachable conduct had secured their release, everything about the daily routine in the camp demonstrated that work and faultless conduct in no way guaranteed liberation.

Somebody starts to run, wants to have his bunk on the ground; somebody wants the spot above, but after an hour or two hours, we was already quiet, sitting and waiting what'll be next. We didn't know
what'll come next.

We knew that Dachau has a reputation as a killing place. We heard
rumors before that Dachau was the first concentration camp in Germany, not far from Munich, twenty or twenty-five miles away, made
for the German socialists and communists, political prisoners.[2] Later,
they made there crematoriums—in the beginning was no crematoriums there.[3] When we came there, the Germans what they was political
prisoners was communists, socialists, clergy, all kinds . . . most of the
German socialist prisoners was like *Kapos,* they was taking care of the
newcomers—Jewish, French, Czechoslovakian, Gypsies, not only Jews
but other nationalities. In that time Italy was no more an ally with the
Germans, so they took a lot of Italian war prisoners, and they brought
them there to Dachau . . . Italian soldiers in the uniforms.

This was already in 1945. There in Dachau was 32,000 prisoners,
and between them was about 20,000 Jewish prisoners. The German
political prisoners was a little better treated than the other nationalities—that's what they said in that time. Every national group had a
different field, and every field had electrical wire that one group
couldn't mix with the other ones . . . one section was a camp for Jewish prisoners; one was a camp for German political prisoners.

The rumors was, in 1945, that they liquidate the ovens, the crematorium ovens, what they use to burn the bodies so that there
should be no sign that there was crematoriums. The rumors was that

2. Dachau was opened on March 22, 1933, for five-thousand "protective custody" prisoners. Himmler's press announcement made it clear that political prisoners
were to be kept in the camp indefinitely in order to nullify their political opposition.
"All Communist and—where necessary—'Reichsbanner' and Social Democrat functionaries who endanger state security are to be concentrated here, as in the long term it
is not possible to keep individual functionaries in the state prisons without overburden-
ing these prisons, and on the other hand these people cannot be released because attempts have shown that they persist in their efforts to agitate and organize as soon as
they are released" (Distel and Jakusch 1978, 46).

3. The first incinerator was built in 1940. When the camp needed to dispose of
bodies at a faster rate in 1942, four larger incinerators were built (Distel and Jakusch
1978, 173). Each oven could hold seven to eight bodies, which took two hours to
burn. In the final months of the camp, there were so many bodies to be burned and so
little fuel that the ovens couldn't handle them all, and thousands were buried in mass
graves (Berben 1975, 8).

they felt that the end was coming, because the American aeroplanes
. . . you couldn't see them, because they was very, very high, but
sometimes we could see like little flies in the sky, and we heard the
sound from the aeroplanes flying past the camp. Was also a rumor in
that time that Himmler gave out an order that the camp from the
32,000 prisoners should be liquidated, and the liquidation meant that
all around they would put bombs to blow up the camp with the
32,000 people.[4] That's what we heard when I came a day or two later.

I wasn't assigned any work . . . just sitting and waiting and waiting to be killed. Nobody was working. I think to sit and to think was
much worse than to be occupied, no matter what you did, an unpleas-
ant thing or a horrible thing. In prison, you still have friends what you
knew them, so was easier to sit and not do anything, from time to
time you could talk to somebody else. But here you couldn't talk even
with somebody else, because you didn't know this person, you didn't
know what to say.

ML: Were you thinking at that time how to get a better position
or how to get yourself recognized as a tailor?

JF: I was a type . . . I took what I could take without a fight. An
example is when they start to run to take a place in the bunk, and I
was almost the last from this line what I was standing. I took an empty
place, the second on top from the bottom, so I took this place, and I
sit on the place without arguments, and that's it. I knew the situation:
if I would start to argue with another one, and he is hungry, and he is

---

4. In the spring of 1945, prisoners widely circulated rumors about the future of
the camp, but because they didn't have access to newspapers, and radio receivers had
been removed from offices where prisoners worked, they were unable to confirm the
progress of the Allies. After the fall of Buchenwald, Hitler told Himmler that no other
camps should be taken over by the Allies, and at Dachau, authorities debated several
plans to murder all the non-Aryan prisoners: put poison in their soup, have the *Luftwaffe* bomb the camp, or evacuate the prisoners. All of these options had problems,
since some authorities were unwilling to take responsibility for a another mass murder
operation at this late date; the *Luftwaffe* didn't want a massive bombing on its hands;
and there was little time and insufficient transportation to undertake an evacuation.
Some leaders wanted the camp handed off to the Allies, but Himmler remained vehe-
mently opposed to this and called for an evacuation, news of which circulated among
the prisoners on April 26. But by April 28, as disorder reigned and the SS sped up their
preparations to leave, it was clear that there would be no evacuation. A rumor then
spread that there were plans to blow up the crematorium and the gas chamber (the latter had never been put into operation). Several trains of prisoners did leave the camp,
but they never reached their destinations. (Berben 1975, 179–94).

barefoot, and his mind doesn't work like a normal person from a normal time—and I considered myself more normal in my mind than the other ones because for a longer time I had a piece of bread more to eat, so my body, or my brains, could think more. That's what I think, to the point that I shouldn't argue with the other ones, but to let go by some arguments, and I think this helped me a lot to be today alive.

———

At night we was lying one near another, very close, you couldn't turn over, you had to manage to turn over from one side to another. One night, a guy hold his arm over my chest, and I ask him, "Please take off your arm. You are choking me." He didn't want to listen to me. He still kept his hand over my chest near my throat. I was afraid again . . . I didn't know who he was next to me . . . it was dark, the middle of the night, and I couldn't turn over, so I laid the whole night with his arm over my chest.

In the morning the bell was ringing to get up for the counting, and he was still having his hand on my chest. I said, "Now it's daytime. Take off your arm. It's about time to go out."

He didn't move; this guy still had his arm lying on me. I had to get up, so I took away his arm with my hands. I felt his arm and it fell down. I pushed him a little bit, and I found that the guy was dead all night.

ML: In Dachau, when it got to the point where there was very little food, do you think that a person's willingness to help another person depended on how physically strong he was and how hungry the person who needed help was?

JF: In Dachau, was no help. In Dachau, became a different atmosphere than in the other camps, because you had the feeling you would not be there very long—dead or alive—because of the atmosphere of what you saw, the planes passing by, listening to rumors that all the German's cities are bombed, destroyed, so you knew that this is only a matter of a short time. The closeness one from another almost disappeared, maybe because in Dachau, you came to a place what you didn't know the other prisoners. They was concentrated from all over. In Vaihingen, we all came from Radom, so was like a community. Everybody knew each other from Radom, except the twelve what we was from Lublin . . . you follow me? In Dachau, was not this kind of feeling, because everybody was like from one to another a stranger; you didn't know the next one. Maybe was two or three what they knew each other from before, but most of the time they was from other camps.

ML: So the condition of being a slave among other slaves, starving among other starving people, doesn't at all create a feeling of unity?

JF: No. Everybody was for himself. Was even a time in Dachau, one stole the portion of bread from somebody else. Was not near me, I was only listening to it. I only saw a guy crying, and I passed by him. I asked, "Why is he crying? Is he sick?" They tell me somebody stole his portion of bread what he was hiding under his head in the night-time, what he didn't eat . . . he left for the next day a piece of bread more, so they stole, and he was crying . . . I can't say too much about this. But that's what you heard there. I didn't hear this kind of stealing in Vaihingen.

ML: Did the sound of the planes and the rumors about liberation also influence how people treated each other?

JF: Was not too much discussion from one to another, because you only discuss with somebody if you know him. If you didn't know him, you have nothing to discuss with him. In that time you didn't think about politics, you didn't think about clothes to wear. The only thinking what you think, or to talk about, was about bread and about soup. That was only the one subject what you could discuss in that time.

ML: And were those pointless subjects for discussion because you only had so much—you only were going to get so much, and there were only a few ways *maybe* to get more? So at a certain point there was nothing more to say about that either?

JF: That's right. Was very little to say. If there was a discussion— "Did you receive a potato in your soup today?"—this was the discussion that one asked another. "Did you receive a little bit larger portion of bread when they cut this bread?" In Dachau, this was only the conversation what you had . . . I didn't take part in this discussion because, like I said before, in this condition people was very, very nervous, and if you didn't answer the right answer, he was insulted, or he would hit you. I never was hit; I stood on the side . . . there was a couple like me—I was not only the one.

ML: Did you gravitate towards that way of acting naturally, or had you observed this many times and decided consciously, "I'm going to avoid these discussions"?

JF: I observed this consciously, and I decide to stay away, because I knew this wouldn't help me too much to get involved more in this, because first of all I was a stranger . . . even in Vaihingen the Jews all came from Radom. I was a stranger from Lublin. I couldn't talk too much to complain, even when I had something to complain about, a smaller portion of bread if it so happened that I received. I knew this wouldn't help me. Would only help me to get hit or to insult somebody more.

ML: Did the other prisoners in Dachau look at each other as things and not as humans? Did they look at them as inanimate things who had something that they wanted, or did they look at them like animate things that unfairly, randomly got something more than they had?

JF: You can say that. One didn't look at the other as human. Especially near the end. The humanity disappeared; you didn't look at the other guy as a human being.

ML: When you say, "Near the end . . ."

JF: What I mean "the end" was the feeling from everybody was it wouldn't take too long, because hearing the anti-aeroplane guns from the ground, the noise from the ground to shoot them down, you heard this every day and every night, especially in the beginning of April 1945. This was almost near the end, a couple of weeks later.

ML: Was this situation where humanity was almost completely gone worse near the end because people didn't think that artillery fire foreshadowed their liberation—it represented that the Germans would liquidate the camp before it could be liberated?

JF: We didn't think what kind of liberation this would be. To be liberated as people or to be liberated with death, if we'll be dead in that time. This was a liberation too, not to go on anymore . . . what kind of life was this? If people still had their minds, if they still could think, they was thinking "What kind of life is this?" They was talking about liberation, but to be liberated not entirely meant to survive. A lot of us was praying that a bomb should fall down from the American plane and to be killed from the American bombs.

ML: So the belief that you would have a better life after being released from the camp was completely crushed because liberation didn't necessarily mean being released from the camp. It could have meant death, or it could have meant an end to suffering.

JF: Correct. The liberation was to be an end from suffering. I felt there's no more to hope for something. It's no more to hope for something that I would gain from being alive, because nobody's with me anymore. I lost everything. I was waiting that this should come to an end, and if this has to be death . . . and I knew there was many times where I was almost dead, so that's it. In my mind, no world ex-

isted anymore, and what I mean "the world," I mean the Jewish
world—that there's nobody from us Jews alive anymore. Going from
one place to another, every time there was less and less and less. So
here we are; we went almost a couple thousand miles from Poland to
Germany, around Germany, and from one camp to another, every
time there was less Jews. In my mind, there was nobody from us, from
the Jewish population, existing anymore. What is the use to be one
person—if I will survive, how will I be able to live by myself in so a
wide world? What kind of life would be for me? But in the same time,
there was a mind, if the war will come to an end, and I'll survive, I
would like to see how the world looks without Jews.

I don't know . . . in one way, I wanted this to come to an end. If
this means death, it wouldn't bother me too much; but in the same
way, maybe there was another way that it should come to an end and
I'll survive.

———

A couple of days later—again I don't remember exactly how many
days—a Nazi came in, one from the Gestapo. No Germans used to
come in the barracks where we was living. Most of the time they was
afraid to come and mix with us—because typhus fever or some other
diseases were there. One day in the afternoon, almost the evening,
they came in, and they said we should prepare ourselves for tomorrow.
Tomorrow we will have to go and take a bath, a shower.

We didn't think too much; sitting on the bunks, we didn't know
what to think. But when I heard this that they are taking us to take a
bath, again my brains start to work. I start to think, "What in the hell
are they talking about us to go out to take a shower? They are not
mixing with us. What do they care if we are dirty or not?" I knew they
always have schemes when they have to kill some of us—and I decide I
wouldn't go to take a shower.

A couple of minutes later, my mind starts to think—I said I
wouldn't go, and what can I do not to go? The only thing I can do is
to kill myself, and this never occurred to me all the time to commit suicide. So this mind passed by. This was in the evening, and I couldn't
sleep a whole night, thinking what'll be the next day tomorrow.

Tomorrow about afternoon, the time came that we lined up to
go and take a bath, a shower there, and I was thinking again, "That's
the end."

They took us in a place where there was many showers. We undressed ourselves, and all of us was thinking they'd put in gas, and they'll gas us.

But instead of gas there came out warm, warm water, and everybody received a piece of soap, and we washed ourselves. This shower took until about five, six o'clock, and after we had our supper, the little water, the soup, maybe about half-past six.

This was in April of '45. After the shower what we took, we was heavily perspiring from the hot water. I didn't have a shower for a long time, and I was thinking—I was very, very pleased—"After so long a time, what'll be the end? At least I am clean. I had a shower; I washed myself."

After the shower, they told us that the next day, we'll get transferred to another camp—we had to be clean to go to there. So I figure out, when we went home, what the shower meant, and what will be tomorrow, and I decide I am not going anymore to other camps.

After we got dressed, they took us back, the same Gestapo guy, without a machine gun, without nothing, because inside camp they was not afraid we will escape. He took us back to our barrack at about eight or nine o'clock in the evening. Everybody went in, and I went in too. I was trying to be the last in the group, from this barrack. I was trying to keep myself behind all of them so they should go in first. Everybody went in, and I was standing in a little hall before an arch what led to the room with the beds. I didn't go in—like I said, I was trying to be the last one.

When I saw everybody was there, the light went out, or somebody shut out the electrical light, and the whole barrack was dark. In the hall, there was the door to the outside, where on this side you could open it to see the view of the camp. And when everybody was there in their places, I took off my jacket, what I was wearing with the prisoner's stripes, and I opened one door a little bit to crack it. The weather was very bad at that time—snowing, raining, windy, in April very terrible, miserable weather. After the shower what we had bathed under hot water, I figure if I would stay by the open door, so windy and so miserable, that I'll get a cold, and I'll have temperature.

To commit suicide I didn't have anything, I didn't know how to do it, so I figure maybe this—if I can catch a cold, to stay near the door . . . I was all perspiring, nude, completely nude by an open door, and the wind was—you could hear the sound from the wind like thunderstorms, the weather was miserable. In this little hall there was an alarm clock what the barrack leader used to call out when it was six o'clock in the morning. I was standing from nine o'clock, ten o'clock, eleven o'clock, twelve o'clock, and nothing happened to me.

At five minutes before one, I start to shiver, and I said to myself, "Oh"—I didn't remind myself to call his name, God, for a long time—I say, "Oh God! I am liberated now."

This was my liberation—to get sick. If I start to shiver, I will get temperature after this—maybe. Maybe this will save me, because I heard rumors when we came to Dachau that the crematoriums were liquidated; they don't burn there. So maybe I'll survive, or I'll die from a disease that I'll catch then.

At that time I didn't feel that I had a temperature because I was still shivering. I was standing for maybe ten or fifteen minutes, I couldn't stand anymore on my feet, and I went to my piece of space, was there empty waiting for me. I put on my pants with the jacket, and I lie down on the *pritsch*, on the bunk.

Lying there for five or ten minutes, I start to feel that I have temperature. The guy what was already there what I squeezed in next to him, he felt I came to lie down there. After a couple of minutes he said, "Move away a little bit! You are burning me up! You are hot! You are burning like hell!"—*"Du brens we ein fajar!"* in Yiddish. He told me this, and I was very happy. In that time, I'm sure I had a 103 or 104 temperature.

I was lying there a couple hours until the day came. Everybody got dressed, everybody got down, I couldn't get down from the *pritsch*. I felt dizzy . . . I couldn't stay on mine feet. But before when we came home from the shower, the German Nazi, the Gestapo guy, he called out that the next day in the morning a doctor will come here, and if somebody is sick, they can go over to the doctor and report that they are sick.

ML: And be admitted to the hospital?

JF: We don't know. He just said if somebody is feeling that he is sick, he should announce himself when he gets up in the morning and go over to the doctor. I was waiting for this moment for when the morning should come. Seven or seven-thirty, a gentleman with civilian clothes came in, with two uniformed Gestapo guys, and the German in the civil clothes, he was the doctor. We all was standing in line, and he looked over the beginning of the barrack to the end in the sleeping hall, and he called out, "If somebody from here is sick, he should raise his hand."

There was two or three, and I was among them so I raised my

hand. In the little hall was standing a table with a chair, like a desk, and he was sitting on the chair, and we should go over to the doctor so he should examine us.

One went over. The doctor took his pulse, and he said he should go back to the line.

The other guy went over. The same thing.

I was the third one, and I saw the other guys. They raised their arms that they are sick, and I am sure that they are sick, but the doctor tells them to go back to the line. In the same moment before I went over to the doctor, my mind was working: it looks like my scheme wouldn't work.

The other guy went back to his line, and the doctor called me over. He took my pulse, and he said I should go to the side, on the other side of the hall, not back to the line. I start to feel a little bit relieved. I didn't know if they'll take me to finish me off, because many from before, when you was sick, they killed you. But in that moment, it didn't matter. Here or there, so long as I don't have to go to another camp.

He was talking, he said something to the two Gestapo guys. The two Gestapo guys called over some *Kapos*, some of the German political prisoners, and he told them something—I didn't know what he said, but then in a minute or two, the two guys came over with a little wagon. They took me under my arms, and they stretched me out on this wagon, and they carried me away from the barrack, from the all other ones. I didn't know where they are taking me—again, if they are taking me to be killed or to the hospital, I didn't know where. But it turns out they took me to a hospital.

A nurse came over, and she took me over to a bed. It was a bed with a white sheet, with a mattress, with a pillow. Since two years I didn't have this. I said, "God—I don't care what will be the next moment, but for one night, to lie in a bed like this, is worth all of this life in the camp."

The next day, in the morning, I was there lying a whole day; they took me to a place where they gave me a sponge bath with alcohol, and a nurse took me back to my bed—like a regular hospital, like a regular patient!

ML: The reason you made yourself sick was simply not to be transferred to another camp. It wasn't because you thought you would live if you were taken to a hospital; it wasn't because you were certain they would kill you because you were sick.

JF: Correct.

ML: So it goes back to what we talked about before: you didn't care whether you lived or died, just to not have to move again.

JF: But at the same time, when I said that I only cared about not going to another camp, I was sure—not always I was right—but I was sure what they'll do in another camp: they'll finish us off. So I cannot say. I said to myself that I shouldn't go to another camp, but I was not sure if this was the reason or the reason was not to get killed in the other camp. Do you follow me what I mean?

ML: No . . . explain it again.

JF: I said I would not go to another camp because I am tired—I don't want to live anymore to go to another camp—but at the same time, I knew in the other camp will come out something from the schemes what the Germans had. They'll kill them, but not always do they kill them. If this was this way, or only not to go to another camp, I cannot explain whether I was thinking this way or the other way.

ML: So you can't explain what you were thinking: if it was because you didn't want to live anymore or because you knew they were going to kill everyone. Instead, you decided to try to do something in which the outcome was uncertain. You didn't know whether they would kill you because you were sick or put you in a hospital.

JF: In that time, I was thinking I had more a chance to live than to die. When I came to Dachau, I heard rumors that they liquidated all the crematoriums, and they weren't killing anymore because they don't want to have witnesses or someone to see what they did. So the mind was, "I don't know where they are taking me," but in the same time the mind was thinking, "I have more a chance to live than to die."

ML: Maybe this wasn't true at Dachau, but from reading about Auschwitz and Majdanek, I was led to believe that people who were sick or weak were killed. Yet I also read that sometimes people tried to get into the hospital because there was more food, a better place to sleep, and it was warmer, but I would have thought if they were really closing down the camp and destroying everything, it would be dangerous to go to the hospital.

JF: Until Dachau, no prisoner from a concentration camp where I was . . . the Nazis never took in a Jewish prisoner to a hospital. If you became sick, you get shot, or you get burned in the crematorium. Even sick people between us, when somebody between us became sick they went to work in order to say they are not sick, because if they say

Liberated prisoners and American journalists view about 200 corpses of prisoners at Dachau on May 4, 1945. The total death count at Dachau between 1933–1945 was 31,591 people. *U.S. Army photograph. Courtesy of the National Archives and Records Administration, Washington, D.C.*

they are sick, they will be killed. In that time it was too late; there was no more camps. Poland was occupied from the Russians already. Yugoslavia, Latvia, Lithuania, Vilna—there was no more camps there. So was only some camps in Germany. In Germany, already many camps the American Army liberated. And the Germans knew already it is too late—the Americans, they are bombing day and night . . . the Nazis was busy to destroy the evidence—not to kill. So they took you into the hospital: if the Americans will come in, the Nazis can show that they was taking in the prisoners, even the Jewish prisoners, into the hospitals.

When they took me to the hospital, there was still over two thousand Jews in the barracks where I was located . . . was five or six barracks . . . over two thousand Jews from all over Europe, from France, from Italy, from Greece, from Turkey, all put together.[5] But the same time when I decide that this was only the one way to get rid of the suffering anymore, when they took me to the hospital, they took out the whole two thousand Jews outside Dachau to kill them. Later I heard, when I survived, they took out the two thousand and they killed about three or four hundred . . . they haven't got time to kill all the two thousand, so they tell them to go back to the camp.

About two or three miles from the camp they took them out. They brought them back to Dachau, and the watch-guys, the SS, with machine guns, start to run away, to hide themselves. After a couple of days later, there came down parachuters to the camp from the air, from the American planes. After when the Americans occupied the camp, they discovered the mass grave.

5. There were 67,665 prisoners altogether in the camp on April 26, 1945; the two largest categories of prisoners were the politicals, numbering 43,344, and the Jews, numbering 22,100. The largest groups by nationality were Poles, Russians, Hungarians, Germans (including Austrians, since they were considered citizens of the Reich), French, Italians, Lithuanians, Czechs and Slovenes (Berben 1975, 213 and 221).

33

The Remains

I HAD A PAIR OF SHOES, but I was wearing these shoes for almost five years. Everybody who was transferred to another camp, they used to take away their clothes and give them new stripes uniforms, and the prisoners who had pairs of shoes that are not comfortable or ripped apart would exchange the shoes or the stripes uniforms what they was ripped. But in all the camps where I went, I never asked them for a change. In my boots, I had a Longenes golden watch hidden in the hard part of the high heel. Also I had there a two-and-a-half carat white-blue diamond, but the diamond I sold in Dachau about two days before they took us to the shower.

There was a Polish prisoner . . . for eight ounces of bread. I said I had a white-blue diamond . . . it was black market—through the electric wires . . . but I couldn't come with him to a conclusion on the deal. He wants first that I should throw over the diamond, because one didn't trust the other, and I want him to throw over this piece of bread first. But he said no. We talked Polish, and he said, "I give you my word that after you throw over the diamond, you'll get your bread." I didn't have no other choice—I was very hungry . . . I don't know what happened with my ration of bread what I was receiving every day—and I felt that if I wouldn't have this piece of bread, I will die, and the diamond I cannot eat. So I took a chance and I throw over the diamond to him, and he throws over this piece of bread. This finished the deal.

I ate this piece of bread the day before the shower. Two days later, they took me to the hospital, and a couple days later the American army came in, and I was liberated. You couldn't have the shoes behind

253

Jacob and Dora Frank. Photo taken in
Lublin, Poland, on February 2, 1940.
Courtesy of Jacob Frank.

your head under the pillow, and I kept the shoes under the mattress.
The nurse didn't know where the shoes are.

I still have the watch, and I'll take it out and show it to you. I
carried the watch for over fifty years. I don't know if it's working or
not; I keep this for a souvenir. This was a watch for my sixth wedding
anniversary—I received this from my wife. The value from the watch
or from the diamond was not important—only to have something to
remember.

I made some pictures in 1940 when we still was living in the
ghetto and I used to go to work to the labor camp. I had three pictures: one picture from me and my wife, and one picture from each
boy. I was figuring out how to hide them. In that time, I still could
carry my pictures in my pocket. Later, when I saw the times getting
worse, I was very much interested to keep these safe—maybe I'll survive, and if they wouldn't survive, I'll have a picture to remind me, to
see them.

I went into the saddler shop on the Lipowa, and I told the man what he was the head from the shop, "I have some leather; maybe you can make me a wallet. I have three pictures what I want to preserve."

He made me the wallet from leather left over from the leather coats what I made for the Nazis; even the color I remember, gray, very soft leather. He made me a wallet by hand, and it was really a beautiful wallet.

When the time was getting worse, I took the three pictures, I put them in the wallet, and I hide them in my shoulder pads from my jacket what I was wearing. In that time I still was wearing my suit, civil clothes.

When they liquidate all the camps, and they took away my wife with the little boy and then the older boy, everybody was dead in that time, so I was glad that I did something that I'll have the pictures. The Nazis made me believe that I'll survive because they needed to use me, so I figure maybe they won't have time to finish me off. But from Lublin Prison, they took me to Radom, and there we had to change the clothes. I always had with me a needle, with some thread; always I was carrying with me if my clothes should get ripped. When they tell us to leave our clothes there, and they took us in for a shower, they tell us to put our clothes on benches. Before I went in to take a shower, I ripped apart the lining from the shoulders, and I took out from the shoulder pads the wallet with the three pictures. I put this under the clothes what I had.

After the shower, they shaved us, and then we have to bring our clothes with us to go in a warehouse, was maybe two hundred feet, to receive our new uniforms, the stripes. In the stripes uniform was no pocket and I didn't have a place where to hide the wallet with the pictures. I had a striped shirt and I put on this shirt with the pants—they didn't give us belts, no nothing. I couldn't sew on; I didn't have anymore the needle with the thread.

When we came into the barrack where we will stay, I was keeping the two shoulder pads on the waistline with the pants on—that's how we was sleeping, with the pants on, with our clothes. We didn't have no underwear to change or pajamas.

I was hiding for a day and night the shoulder pads. The next day in the morning they called us out, and they count us. I saw some from Radom what they was there for a long time, for years, so I asked somebody maybe he can get me a needle with some thread.

"My pants are ripped apart," is what I told him.

He said, "I'll take care." A couple of hours later, he brought me a needle with some thread, and I sewed on the shoulder pads into the shoulders from the striped jacket.

I kept the shoulder pads with the jacket. In many camps . . . from there I went to Tomaschow, from Tomaschow they took us to Auschwitz, and Auschwitz we stood only one day, and they took away the women with the children, and they took us from Auschwitz . . . only the men—the women with the children they took away to the crematorium. From Auschwitz they put us on cattle trains, and they took us from there to Natzweiler.

By the gates from Natzweiler when they let us in, I saw a big basket and was a sign hanging in German, that everybody what they have some papers or documents or pictures, should throw everything in this basket. If they'll find by somebody any piece of paper what this is written, doesn't matter what this is written there, they'll be shot right away on this place. All the prisoners what I could see around me, what they have some documents or pictures or papers, they throw in the basket. I risked my life because the pictures was sewed in the shoulder pads in the jacket, and I was wearing the jacket. I passed by the line, and I went into the barrack—they didn't search us.

I kept the pictures till when I was liberated. But unfortunately in the time when I was here in the United States, I moved from one place to another. At first, we lived with an aunt and uncle from my second wife, and then the uncle bought a house, and he gave us a five-room apartment. From the moving I lost the pictures from the children. The picture from my first wife, that's what is left from all from sixty-four people from my family: my father, mother, six sisters, their husbands, their children, my wife, and two kids. That's what is left from all of this.

34

The Reversal

Late April 1945 [1]

WHEN THE PARATROOPERS CAME down and they occupied Dachau, I was lying in bed, and in that room where I was in the hospital was about thirtysome patients, thirty beds—most of them was very sick with typhus. Some of them, the nurses had to feed them, with water or something, I don't know. By me was a little table, also like in a hospital; was some water there and they asked me if I want, and I said I can drink by myself, so looks like I was not so sick like the other ones.

I heard a noise outside, but inside was like before—nothing. Of all the thirty patients I was only the one to raise my head a little bit from my bed. All the patients, they are lying like dead. When I turned around, I saw the next patient to me was a face what I know him, he was in Radom—he was with me in the camp. They took him to the hospital before they took me . . . he didn't have to go to the shower when they took me—you remember this story? He was there for I don't know how long . . . three or four or five or six days. His first name was Moishe—I don't remember the other name—and I said, "Moishe, something is going on. I hear a noise, shooting outside."

The noises went around, and I was standing by the glass doors or the windows to look out . . . I didn't know what happened.

I talked to him, and he couldn't understand what I am talking to him because he is very sick. In fifteen minutes or twenty minutes, I saw a couple of guys, soldiers, came in with masks, their whole bodies was with mud, dirt, very dirty. I raised my head a little bit higher, and I saw the guys was wearing uniforms . . . they looked to me different

1. Possibly April 29, when thousands were liberated (Berben 1975, 194).

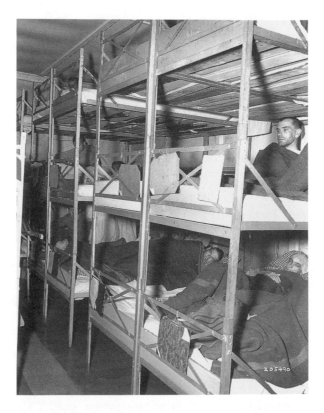

The hospital at Dachau, which had three tiers of bunks. Frank (not pictured) was in a Dachau hospital just before the camp was liberated. This photo was taken by the U.S. Seventh Army on May 1, 1945. *Courtesy of the National Archives and Records Administration, Washington, D.C.*

than the German uniforms. One guy came over near this bed, not very close, but away, and he talked to me. I didn't understand a word of English, so I didn't know what he is saying. He start to talk to me German . . . looks like the Army sent over soldiers what they was from German descent what they can speak German too. But how he talked to me German was not the German what I learned in the almost six years in the camps . . . was some words like Jewish, was like a Jewish-German, like Yiddish. When I heard the couple of words what sounds like Yiddish, I ask him in Yiddish, "Are you are a Yid?"

He said, "Yes. I am a Yid. You are a Yid?"

I said, *"Yoi, ich bin a Yid."*

And he talks to me German, a German-Yiddish, and I talk to him Yiddish maybe about ten minutes or fifteen minutes . . . looked to me like a very long time, and I couldn't keep my head up too long, so I put my hands under my back to support my body. He ask me how long I am here, and I tell him the story what you have here, how this was two days or three days ago when they want to take us to have a shower, and I became sick, so they took me to the hospital. I didn't tell him that I undressed myself, you know, to catch a cold or something.

He said to me, "You lie down, and I'll be back to talk to you." The other guys was busy in the hospital room, attending the other patients, but they saw that he is standing and talking to me for a longer time. He went back to the comrades, the soldiers, and looks like he told them the story from me.

They all went out; I laid down to take a nap, and then he came back and told me, "You are liberated. I am a Yid from America."

He is a Jew from the United States; he is a soldier in the army: "You are liberated; you are free."

He start to talk to me very friendly, that was the feeling. The conversation went for a long time—he told me all kind of words . . . I felt that I was like I was just born again, this feeling, a grown man that I just was born. So much joy with so much—I didn't have no food, nothing to be so happy, but the happiness when he told me that I am free, that he is an American.

He said, "You lie down; take it easy"—like the Americans say "Take it easy." About an hour or an hour and a half, he came back with two soldiers and one woman, a nurse . . . the French Army was with them. They took me out in a field bed in like an ambulance, and they took me away two miles or three miles to a military hospital. Two nurses start to give me a bath, a sponge bath with some alcohol to make me clean, and they gave me a new shirt, and then the captain came in to visit me and said, "How do you feel? You look different now."

I was there in this hospital maybe about ten days, and the next day they start to feed me with food . . . a matter of fact, a doctor came over, and he told them in German not to feed me too much, because a lot of the prisoners, I found out later, they was falling like the flies dead from the food what the soldiers start to throw them, to give them. It was too much food for them . . . a lot of them died from this.

ML: Was that because the food was contaminated?

JF: No, no, was too much food. Their stomachs was like holes. They couldn't digest the food. It was good food, delicious food. But a lot of them died, from . . . what do you call this? From diarrhea, from dysentery.

———————

They gave me an American uniform, a pair of trousers with a shirt. In that time it was already spring; it was warm, so I went around with a pair of American military shoes. I start to go around almost the whole camp in Dachau. It was barracks, and from the electrical wiring they disconnected the electricity from the wiring, and they opened from one field to another—before, everything was closed. Was there all kind of nationalities, not only Jewish, was over thirty-two thousand people. Everybody went around looking, wandering. My barrack was Barrack 9, so I went to see my barrack; then I went to the entrance from the camp.

Was iron gates there . . . I still remember the sign *"Arbeit Macht Frei."* I was reading this maybe a thousand times, just one word, *"Frei, Frei, Frei."* I didn't see the other word, I didn't want to see the other word, *"Arbeit"* but over and over I read the sign like a crazy nut. Some of the prisoners passed by and saw I was saying over and over: *"Frei, Frei, Frei."*

ML: Because you were so exhausted and starved up to the time when you were in the hospital, and you described that before you made yourself sick, you wanted everything to end, whether you were freed or whether you died, I was surprised to hear that when the American paratrooper came in and said you were free, you felt that upwelling of joy.

JF: Didn't I answer you this question? Everything what I said before, everything disappeared in one moment. When I heard these words, "You are free; I am from America; you can do anything and everything what you like. Nobody will hurt you here, and we'll take care of you"—with this couple of words in a broken Yiddish, was like between German and Yiddish, but I could understand every word, and he repeated himself maybe twice or three times, and he asked me if I understand, and I said, "Yes"—from this moment, the whole thing what I was thinking before, I didn't remember nothing at all what I went through. Everything disappeared.

Another thing . . . I will take a rest after this because it makes me a little bit tired just to remember this kind of happiness.

Two photos of Frank with other survivors, taken in the Dachau concentration camp three to four months after the liberation. Frank has a check over his head in both photos. The man wearing the dark military uniform and tie was the American captain who found Frank in the Dachau hospital. *Courtesy of Jacob Frank.*

When I start to live like a real human being, the same American
. . . the rank by the way, later I found out when he was dressed different, not in the field outfit, he was in the rank a captain . . . he talked
to me about houses outside the camp. The camp was with a wall all
around, and outside was little houses, with two floors, each with an
apartment. Officers from the camp and their families was living there,
what they supervised the other watchpeople from the camp. After a
certain time, eight or ten days, I was completely back to my health like
before. The captain came in, and he said, "I have a room for you,
what this was before from the SS, what he was living there when he
was off duty." This was a very large room with a toilet, with a bed,
with all facilities. Was for me like a castle there. "Temporarily you'll
stay here," and I received special food from the army, good food. Like
I said, I start to feel that I am newborn. In this room, I was living
there not too long, two weeks, I think.

All SS, all Nazis, they all was under arrest, under the watch from the
Americans—they took over the whole camp, and the MPs was standing
outside and inside the gates. The captain, he has an office outside the
camp, and he came in after a couple of weeks, and he told me he talked
with the general and told him the whole story that I made a leather coat
for Himmler; I was the tailor from the big Nazis from Poland, and I tell
him the whole story what I went through in my life in Poland.

He said, "There is an empty house where a Nazi general was living, and now he escaped. I spoke with the American general, and he
agreed. By the way," he asked me, "if you should move in there and if
you will be established there, would you like to make a uniform for
the American general?"

I went out with him from the camp, and he showed me the apartment in this house. Was on the second floor; there was six rooms
there. There was hanging paintings on the wall, Rembrandts, other
world painters. Today, when I see so a painting, I'm sure this was
worth millions of dollars. Everything what was there was robbed from
all the museums from Europe. The Nazi general ran away, left everything. Everything was electric, with push buttons—I didn't see something like this until a year later, in the United States. China, furniture,
light fixtures. I would never be able to live in so a luxury, what this
house was, and he told me, "This is your home."

Two or three hours later, a soldier came up with packages, all kind
of food, with biscuits, even a bottle with liqueur, chocolates, cigarettes.

"And if you need something, over there is my office; you come in just to tell me what you need."

"I have everything what I need. What I'll do with this everything?"

"Take it easy, and you enjoy yourself," like you say in English.

After five or six days, he came up, and he tell me the story again about what he was talking with the general, and the general ask if I would like to make a uniform for him. And I said, "How? I don't have no machines."

He said, "Don't worry about this. You don't have to do anything. We have Nazi tailors, machines. We'll bring you up, you tell me how many machines you need and how many tailors you want to have to the fitting room. You don't have to do anything, only to show them how to sew. You speak German to tell them what to do, and they will do the work.

I said, "I'm very happy to do this."

The next day, there was two machines and five Germans with an MP—he didn't have the machine gun like the Nazis used to take us for a march, but he had his rifle on his shoulders, and he brought up five Nazis.

ML: Did you know them?

JF: No, I didn't know them. The four was tailors, and one was to clean the apartment. They came with a little truck, and they brought up the machines, and they took away one room from the six rooms, and they made there a table with the machines, with chairs. "They'll come everyday, and you tell me what time you want to have them there." They came everyday, and the captain brought me the material, and he took me to the general to take a measurement—again, like the old times, I am taking a measurement from the general, like what I used to take from the general from the Nazis. But this measurement was a different feeling in my body, in my heart, with love, with satisfaction, and with thankfulness. They gave me a pass to the officer's casino to eat there, and I was living there, and in a week or in ten days, I brought the uniform down to the general, and he tried it on, and he said in English, and the captain translated it for me in a German-Yiddish that the general says that it's no wonder that Himmler let me live, because of my work what I am doing. Came back all my talent what I had before the war, and I put in this uniform.

When I brought in this uniform, the general asked me how much he has to pay me, and I said, like you say here, "This is on the house."

He said, "No way. This is not our system. You was working. . . ."

I said, "I didn't work. The Germans was working."

"Never mind," he said. "You tell me how much should I pay you."

I didn't want to take money, but he gave me some money—I don't remember how much. When I came to the United States, I came with $310 what I kept, not just from what he paid me, but from other work . . . I made something for the captain's wife what they paid me; I made for another officer. So all together, I accumulate. Over there, I didn't spend no money; I had everything for free. You know, in that time, $310, today the value would be much, much more. This was in 1945.

ML: What was it like to supervise those German tailors?

JF: Well, to supervise, I just tell them what to do in the work. They was good tailors—as a matter of fact, they know their trade very well. When I told them what to do, they carry out exactly what I told them. They didn't say anything, but for one word what they had for me: "*Jawohl* and *Jawohl* and *Jawohl*"—this was the whole time. I didn't make for them any trouble, because when I start to go out from the hospital to take a walk, after the liberation, I saw a lot of the Jewish prisoners, now they was free; a lot of them start to take revenge on the SS, on the Nazis. They killed them with a pipe of iron over their heads, or over their neck, or over their back. They killed a lot of them. And the American soldiers, they looked away. But after two or three days, there came out in an order in English and in German that no prisoner, no ex-prisoner, is allowed to hurt any German, because we have now a different system, not to do what the Germans did. It has to be law and order, and they don't let them hurt them. The Jews what they survived, some of them what they felt a little bit stronger, they want to take revenge, and they didn't let them—a lot of them was a little bit unpleased with this order. But they carried out what they had to, because they was already used to carrying out orders.

35

———

The Mob

THERE WAS A COUPLE HUNDRED Jewish women from Bergen-Belsen what they was liberated by the English army—I don't know how many hundreds, but was a lot of Jewish women what they was there in the camp. Jack Silberstein [1] received two rooms in Dachau for his sister-in-law and for other two women—one was an older woman in the late fifties, or sixty years old I think, and she was the "mother" from the two girls . . . they called her "mother." Jack Silberstein visited his sister-in-law in Bergen-Belsen, and when he came into the room with her they start to talk; they cry, they laugh:

"You are here, and you have nobody, except I survived. I have two rooms in the Dachau camp. How's about to go with me to Dachau? I have there a friend, Jacob Frank—the American Army gave him a luxurious apartment. He has five or six rooms, and he's by himself. I'll talk with him—maybe he'll give us a room or two rooms, and we'll move in with him there."

She was listening to him, and she said, "I would be willing to go with you, but there's one thing what I have to tell you. I have a girl-friend what I was with her all the time in Auschwitz, and then later they send us to Plazow, to the camp near Krakow"—I think this was before they send them to Auschwitz.

She told him that she will go with him, but only if he can take her friend who was together with her in all the concentration camps, in Auschwitz, in Bergen-Belsen. Without her, she would not go.

---

1. Jack Silberstein first appeared in Chapter 30, " 'This Is the Last Stop of Your Life.' " His wife and daughter were killed in Auschwitz.

265

He said, "The Volkswagen is very small. There's only space for one person, not two."

She said that she's sorry; she wouldn't go.

The end was that Jack Silberstein should try to take her and her friend to Dachau some other way. It took him about ten or twelve days to come back to Dachau, and she was with her friend from the *lager*, in the room what the American Army gave him.

By the way, when Jack Silberstein came home, he found out that two sisters from him survived in other camps, and they brought them over to Dachau and told them their brother is alive, and he has a room in the concentration camp where he was before a prisoner. So was there already four women, and he was one man.

In a month or five weeks, Jack Silberstein went to the city Dachau. The camp was about five miles from the city, and he found an apartment from a German doctor. In that time, the Germans was very polite, and they was very glad to take in a Jewish family. The apartment was four rooms, and he and the four women moved in. In another three weeks, after almost two months from leaving the camp, Jack came up to me in my apartment. I took in two friends what I was together with them in the concentration camps, and also two older women what they was living in the camp in a very small room. I had such a big apartment for myself, so everybody had a room for themselves. It was a little bit more pleasant to be with somebody, not by ourselves.

But a few weeks later, Jack came up, and he said he has something to tell me and to ask me something. I said, "Alright, I'm listening." He said he's getting married to his sister-in-law, but she doesn't have anything to wear to the wedding. Maybe I can make for her something.

I said, "OK, this is no problem," because I had some material left from what the American officers gave me to make slacks and uniforms. It was beige material, and I made for her a suit for the wedding.

She married him, and by the time I made for her the suit, she asked me, "Jack, I have something to ask you, but please don't refuse me. You made a suit for me, how's about to make a suit for my friend Deana?"

I said, "Here I'm not a tailor, just for the American officers." She start to persuade me, and I made for her friend also a suit. Her friend Deana, she became my wife a couple months later.

We started living together in this house, already as husband and wife. After three our four days, my wife told me, "You have a lot of guys what you was with them before in Vaihingen or in other camps; they survived, and they are in the Dachau camp. Let's take a walk—maybe you can find a nice guy that my friend Adja shouldn't be by herself, so maybe she'll have a friend."

I said, "OK, we can try." We went into the camp, and we find there a guy named Brik, what I knew him . . . I didn't know his way of life, how he was before he came to Dachau, because he was in a different labor camp somewhere. I didn't even know if the labor camp still exists, but was a big labor camp there, a couple of thousand Jews, and he and some others, maybe about forty or sixty, survived from this camp. They was liberated, also by the Americans. They brought them to a *lager* what the name was Feldafing, not far from Dachau, about fifty or sixty miles; I don't know exactly. The *lager* Feldafing was under the jurisdiction of the Jewish community, especially from New York—I think the name was Joint and the Hias. They supplied the food and clothing and the other things what everybody needs. Was also there some women survivors from Plazow, where Göth was the commandant.[2] They brought all the Jewish survivors from all the labor camps and all the concentration camps to the camp Feldafing, and was there a synagogue with a Jewish rabbi. They start to carry on with a Jewish life, with the conditions what was there. It was not like before the war, not so bad. A family had a separate corner somewhere with little houses, with little tents . . . I don't know how this was; I never was there. I just heard they was very satisfied after so a hell what everybody went through.

We introduced them; we start to talk, and the Brik start to talk with Adja, my wife's friend from Radom. But after a couple of days, came out a *melding,* a poster, in the *lager* in Feldafing, that there was a trial from the head Nazis from the Dachau concentration camp, and they would send them to death by hanging.[3] I think it was about three or four of them. Everybody from the Jewish prisoners want to see this to have a little revenge for all the torturing, for all the dead families what they lost. The Hias with the Joint, they supplied the trucks for the transportation to the concentration camp Dachau, to see how they hang the Nazis.

2. See Chapter 16, "The Maven," for a story about Göth before he became commandant.

3. Forty-two SS men, a Nazi doctor, and a camp commandant were tried by an American tribunal in November and December 1945. Thirty-six were sentenced to death by hanging (Berben 1975, 200).

I was in the house with my wife . . . all of a sudden, we hear a noise from downstairs, through the window. Somebody is running. I look out from the window, I see the Brik, the friend what we introduced him to the friend from my wife, and he is running to my house, to my apartment, and when he came near the house, he saw me through the window and he called me, "Jack, save my life, save my life! Let me in!"

I didn't know what this is going on, so I opened the door; I ran down the stairs, and he ran up, and I locked the door. There was maybe about twenty or thirty from the survivors, and one finds out that I live upstairs, and they call out my name: "Mr. Frank! We want you to give up Brik. We know that you are hiding him in your house. We have nothing against you, but he was a *Kapo* in the camp in Budzyn"—he was head of the shoemaker shop there.

"He was a *Kapo,* and through him a lot of our friends was tortured from beating there."

In the apartment where I lived, you could go out from the window and get to a little roof what you could stay outside the apartment. Do you follow me? A little ledge. When they called me to give him up, I told him to run out through the window and to hide himself there. They told me he was a *Kapo,* but still, he is in my house; I knew that they'll kill him, so I said that he is not here. And in that time my wife was already pregnant with my daughter, and I was afraid for her too. There was twenty or thirty, and I locked the doors, and they say that if I wouldn't give him up, they'll knock down the door, and they'll come in. Like I said, I was afraid for my wife, but I opened the door, and I said, "This is wife." All the stairs was occupied; they let her through. She went out from the building, and she crossed the street . . . was about 150 or 200 feet. She went out to the street, and she was calling the Americans for help.

In a couple of seconds or a minute or two, help came in, and the MP or the American police took him out from my apartment—they saved him not to be hurt by the mob, and they took him into the camp.

After the police came, I went down from the apartment to where my wife was waiting by the police station. The same time what I was not in the house, the mob demolished the apartment, all the furniture, everything was broken. The pictures they didn't touch, but there was a lot of material for the Americans what I had to make suits, the uniforms. They took everything in trucks—there was two trucks with them that brought them to the camp. They was so busy with this guy that they didn't attend the hanging what they came for. In the meantime, they hang four or five Nazis. When I came back, the whole apartment I didn't recognize—was in shambles; it was destroyed. The tables with the chairs . . . most of them was demolished.

I came down . . . I don't think this story is very important . . . I came down to ask them, "Why did you demolish my apartment?"

There was one standing on the truck, and he said, "This is Mr. Frank; he is from Lublin. Don't you remember from Radom what we went with him to Tomaschow? This is Mr. Frank."

When they heard that I am Jack Frank, everybody start to dig out the all bundles what they robbed from the apartment, and they brought back everything what they could. This was the story what I said I didn't want to have taped even.

ML: Did you ever see any of those people later?

JF: No . . . this was not important so much for me, because after the all luxury what I was telling you, I decide not to live there, even with the all things what I need. Being there and to look out through the windows and to look out how the Germans—the SS was now prisoners—when they walked out from the camp and to see the picture from the concentration camp where I was before, I couldn't live with this memory from before, so I decide to leave this whole luxurious thing what we had in this apartment and to go and look in the city.

Me and my wife went to the city and looked around, and found an apartment by a doctor there, and he gave us three rooms. This life, day and night, we start to always talk about the past, what happened with our families, but now we start a new life. We tried to forget, but who can forget what we went through? But life is very strong, and we start to live more or less like a normal couple before the war. My wife was pregnant, and when I found out, I start to think in my mind I didn't want to have a child on the German soil, and I start to talk with the Americans what I was working for them—the captain became a good friend of mine. Maybe there is a way to go to the United States; maybe he can talk to the general or some other way.

He told me he'll try, and he'll let me know. Later I went into the office, and I talked to him, and he said the army can't do anything, but if I have somebody in the United States then they can sponsor me.

I didn't have nobody in this world. Everybody was dead. Before I left Poland, I knew I don't have nobody. But my wife says she has an uncle, her father's brother . . . before the war, he used to communicate with them, but after almost six years, she doesn't remember the address—also he changed his name. He used to be Razhitsky, and when they used to receive the correspondence from him, there was a different name, and she doesn't remember the change.

I told this story to the captain, and after a certain time, the captain came up to the apartment across from the camp, and he told me he talked with an adjutant, a major who works under the General from the Third Army, and he is going on vacation to the United States. He gave him the old name Razhitsky; maybe he can find out something. After five or six weeks, he said he looked around in the telephone books for the name Razhitsky, and he called all of them, and he found a name that is her uncle. He changed the name to Rose, and he lives in College Point, New York. He went over to him . . . I think the major was from Pennsylvania . . . and he told my wife's uncle the story. If he will sign some papers, there's a possibility we can come to the United States. He signed, and almost to the year we came on a military ship.

The uncle with his wife came to the ship, and they took us to their home, a private house they owned, and we was there a couple months. Two weeks later, I received a job as an assistant designer with a nice salary. Living there in the uncle's house, they gave us a room; my wife was already in the seventh month—knowing my wife will soon have the baby, living with the uncle and aunt, this will be very uncomfortable. This was a beautiful home she had, and in the end, she start to talk with her husband . . . they didn't have any children, and she didn't want to spoil the beauty from her house with a little baby. So the uncle bought a two-family house, and he gave us a five-room apartment, and about two months later our daughter was born, and we start to live like human beings again.

I had a beautiful job with a nice salary, designing ladies' suits and coats. After about five or six months, I saved almost $4,000. In that time, everything was cheap, and I was making over $1,000 a month, and in that time we paid the uncle $45 a month rent for the four rooms. Food was very cheap, so I saved. All of a sudden, I start to feel sick . . . I don't know if this was too much responsibility from the work what I was doing, because I was very good on my job. The designing put a lot of responsibility on my shoulders. I start to go to doctors; I start to lose weight, I couldn't sleep, and when I eat, I threw up, so with one word, the whole good time what I was feeling start to change for worse. I couldn't carry out anymore the work what I'm supposed to do, and the doctor couldn't find out what was wrong with me. He sent me to a medical center in the Bronx. A lot of doctors start to examine me with all kind of X-rays, and they came to a conclusion that all GIs and displaced persons, they all are complaining about the same sickness . . . they call this a nervous stomach, and I have to stop work and take some medication what they prescribe and to take it easy. If I wouldn't do this way, I'll have a serious sickness. I stopped working, so I had to break the contract for three years what I had with this firm. They released me because of the doctor's report that I cannot work, and I have to give up my job.

After a month or six weeks, I start to feel a little better, and that took me about two-and-a-half months. I start to eat a little bit more; I start to gain weight, but going around I already had a child to support. We didn't want to bother the uncle and aunt, because I still had some money what I saved from the six months what I was working, so I was trying to think about something to do with myself. There's no way to sit and to do nothing, because the dollars will disappear and I didn't feel I should take from her family what they brought us over.

The aunt took my wife to Flushing for shopping, and she took her to a Jewish butcher to buy kosher meat. My wife told the story to the butcher about the job what I had, how I made a nice salary, but then I got sick, and maybe I should go into business, but we don't know where to go, what to do, because we've only been here for a short time. The butcher's wife said she owned the building and said she had an empty store—if this is all like I said that I am a good craftsman and I want to go into business, she would rent me this store and would recommend me to customers buying meat there. My wife came home; she told me the story, and I said, "Let's go right away to Flushing and see the store."

I rented the store, and I took out almost $4,000 from the bank what I saved up, and I left $200 in the bank. I decorated the windows; I painted the store; I bought a machine, a table, press-irons, and fixed it up so the back was the shop and the front was the showroom. But I was sitting for twelve or thirteen weeks, and nobody came in. I went out and yelled I am King Solomon; I am the best tailor, but when nobody knows you . . . so here I spent the money, and I didn't make a dollar. I owed the landlord a month's rent, and I didn't have the money—in that time, I paid $110 a month for the store. The landlord came in and said that I shouldn't worry; she wouldn't evict me; they'll give me some work to do for her five children. She'll try to talk with the women what they are buying the kosher meat.

A couple days later, a woman came in to buy some meat, and she start to talk with her. She didn't need a suit, but for pity, she talked her into going into me and ordering something. She said she saw a suit in a window of London-Paris on Madison Avenue and she'd like a copy made.

I said, "No problem. I'll give a look and make one of the same style and same material." This was a grey flannel suit. She took me in her Cadillac convertible to New York, and I looked at the suit in the window, and in the back was also a window, so I could see the suit from the back and front. I went downtown, I bought some material, and I made for her the suit.

She loved the suit, and she asked me how much she should pay, and I tell her, "I don't know the prices here. What you feel to pay me, I'll be satisfied." She told me she bought a suit at Fisher Brothers, and she paid $110. Because this suit is much better made, handmade, and fits her so beautifully, she'll pay me $125. In that time in 1946, $125 was a lot of money. Her name was Wallach, and she was the president from the Hadassah.

36

The Consequences of the Gela Later

JF: YOU ARE GOING HOME SATURDAY . . . I didn't want to tell you this, but from the time when we start to make this, to write about everything, 75 percent of the time from the night, from all nights, I am living through this everything again. The dreams are not horrible . . . last night I had a dream about my father. I remember in the beginning when I became the head from the tailor shop, and I start to organize the tailors to work with me, and then we received the *Verpflegung* cards, the rationing cards to get food for the families. If you didn't have so a card you couldn't buy food except maybe on the black market, what was ten times as high—this was in the beginning. Later was no black market at all.

Was in 1940 they start to catch Jews with beards on the street and to make fun from them and to cut them with scissors or rip them with their hands. My father had a little beard—not a very, very big one. He used to cut his beard every week, a little bit. He was a very religious man, Talmudic.

When I saw what they are doing with the people what they catch them on the street with a beard, I told my father, "How's about to shave off your beard, because you are endangering yourself if you go out." Even he didn't go too far, he went from the house to the synagogue to make the morning prayers or the evening prayers, but you never know when a Nazi will pass by, and he'll cut you.

But he said he'll never do this.

"Don't talk with me anymore about this. Never mention this because I'll never do this."

Alright!

So with the time, I asked the commandant from the labor camp—the commandant in that time was Riedel—if I can take my father into the shop. I told him, "I have some relatives what they are very good

273

tailors." My father was not a tailor . . . he made hats from fur what the very religious Jews wear—but I tell him he is a tailor. Riedel agreed, "Yes, we need more tailors."

I took my father with one brother-in-law . . . he was a musician . . . so happened he was a very, very good one, an artist—he played the flute. He had four children, three sons and one girl, and all three boys—one was eighteen or nineteen, the others was sixteen and fourteen, and the girl was twelve—they all was playing instruments. Was a whole orchestra in my brother-in-law's house. They was very fine boys, and also this girl . . . her name was Pearl. And I took them all on the Lipowa to be with me. They was not tailors, but I arranged with Langfeld, the Nazi what he was above me in the tailor shop, that they'll do the cleaning or to hand over the bundles to the operators on the machines what they was sewing the uniforms. Also my father had work there . . . I was a little bit relieved that I have them all with me together.

But once, I don't know the situation exactly, my father went out to the toilet. Riedel saw him, and he didn't like his beard. He called him over, and he asked him who he is—he didn't know. When I said, "Can I bring over my father?" he didn't see him, he didn't have his picture to know that he is my father. My father told him, "My son is the head from the tailor shop."

Riedel said, "If you want to work here, you cannot work here with a beard. You have to cut off your beard."

In the evening—in that time we still was allowed to go home to our homes; we still was with our families . . . this was very early in 1940—my father came in; he told me the story. I start to talk with my father about the beard to cut off . . . because the Yiddish book says you shouldn't shave, but there is not there written that you cannot with a pair of scissors cut your beard off—just not with a razor.

"You don't have to raze off with a razor, but you can cut off with a pair of scissors that should be very close to your skin."

He said, "I won't do this."

I told him, "Dad, better a Jew without a beard, than a beard without a Jew."

He said, "You know how to give the right expression, my son, but this is not about the beard. Now he sees the beard bothers him. Later this'll bother him that I am too old," and he was not an old man in that time, fifty years old, forty-nine I think.

He decide that he wouldn't go anymore there. I couldn't sell him this kind of thing, that he should cut off his beard. The end was he resigned from going to the Lipowa to work, and he was in the house until about a year later in 1942 when they liquidate, and they all went together. The boys and the girls even, my brother-in-law's and my sister's children what I said they was playing all the instruments; they want to all be together, and they went all together. I never saw them again.

So in the dream I had yesterday night, I was fighting with my father about the beard. When I woke up, I couldn't remember the whole dream, but I tried; I didn't want to fall asleep so I remember just this what I am telling you—I was fighting with him that he should take off his beard, and he was telling me, "This is not just the beard what they'll take off. Later will be something else."

ML: Do you interpret his answer as meaning "It's useless to shave off my beard, because they'll only keep me alive here temporarily?" Or is he saying, "As a Jew I refuse to shave off my beard?"

JF: I don't know in his mind what this was, but I figured out that he knew in his mind . . . he was smarter than I was, or than I am now, and he knew this is the end from the Jews. He was more mature in life, he knew there is no way to escape. If you feel bad where you are, you can move somewhere else. In Poland in that time, even if you move somewhere, if you escape somewhere, the Polish guy will catch you and give you over to the Germans. There's nowhere to escape.

When you talked to him, he was a very religious man, and I was brought up in a very religious home . . . but seeing what is going on, I ask him, "Where is God? Where *is* God? You said we have a God here upstairs, and he is watching what is going on down on the earth, and he doesn't do anything?"

And he said, "My son, don't ask this kind of questions."

ML: Was that in the dream, or you actually asked him that?

JF: No, I ask him when I came home from work with him.

ML: Do you think he said not to ask that question because it was challenging his faith?

JF: Yes. In that time, the religious Jew said, "You cannot ask questions." I found out that today the Jew, even the rabbis, have to question God if you feel something, if you have a question to ask. In that time, when I was a little boy, I couldn't ask this question, because this was a sin to ask so a question. So, "God wants it this way." And another thing, the religious Jew had an excuse for why this is happening . . . the other Jew has done something what he shouldn't do—he doesn't put on the prayer shawl in the morning; he doesn't put on the *tefillin,* he doesn't do what the Jewish law says; he doesn't eat Kosher meat. He does all kind of things, so that is the punishment.

But I cannot see that I have to be punished for what the other guy is doing, what he is not doing the right thing. But in that time, you couldn't see it that way.

ML: I think that kind of explanation for the Holocaust—retribution and punishment—is a justification for deeply rooted historical events. Those people are seeking an answer, but they're inventing a reason. I can't see the defense in taking so tenuous a concept as some kind of cosmic deity or force, the creator of the universe and the giver of the law, and justifying the legal actions against the Jews, ghettoization, mass killing.

JF: What everybody is doing, that's what they do in the name of God. The Germans did in the name of God too. On their buckles was written "God is with us," but Hitler was their God. Even if you want to go into the biblical times, when God told Moses that he cannot go into Israel, to the Jewish land, and he chose his general Joshua, and Joshua was a very mean general. He went into Canaan, and he gave an order to his army, "Everybody, men, women, children, animals, everybody has to be killed, has to be liquidated." This was also in the name of God. God told him to kill. But the difference between Joshua and Hitler was—Joshua gave an order to the army, if you give an order to the Canaanites, the population there, and they will abide the order, you don't have to kill them. But Hitler didn't give you any way to escape death. The same with the Spanish Inquisition—people what they convert to Catholicism, they could escape death. They could escape being burned. But everybody is doing what they are doing in the name of God.

ML: At the time when you were the leader of the shop on the Lipowa, was your father still continuing to study the *Talmud* every night?

JF: Yes. On the contrary, he was even more religious. He prayed even longer. And I'll tell you something: you asked me if my father in that time was more religious or less religious. When we was liberated in Dachau, 90 percent or 99 percent of us what we survived—was about seventeen hundred or eighteen hundred from all of Europe—the first thing what we did, we opened a synagogue. We took over a little house from the Germans; we found a *Sefer Torah,* what the Germans saved or from the Joint Distribution Committee in the United

States . . . the first thing what we did, instead to take revenge on the Germans, we opened a synagogue to pray to God.

ML: Did the synagogue in Dachau serve a religious tradition, or was it to show thanks to God for the liberation?

JF: The synagogue is the Jewish tradition, no?

ML: I could see setting up a synagogue to continue the Jewish customs, but maybe many of the people there no longer believed or were uncertain in their faith.

JF: There are many what they believed even more. There was many between us what they was free of the Jewish way of life, and they became very religious after the war. Very religious. I had a man working for me here in the United States, a survivor, what he survived in Dachau with a son. I started to be busy in my shop; I put an ad in the Jewish paper that I need some help. A man showed up, and he said he was a tailor; he was a survivor, and he was looking for a job. I said, "OK, let's see what you can do." He knew his business; he was working, and in the evening, before it became dark, he asked me if I will allow him, he likes to go in the side, out from the showroom . . . he wants to make his evening prayer. You call this *mincha*. I said, "Sure, go ahead." He took off time, and he said the time what he is taking off he'll work a little bit longer. I said, "It's OK. Don't worry about it." That's what he did every day.

After working a couple of months . . . I had the shop one block from where we used to live . . . so my wife brought in lunch for me. When my business was just in the beginning, and there was only one helper, so she brought in lunch for him too. He refused; he didn't want to eat because he was not sure if this was Kosher. And I didn't blame him for this.

But after a couple of months, when he was working, I ask him, "I was more religious than you are, what I can see, and now I am not a Kosher *Yid*, and I don't even make the prayer every day, in the evening." And I tell him the cause. I ask him, "Was you all your life this way, when you was a youngster?"

He said, "No." He didn't know from *Yiddishkeit* at all.

"So what made you do this kind of thing, now to be so religious, not even to want to taste the lunch what my wife brought for you?"

Then he told me the story. In Dachau, he had a son about seventeen years old. He survived, and after the liberation, about twenty or thirty miles from Dachau, the army had a baseball game what they play against the navy. And the officers from the baseball players, they brought five or six military trucks, and they took all the civilians what they want to go to the game. We all in that time was young—the survivors. His son was the last one in the truck, and the end of the truck was the part what was open, the gate. He was sitting on the edge; the gate opened, and he fell out from the truck and was killed. So from that time he became so religious.

What I want to bring out is all kind of things what happened with people, some of them what they survived became very religious till today, and some of them, like me, for instance, I'm confused. I am not entirely free, because I go to synagogue Saturday, but this is not a thing what I use this because I am so religious.

ML: That's why I was asking about the synagogue in Dachau, because I wanted to know if there were many people like you who didn't go to synagogue because they were so religious or they held all the theological beliefs, but they were going for other reasons.

JF: We didn't know why we go. We didn't have nothing . . . we didn't know what to do in that time. "Why," I asked myself, "Why me? Why did I survive? Was I better than my father, than my cousins, than the other people, the Jews like me? Why did I survive?" In that time, you don't know what to think about why you survived. In the end I found out this was just an accident. Just an accident, not because I was better or because I was Himmler's tailor or another's tailor; just an accident. They didn't have time. And I tried to do something when I undressed myself to get sick, you know—I tried to do, but was an accident.

ML: Do you think a lot of survivors couldn't face that truth that it was an accident? There were thousands of reasons why they survived, and there were thousands of reasons why they might not have survived?

JF: Was only one reason: they didn't have time to finish us off. In the time when they took me to the hospital, was almost twenty thousand Jewish prisoners from my barrack; was thirty-two thousand prisoners in Dachau, all nationalities. They took the Jews outside to kill them. But the planes start to go over them, so they kill a couple of hundred, and the Gestapo or the SS what they took them out to kill them, they escaped. They escaped from the bombs, and the other sixteen hundred Jews—I don't know how many they kill, there was no watchmen; they was in the middle of the field—they went by themselves back to the camp. So it was an accident. The planes was over their heads, and the Germans escaped.

ML: Do you think there are some survivors who won't face that it was an accident?

JF: They are facing that. They know this was an accident.

ML: I was under the impression that many people who try to understand what happened want to invent reasons why people survived.

JF: What do you think? What is the reason they survived?

ML: I see it somewhat as you do, that there were no reasons. I think there were cases when someone was in an advantageous position or something beneficial happened to the person, but other times there were people in the same positions or better positions who were killed. The reasons that someone was stronger, smarter, had more hope, more deeply believed that he could continue or that he understood the power of life or he refused to be smashed under the starvation and the discipline—I don't think that had anything to do with it. I think both prisoners who lived and died might have felt those things or been able to use those attributes in some instances, but many of them weren't able, and they might have felt the opposite. They might have felt, "It's all over. It was all over in '41 or '40."

JF: There are some, but the way what a person thinks most of the time is with hope—"Maybe, maybe." But there are some what they see no hope. There are some what they poisoned themselves in the beginning; they killed themselves. But I don't see another way how I survived, and I don't see another way how the others survived. Was only an accident, because the whole plan—what I learned, because I had time, and I had the opportunity to be with the biggest henchmen, and I could learn a little bit; in that time I didn't have time to study, but after the liberation, more or less, I learned from them what they are thinking, what they have in their minds—and I found out what they have in their minds was to liquidate everybody. The main thing what they was thinking was not to leave no witnesses. Even with the survivors, there are about 15 percent or 20 percent of Americans who think there was no Holocaust at all. The whole policy from the Germans was to kill everybody so when the war will come to an end, even if they should lose, you shouldn't have somebody to say there was a Holocaust. So if this was their plan, how can I think different that it was only an accident that we survived? How can I think different? It's only the one way what I learned, and I had the opportunity to learn more than someone else what he survived, because I was with them, the heads from the henchmen, for five years and nine months.

ML: The fact that you saw that they had every intention to exterminate everyone, and you learned that from being around them for five years and nine months, was that because you saw the orders they gave, how they behaved?

JF: That's right, but in that time, I didn't have time to study what they are thinking, what their mind was. Later, after the liberation, I start to put together many instances, when they gave me the order, how they act, how their faces was, and how they look, so I can make the decision what I learned from the time I was with them.

ML: Most of the time, when I sit here talking with you, I already have many of the overarching ideas and outlines in my mind for this historical period: a world war and a systematic genocide against the Jews, Gypsies, Slavs, and it was probably going to extend to other European peoples—so when I ask you questions, it's from the point of view that the systematic killing in stages was obvious, but you're now pointing out that it was only after the liberation that you put together what all of the stages were and how the orders were given, that you could see the final goal. It wasn't clear to you from 1939 at all. We know this now, but it reflects our reconstruction of history, our hindsight.

JF: You see, in the beginning, sure, it was not clear. Before the Germans came in, this is impossible what people are saying about them, that the Germans will do things like we found out later, impossible that people was right what they told us. But to your mind, this is impossible to think that people can come to such a stage to do something like this, to take children and to throw them to a brick wall, or to take women that they should undress themselves, and they should kill them naked, or to throw a live human being in an oven, in a gas chamber. Your mind couldn't swallow this. It was impossible.

It reminds me . . . in 1938, the Germans took some Jews what they was born in Poland, a couple of thousand, and they throw them over the Polish border. Some of them came to Lublin, a couple of hundred or a hundred, I don't remember exactly. So happened my father took in a couple with a little child. They was not too long with us. They had some money, and they rented an apartment later, but most of the people from Lublin took in the Jews from Germany.

Between the Jews was a Jewish actor, Granach. He was one from the best actors from the Yiddish stage in Germany, and he wrote a play in 1938, the name was the *Gela Later*—this means the yellow patch what we was wearing in the camp. He showed in this play *exactly* the things what I went through the whole time from the war. He showed us when the Nazis came into a Jewish home, they took out the Jewish family, and they had ready concentration camps, they separate this wife and this child, they burned them in the gas chamber, and the man they took away. He was young, he should work, and later when he became weak, they killed him.

I saw this play, with many friends, with my wife. We went out; we said this guy is crazy. How is this possible something like this could be true? And exactly three, four-and-a-half years later, I saw this play was exactly like what this was in the time from the concentration camps, and he knew to produce a play from what will be four or five years later. Nobody wanted to believe. What I want to bring out is the human mind couldn't understand that people can do something like this . . . people like the Germans, a cultural nation, with the music conductors, the poets, a nation with culture, and they turned around the culture to make an evil turn.

37

Final Words and Thoughts

ML: I'VE OBSERVED THAT MOST PEOPLE have a very limited contact with death, and when they do have contact with death, it's through our customs: we visit people in hospitals; we go to funerals; we have religious practices to extract certain meanings from death, to regard it in a certain way, and to grieve in a certain way. But you've mentioned before to me that you saw many instances where human life was as short as a fly; you've seen that side of death, as well as mass numbers of people killed. How has that affected you in later parts of your life—your understanding of death, the death of your friends, other people in your family, from your seeing these other sides of death that we normally don't see?

JF: From the time when the killing went on, you was not thinking too much about this, because the Nazis didn't let you think. They kept you busy with beating, that you have to run from one place to another, from one barrack to another. The SS, the guards in the labor camps and in the concentration camps, when the killing went on, they didn't give you time to think; you couldn't think too long, maybe a minute, maybe a second. They found ways to stop your brains from thinking.

But later when I was liberated the first day, the first couple of days, you felt very good, that you are alive, after when you saw everything what happened a couple of months ago or a couple of weeks ago before the liberation. You saw that you survived, so was a couple of days you lived with enjoyment . . . you enjoy the time, the day, the night. This was with everybody, with most of us. After the liberation, when we saw the American troops, when I went out from the hospital, I start to take a walk in the Dachau camp, and I saw all the people what a week before was prisoners, and now we are free—we almost danced for joy. Many took the arms and the shoulders and to hug the people what they was together in the same barrack.

But I personally start to have a little bit better than the other ones. The apartment what I received from Americans, comparing from before when I was in the camp . . . not even comparing from before, but comparing to private life from before the war, I didn't have so a luxury life what I had when they gave me the apartment there, with chandeliers, with paintings what they stole from all the museums from Europe, with china, with carpeting, with rugs on the walls. But being there a day or two, I took a walk . . . this was on the other side of the camp . . . I went to meet some what I was with them in Dachau from before, so a whole day I was busy walking around, to look, maybe I'll meet somebody from the thirteen what I went from Lublin to Tomaschow, and then to Auschwitz, and then to Natzweiler, and to Vaihingen. I couldn't find nobody from the twelve what they survived, because the Ladermans what they survived, they was in another camp. When they liquidate Vaihingen, they took them away to another camp, and I didn't see Laderman again.

I was alone, with six rooms, with all the luxury. Start to get dark, and in the evening, I start to look for a newspaper what I received from some soldiers . . . I couldn't read English, just looking at the pictures in the paper. I went to bed . . . I was lying an hour, two hours; I couldn't fall asleep. I closed my eyes, but I was not asleep—I was dreaming with my eyes half-open. I start to dream about the nearest from my family, two little boys and a wife, a father and a mother, and six sisters with their husbands and their children. This went on every night. After the liberation was even worse for me than in concentration camp, because in concentration camp, like I said, they didn't let you think, and even if you was thinking about the tragedies what happened every day, every hour, a moment later you had to run because the Nazi was after you all the time. You didn't have time to think even. After this happened, they took away one part from your body, until they killed you entirely.

And here, after so a hell what I went through, I am lying in a luxurious bed, talking to myself, "Why you? Why me? Everybody from sixty-four, from my family, from my wife's family, why I am alive to live in so a luxurious place?" This life was much worse than to be in concentration camp. Over there, I knew I had to die. Here, I couldn't live, and I couldn't die. My living was a whole night dreaming from all the people in my family, and after the dreams, I woke up in the morning, I received *Verpflegung* from the Army, and later, I received a pass to eat in the officer's casino with the American officers.

I went down; they served me delicious food, but I couldn't eat, and many times, what I ate, I threw up. This went on for maybe two months. In the meantime, I met one in the camp; I knew him when I was in Vaihingen, and I invite him up to my house. He couldn't get over the all luxury. I start to be with him very close, so I found a friend . . . it was a little bit easier. In the meantime, there was a Jewish chaplain in the army; he start to organize us on one place, and he start to talk to us, and it start to be a little bit easier to live, listening to the chaplain.

ML: How did you grieve for your family? Do you remember what stages or what changes you went through in the years following?

JF: You didn't have too much time for your family, because they took away some of them, and some of them, they left, so you don't grieve too much, too long, because, in the beginning, you didn't know where they are taking them. They tell you they are taking them to a different camp. Even when you find out that they are killing them, you didn't want to believe. How can they kill thousands and thousands of people, women and children? It was unbelievable. So you didn't know to grieve—maybe they are alive, you didn't know. Later, when they finished off everybody, again psychologically, they kept you not to have time to grieve.

ML: Beyond that, what were further stages of grieving?

JF: Later, after a couple of months when I met my wife,[1] you was involved, you want to start a new life. My wife became pregnant with our first child, so you start a little bit to forget what this was—you're starting a new life. The whole thing disappeared, and comes up a new thing to think about.

ML: But then it never really permanently disappears.

JF: Never disappears. Sixty-four people what they was alive and they was killed—you can never forget this so long as you live. But in the other way, you have to think now about the living ones, the new family, the new children, the new grandchildren. It's a very hard question to answer you. You can never forget something like this, but you can also not remember all the time because you have a new life what you brought to this world.

ML: Did you ever feel that you were between the two lives, neither wholly in one nor the other?

---

1. Frank is referring to his second wife. Originally from Radom, Poland, she survived Plazow and Bergen-Belsen.

JF: No, I never felt. I felt that I have to separate the whole thing what this was. This is dead, nothing can help, I can do nothing to bring them back. The new lives are here, and I have to think about what is here now. The remembrance is only in a holiday, in a *Yahrzeit*, one day when I mourn them. From time to time, I see them in my dreams, talk with them. You can never forget, but again, you have a new generation—they are young and they are growing in a new world. Life is very strong, and you have to go on with your life.

ML: It sounds to me like your decision to separate the two absolutely was almost like a decision where you had to bend iron to achieve it, only permitting yourself one grieving day out of the year.

JF: This is a hard decision, but the whole world doesn't die. There's only a part of the world dying, and another part is born. Good or bad, life doesn't stop, goes on. That's the decision what I made, if I start a new family, then it's a new life. I came to the United States, I saved up from the American officers what they paid me for the work what I did, about $300. My wife was pregnant, she had here the first baby—you have a child, you need money to raise this child, and then we had another one, and you had to think about how to make the dollar to educate them, to feed them, to house them. This was a new life to build. That's the decision what I had to make to live, because life is going on.

ML: Going back to the influence of these experiences with death on your own natural death, when your death comes, do you think it will be a natural process? Do you think about that consciously, compared to all the deaths you saw which happened suddenly and under violent conditions?

JF: Today in my thinking, I am not afraid for death, because I know we all are born to die, sooner or later. When you are asking what I am thinking, my thinking is, when death has to come, I hope I wouldn't have to suffer too long, because suffering is worse than dying. What I learned from the past, dying is really not so bad. Bad is only before you die. Not even talking about the bad things before death what the Nazis did to the Jews before they killed them, but even today, God forbid if somebody is sick, and they have to suffer from a disease for months and months and then they have to die, then this is the worst time. But death itself—life is like a fly. Now you live, and when you're dead, you're dead, takes a minute or two. You don't feel anymore. It's over with the pains. That's the feeling what I have now. I only hope, a little bit afraid . . . I had a good life here in the United

States . . . was not so easy in the beginning, but even the uneasiness what I had, when it was not so good, I remind myself what I had before I came here, and compared to that, I still was living in a paradise. Later, when I had my children . . . we didn't expect to have any more children, especially the women, because when they was in the concentration camps, the Nazis put in special things in the food, so they wouldn't be able to have children. We had two lovely kids, I worked very hard to give them an education, they're professionals, and I had a good life here. In the meantime, it so happened that death came to my wife, and in a way I was feeling very lost. When she died, she died with a death that when the time will come I hope I will die in so a way—she went to sleep and she didn't come up in the morning. So long as I am here, I am trying to enjoy my life. No matter what time, good or bad, the bad things I hope will pass by quicker, and I wait that the next moment will be better. That is what my thinking is today.

ML: This is interesting to me that you hope the bad things will pass by more quickly and the good things will be prolonged, because I remember that you told me that often you felt like you couldn't feel too much joy, and when you did feel that way, you caught yourself from having too much pleasure or enjoyment, not to indulge yourself too much. I took that to be a kind of regulation of your emotions, because you told me that whenever you felt too much joy, you would remember those of your family who didn't live, and you felt that it wasn't right to feel so high. Is that a kind of inner regulation, is it your conscience, or is it guilt?

JF: What you was talking about that I sometimes feel I shouldn't enjoy so much pleasure—this was in the beginning, a certain time after the war. When the children was born . . . not willingly, what I want or I didn't want, I don't know . . . but this came by itself: I have to make the best. The whole thing what I was thinking before, this disappeared. Later from time to time, if even you remind yourself of certain things what you don't want to think about . . . you are not born from a stone, you had a family. What happened with them? When it comes to the high holidays, every child, if they lose their parents, they go to the cemetery. Every parent what they lost a child goes to the cemetery. Sometimes when I am thinking about this, I have nowhere to go to look for my nearest. You have a moment when you think this way, but after when you go out from the synagogue, you made the prayer *Yizkor,* you think about the living ones. You have a new family, you have to think about their lives, to enjoy. I was brought up in a house what was more *Yiddishkeit,* even if I am not observing all the things what I learned when I was young, but still, if you're born with something, it is in you. The Jewish way of life is: Don't laugh too much when your life is going so very high, so very good, but don't cry too much when your life is down and going very bad. You have to live in the middle. I don't know if you understand what I mean. That's the Jewish way what my father taught me.

ML: And do you think that's become more clear to you from experiencing many, many tragedies? Otherwise, you might not be so concerned with the present, because generally in this era, people are very concerned for the future, what they may have tomorrow, where they want to be and how they want to be recognized, and the present moment is diminished. They're not concerned with the mid-stride; it's where the stride will take them.

JF: You have to think about the future. But the future, you have to do the best what you can do for the future, but not to overdo. By overdo, I mean, if there is somebody somewhere else what they are not doing what your vision is for the future, and you go there and kill them, destroy them. Not always the future will come the way what you want, what the other one wants, or what the third one wants.

ML: Would you agree with me that even with a complete understanding of the past, and a greater understanding of history than we have, people would still not set up rules or practices for themselves that would prevent them from killing another group? It requires more than an understanding of the past?

JF: From other people what I am talking with them, I don't ask them their way what they are thinking. My way of thinking today is: the past was no good. I mean the past even before the Second World War, being born in Poland. I understand there has to be a better way to get along with other people, how to live together.

This is my way without a scientific thinking. If something is no good, you have to change, and the change is, in my mind, to live with people in a nicer way than this was before. The policy from the world, from the world's politicians, and maybe today too, is to help to build up the monsters and then to destroy them. Hitler wouldn't have come to power after the First World War if the German hadn't felt that he is so down that he has pay for losing the First World War. Hitler said to the German, "Look, you can't even buy a gallon of milk for your children. You cannot even buy a pair of shoes for your children," and that's the same thing what I, as a layman, observed by the Germans. When I made a German a suit, was like to him that he won on the lottery a million dollars, so happy he was. "Make me another suit. Make my wife a suit." Looks like he never had a suit to wear before he came to power. And even when Hitler came to power, the German still didn't have anything. Later, he told them you should take away all this richness what the Jew took away from you, and this is only the one what you have to kill. And this went on, day in and day out, through the propaganda, through the radio, and that's true in many instances even today.

ML: We've talked before about the constant propaganda influencing attitudes of resentment about social upheaval, but as I thought about our conversations, I observed that there were guards and officers who went far beyond hating. They enjoyed killing, they felt some kind of release or power from that, that can't just be explained by the propaganda they were told, because they went far beyond carrying out orders, or acting as robots. What were those people like in your view?

JF: In my view—not in my view, but I learned this personally in many, many instances—the first time what a man is killing another man, even if he has the order to kill, is very hard for the killer. But after two or three or four, he's never carrying out orders, but comes a satisfaction that the whole power from the world he has in his hand. He can do anything, and bad things are much easier to learn than good things. And he learns this very quick. Especially the German, because the German from nature is to carry out orders exactly what they tell him. You don't have to repeat them too many times. If he gets an order to kill Jews, so he killed.

ML: What about the ones who weren't merely following orders in the death factories but felt like engaging in target practice, or felt like beating people that day, or felt like killing a few extra? It might not even have had to do with their hatred of the Jews, but the intense enjoyment they felt.

JF: That's why I said when he feels he has the power, to use his power that he feels himself on top of the world.

ML: And is that not only a power to destroy life, but a power of being beyond the human law?

JF: That's right. That's the way of thinking from the killer or the torturer.

ML: But at the same time, what I can't understand is that many of those people must have known that the situation where they were beyond the human law, and they could follow their heart's desire in this world, wasn't going to last forever.

JF: I cannot answer this question. You just said you cannot understand. I went through this everything, and I saw this everything what you are writing for weeks now, and after being there five years and nine months in all concentration camps and prisons, and all the torturing and killings what I saw, after today, fifty-one years after, I still cannot understand how this could happen, and especially with a cultural nation, from poets, from music conductors, from music writers, from professors. Even before the war, when I was in Germany in 1932 in Munich to finish a course from the designer's school, I saw the difference between a Polish man and a German man. Was like two other worlds. The Polish man was common, and the German was intelligent, but what they did with their intelligence, this is something else. After fifty years—I am more than three times as old as you—and I cannot understand how this could happen.

But this happened. If people let themselves go so far to choose a leader and to go with him a certain distance, to let them do this, so if the leader has the power, it takes one man. He took 63 million people, he made them 63 million killers. One man. Maybe I'm exaggerating 63 million killers, maybe was a half a million or a million decent Germans between 63 million, but most of the Germans' mothers, when the sons came home with golden earrings, with diamond rings, with golden teeth, the German mothers didn't ask, "From whom did you take the teeth?" So the majority was killers; the majority had the knowledge what Hitler gave them for six, seven years.

ML: I can see you're thinking that one man made a whole collective nation a group of killers, but I also think there was a great deal of complicity because people acquired material things which they wanted, and they were also seeing themselves rise . . .

JF: And this was the policy from him.

ML: So I can find many historical and sociological explanations why there were transitions and people were led to act with complicity during the period. I think what's harder for me to understand is how the individual killer could be so certain that he could escape without any penalty, even if the Nazis had won the war. Maybe I have an incorrect idea of this type of criminal figure, but I think even the criminals who meticulously plan out their crimes aren't concerned with totally eliminating the evidence; they're concerned with reducing the evidence so someone won't know what they've done, and I think it's

clear that at certain points the Germans made an overture to destroy
the death camp apparatus, getting rid of the bodies, getting rid of the
bones, so that much later, there would be no evidence. But it seems
easy enough to think that logically there will be one or two people
who will survive, and it's impossible to get rid of all the evidence on
this enormous scale. I can't see that with such technical execution of
genocide that they really believed that they could succeed. Maybe that
wasn't the point to succeed, but to go on as long as they could.

JF: I'm sure your thinking has nothing to do with age, but I study
my life, really life what I saw, and I saw that if you have power, if you
became powerful, you don't think. You don't think what the next day,
what the next month or the next year, if you'll win the war or lose the
war, what'll be with you. You use out the moment when you have the
power, whether this is killing, robbing, torturing, or rape. You think
one thing: to take more for yourself what you want with your power,
what you have in your power to do.

ML: So power would never have a conservative approach where
one would want to set up an intricate system to take as much as one
could for as long as one could? Only aggrandize now?

JF: Not only now. You think this will be forever. You don't think
there'll come a time when it will not be forever. You don't think about
change. You're so powerful that nobody could destroy you. Even if,
like you said, you have one or two survivors, or ten what they came and
they tell the world what you did, the world doesn't think. All the books
what you read and what you write, what is the world doing about this?
Nothing. Look what happened this week in Haiti. They send away the
UN observers that they can kill more, not to have witnesses. It's the
same thing. So what are you thinking about the guy who's shooting?
That's what you understand and I understand, but the powerful guy
doesn't think this way. He thinks all the time that he'll be alive, he'll
use his power. When it came to Hitler that he lost the war, he gave an
order to open the dams that was keeping the cities from overflooding.
He said to open the dams and to drown all the population, so if he cannot win, he wants to take with him the whole world, the whole Germany. And if he had the power over the whole world, he'll take the
whole world with him. That's the thing from the powerful guy.

References

Apenszlak, Jacob, ed., and Jacob Kenner, Isaac Levin, Moses Polakiewicz, co-eds. 1982. *The Black Book of Polish Jewry: An Account of the Martyrdom of Polish Jewry Under the Nazi Occupation*. New York: Howard Fertig.

Arad, Yitzhak. 1987. *Belzec, Sobibor, Treblinka: The Operation Reinhard Death Camps*. Bloomington: Indiana Univ. Press.

Arendt, Hannah. 1976. *Eichmann in Jerusalem: A Report on the Banality of Evil*. New York: Penguin.

Bauman, Zygmunt. 1989. *Modernity and the Holocaust*. Ithaca, N.Y.: Cornell Univ. Press.

Berben, Paul. 1975. *Dachau, 1933–1945: The Official History*. London: Norfolk Press.

Bronowski, Alexander. 1991. *They Were Few*. Translated by Murray Raveh. New York: Peter Lang.

Browning, Christopher R. 1993. *Ordinary Men: Reserve Police Battalion 101 and the Final Solution in Poland*. New York: Harper Perennial.

Canetti, Elias. 1984. *Crowds and Power*. Translated by Carol Stewart. New York: Farrar, Straus, and Giroux.

Delbo, Charlotte, 1968. *None of Us Will Return*. Translated by John Githens. New York: Grove.

Des Pres, Terrence. 1976. *The Survivor: An Anatomy of Life in the Death Camps*. New York: Oxford Univ. Press.

Destexhe, Alain. 1995. *Rwanda and Genocide in the Twentieth Century*. Translated by Alison Marschner. New York: New York Univ. Press.

Distel, Barbara, and Ruth Jakusch, eds. 1978. *Concentration Camp Dachau*. Translated by Jennifer Vernon, with Jakusch and Distel. Brussels: Comité International de Dachau.

Feig, Konnilyn G. 1981. *Hitler's Death Camps: The Sanity of Madness*. New York: Holmes and Meier.

Fest, Joachim C. 1970. *The Face of the Third Reich: Portraits of the Nazi Leadership*. Translated by Michael Bullock. New York: Pantheon.

Frankl, Viktor. 1963. *Man's Search for Meaning: An Introduction to Logotherapy*. Translated by Ilse Lasch. Boston: Beacon.

Goldhagen, Daniel Jonah. 1997. *Hitler's Willing Executioners: Ordinary Germans and the Holocaust*. New York: Vintage.

Gruber, Samuel, as told to Gertrude Hirschler. 1978. *I Chose Life*. New York: Shengold.

Hilberg, Raul. 1985. *The Destruction of the European Jews*. New York: Holmes and Meier.

Investigation of the SS and Police Leaders in Lublin, 208 AR-Z 74/60. Ludwigsburg: *Zentrale Stelle der Landesjustizverwaltungen zur Aufklärung nationalsozialistische Verbrechen*.

Krakowski, Shmuel. 1984. *The War of the Doomed: Jewish Armed Resistance in Poland, 1942–1944*. Translated by Orah Blaustein. New York: Holmes and Meier.

Kuper, Leo. 1989. *Genocide: Its Political Use in the Twentieth Century*. New Haven and London: Yale Univ. Press.

Langer, Lawrence L. 1991. *Holocaust Testimonies: The Ruins of Memory*. New Haven: Yale Univ. Press.

Levi, Primo. 1986. *Survival in Auschwitz and the Reawakening*. Translated by Stuart Woolf. New York: Summit.

Levin, Nora. 1973. *The Holocaust: The Destruction of European Jewry 1933–1945*. New York: Schocken.

Lifton, Robert. 1986. *The Nazi Doctors: Medical Killing and the Psychology of Genocide*. New York: Basic Books.

London *Times*. 1974. July 27, 1A.

Marszalek, Józef. 1986. *Majdanek: The Concentration Camp in Lublin*. Warsaw: Interpress.

Reck-Malleczewen, Friedrich Percyval. 1970. *Diary of a Man in Despair*. Translated by Paul Rubens. New York: Macmillan.

Willenberg, Samuel, and Wladyslaw T. Bartozweski, ed. 1989. *Surviving Treblinka*. Translated by Naftali Greenwood. New York: Basil Blackwell.

Yahil, Leni. 1990. *The Holocaust: The Fate of European Jewry, 1932–1945*. Translated by Friedman and Galai. New York: Oxford Univ. Press.

Index

Italic page number denotes illustration.